The Profession and Practice
of Adult Education

Sharan B. Merriam
Ralph G. Brockett

JB JOSSEY-BASS

The Profession and Practice of Adult Education

An Introduction

1807
WILEY
2007

BICENTENNIAL

John Wiley & Sons, Inc.

Published by Jossey-Bass
A Wiley Imprint
989 Market Street, San Francisco, CA 94103-1741   www.josseybass.com

Jossey-Bass books and products are available through most bookstores. To contact Jossey-Bass directly call our Customer Care Department within the U.S. at 800-956-7739, outside the U.S. at 317-572-3986, or fax 317-572-4002.

Jossey-Bass also publishes its books in a variety of electronic formats. Some content that appears in print may not be available in electronic books.

Library of Congress Cataloging-in-Publication Data

Merriam, Sharan B.
    The profession and practice of adult education : an introduction
        p. cm. — (Jossey-Bass higher and adult education series)
    Includes bibliographical references and index.
    ISBN: 9780470181539
    1. Adult education—United States. 2. Adult education—Canada. I. Brockett, Ralph Grover. II. Title. III. Series.
    LC5251.M456 1997
    374'.97—dc20   96-22517

Printed in the United States of America
UPDATED EDITION
PB Printing 10 9 8 7 6 5 4

The Jossey-Bass
Higher and Adult Education Series

Consulting Editor
Adult and Continuing Education
Alan B. Knox
University of Wisconsin, Madison

Contents

Preface

Adult educators are everywhere—in the community, in the workplace, on farms, and in hospitals, prisons, libraries, colleges, and universities. They plan and administer programs, and they counsel and facilitate learning in subjects as diverse as ceramics, computer training, nutrition, job skills, literacy, continuing medical education, and environmental awareness. The growing visibility of adults engaging in education (reflected in movies, news stories, and television shows), however, is offset by the fact that many educators of adults remain unaware that they are part of a cadre of thousands that constitutes the field of adult education. This book is meant to broadly outline this professional field of practice.

Nearly fifteen years ago, Sharan Merriam published a coauthored book on the foundations of the field of adult education (Darkenwald and Merriam, 1982). That book, and the later edited *Handbook of Adult and Continuing Education* (Merriam and Cunningham, 1989), have been the only major sources providing comprehensive overviews of the field.

On the doorstep of the twenty-first century, we believe that the timing is right for an updated introductory text on adult education. *The Profession and Practice of Adult Education: An Introduction* describes and interprets the broad and rapidly developing field of study and practice. It is something of a "snapshot" of adult education in North America at this point in time.

As with any introductory text, we have had to make choices about what to include and what to emphasize. This is not a book about how to plan programs or teach adults; instead, it is about what constitutes professional practice. It is not our intent to give detailed scenarios about specific practices or individual practitioners, but rather to frame information by providing a conceptual map of the field. And while we attend to international, community-based, non-formal, and informal adult education in various chapters, the emphasis is on North American adult education, as well as formal, organized delivery systems.

Audience

The major audience for *The Profession and Practice of Adult Education: An Introduction* will be practitioners working in adult education in various capacities and in a multitude of settings. Some of these practitioners will also be graduate students enrolled in more than a hundred North American master's and doctoral degree programs. In these graduate programs, an introductory course often affords students the first realization that they are part of a larger community of adult educators who have much in common; such a course is thus an important socializing mechanism for building the field of adult education while providing a base for other courses in the curriculum.

Other practitioners who discover that they are involved in adult education, and who are interested in becoming better acquainted with the field, will also find this book helpful in gaining a basic understanding of adult education.

Finally, our experience with past introductory texts would suggest that practitioners and students in other countries will also make use of this text.

Overview of the Contents

The Profession and Practice of Adult Education: An Introduction is designed to (1) provide a descriptive overview of major dimensions of the adult education field, and (2) raise awareness of the critical issues and tensions inherent in the practice of adult education. We anticipate that many readers are knowledgeable about their particular aspect of practice but new to adult education as a whole. Acquiring a basic understanding of the entire field—a map of the territory—is a necessary first step to situate one's own base of practice within a larger framework. Hence, eight of the book's eleven chapters are primarily descriptive.

With regard to the second goal of raising awareness of the critical issues, three chapters specifically examine issues and tensions of the field. Rather than being grouped at the end of the book, these three chapters are strategically placed to focus on the topics of those chapters immediately preceding them, and they attempt to help you stand back to critically assess issues challenging the field. In so doing, we hope that you will see the potential for becoming reflective about your practice, and about who will take an active role in shaping the future of adult education.

To highlight this dual focus of description and critique, the chapters of the book have been divided into three parts. Part One, "Foundations of Adult Education," contains four chapters. Part Two, titled "The Organization and Delivery of Adult Education," includes four chapters. The three chapters in Part Three are devoted to the topic of "Developing a Professional Field of Practice."

Chapter One sketches the broad outlines of the field in terms of its definitions, major concepts, goals, and purposes; and it asks readers to situate their practice within this framework. The underlying theme of the chapter is that what "counts" as adult education is determined by the context and where one stands in relation to the field.

Chapter Two explores the philosophical foundations of adult education. We discuss major schools of educational philosophy and present a rationale for engaging in philosophical inquiry.

Recognizing the impossibility of covering the history of adult education in a single chapter, we wrote Chapter Three as an examination of how the history of the field has been approached and interpreted. As with philosophy, we present a number of arguments for studying history.

Part One concludes with a chapter that outlines three critical issues related to the foundations of adult education practice: whether we should strive for unity, whether we should align with the rest of education, and whether the primary focus of our activity should be the individual or society.

In Part Two, Chapters Five through Eight center on the organization and delivery of adult education. Chapter Five outlines how agencies and organizations deliver formal adult education in the United States. In addition to institutionally based typologies, we map the field by content area and personnel. We also address the process involved in delivering programs.

Chapter Six focuses on the learner in adult education, addressing who participates and why, what they are studying, and so on. We also cover some basic information about the nature of adult learning.

Chapter Seven shifts to a global context. We first describe what adult education is like in other parts of the world, then attempt to conceptualize international adult education as a forum for exchanging ideas and experiences. We also discuss international adult education as a part of the academic discipline of comparative studies.

Chapter Eight focuses on the issues related to the organization and delivery of adult education. Here we focus on the troublesome issues of opportunity, access, and participation. Since the barriers and responses are common to most countries, this chapter is written with a global perspective.

Part Three contains three chapters related to the development of adult education as a professional field of practice. Chapter Nine examines current aspects of the professionalization of adult education. We look at three elements of what constitutes a profession: professional associations, literature and information resources in the field, and academic preparation.

While many important developments in the adult education field are linked to professionalization, a vital element of adult education takes place outside the mainstream. In Chapter Ten, we explore this "invisible" side of the field by looking at who these educators are and what they do. A major emphasis of this chapter is on efforts to promote adult education for social change.

Chapter Eleven serves to bring closure to the book by addressing some of the tensions and issues related to the very different visions of adult education offered in the previous two chapters. The chapter closes with a discussion of possible future directions for adult education.

Acknowledgments

A number of people have contributed their time and expertise toward making this book possible. To University of Tennessee graduate students who offered comments on earlier drafts of Chapter Three, and to University of Georgia doctoral students Emuel Aldridge, Lilian Hill, Patricia Reeves, and Debra Templeton, we thank you for the many hours you devoted to editing draft chapters, tracking down references, and helping us assemble the final manuscript. A special thanks goes to Lilian Hill for her long hours of work on the index, and to Patricia Brockett, who assisted in the final preparation of the index. Our grateful appreciation also goes to colleagues Ronald Cervero, Carolyn Clark, Tal Guy, and Arthur Wilson, who critiqued the book's organization and draft chapters. Your suggestions did much to strengthen the book. To Arthur Wilson, who also served as a manuscript reviewer for Jossey-Bass (along with Adrianne Bonham and a third, anonymous reviewer), we thank you for your detailed reading and helpful critique. Finally, we want to acknowledge family members Robert Rowden and Patricia and Megan Brockett, who lovingly endured the absences, stresses, and anxieties associated with our writing this book.

August 1996   Sharan B. Merriam
                                                     Athens, Georgia
                                                     Ralph G. Brockett
                                                     Knoxville, Tennessee

Preface to the Updated Edition

In the ten years since the original publication of *The Profession and Practice of Adult Education*, our world has witnessed many profound changes. Stimulated by geopolitical realignments, increased terrorism worldwide, globalization, natural disasters, and environmental crises, today's world is very different from even a decade ago. At the same time, technological advances have drastically changed how we work, how we communicate with others, how we keep in touch with one another, and how we are able to maximize opportunities for learning. All of these changes have impacted the profession and practice of adult education.

Former U.S. Secretary of Labor Robert Reich, in his book *The Future of Success*, characterized American society today as being in "the era of the terrific deal" (Reich, 2001). By this, he meant that so many of the accoutrements most people in the U.S. and other developed nations have come to take for granted can be had at a much lower financial cost than at any other time. Furthermore, we are caught up in what Barry Schwartz calls the "paradox of choice" (Schwartz, 2004). According to Schwartz, the paradox of choice refers to the notion that in today's society, the range of choices available in nearly all aspects of life are virtually unlimited. Every day, we face choices about which food is good for our health, which books we wish to read, which career move is best. Schwartz claims that while choice can be a good thing, *too much* choice can have a negative impact on the quality of life because there is a risk that people will keep looking for the "next best thing" and, hence, be unable to be satisfied with the choices they have made.

In adult education, as in society as a whole, the growth of new opportunities for learning has mushroomed. Online learning and other distance education opportunities have blurred the geographical boundaries that an institution can serve. In addition to the rise of online degree-granting institutions, most higher and continuing education institutions are offering courses and some degrees online as a standard part of their curriculum. Similarly, the need and the opportunities for learning in the workplace continue to expand. The percent of U.S. adults participating in adult education programs of any sort has increased from an estimated 14 percent in 1984 to 46 percent in 2001 (Merriam, Caffarella, and Baumgartner, 2007). Add to this the large number of informal adult education activities and self-directed learning efforts undertaken by adults, and it becomes clear that the *practice* of adult education is thriving in the early twenty-first century.

At the same time, the *profession* of adult education has faced some challenges and even setbacks over the last decade. Perhaps this is best illustrated in difficulties that have arisen in efforts to maintain a thriving "umbrella" adult education professional association in the U.S. In 1998, the American Association for Adult and Continuing Education (AAACE) faced a major financial crisis, and a year later, the Commission on Adult Basic Education, one of the largest groups within AAACE, voted to leave AAACE and establish itself as a separate entity. Since 1999, AAACE has faced declining membership and attendance at its annual conference. Yet, the association continues to produce two of the most influential periodicals in adult education, and the annual conference still serves to meet the professional development needs of those who attend.

Despite the many changes taking place in adult education today, we believe that *The Profession and Practice of Adult Education: An*

Introduction continues to serve as a timely introduction to the adult education field. The discussions of topics such as what "counts" as adult education, philosophy, history, providers of adult education, and the background on professionalization of adult education still reflect the essence of contemporary adult education. With our wish for the book to continue to serve its purpose as an introductory text, we have worked with Jossey-Bass to make the book more readily available by producing it in a paperback format. We have added a completely new Epilogue that strives to capture some of the major changes since *Profession and Practice* was first published. In this Epilogue, we consider developments in five areas that have had an impact on adult education over the past decade: globalization, the interface between human resource development and adult education, holistic conceptions of learning, critical adult education and diversity, and the current state of the adult education profession.

Acknowledgments

We wish to offer a special thanks to David Brightman, our editor at Jossey-Bass. David has been an enthusiastic supporter of our work, and his involvement was vital in bringing this paperback edition to life. Also, we wish to thank our spouses, Robert Rowden and Mary Brockett, for their love and encouragement. Finally, we would like to acknowledge the many students and professors who have used the book over the past decade. Their support is what gave us the impetus to find a way to keep the book in print and relevant to the early twenty-first century. We hope that through this updated edition, *The Profession and Practice of Adult Education* can continue to serve the adult education field and those who study and practice it.

May, 2007

Sharan B. Merriam
Athens, Georgia
Ralph G. Brockett
Knoxville, Tennessee

The Authors

Sharan B. Merriam is professor of adult education at the University of Georgia, Athens, Georgia, where her responsibilities include teaching graduate courses in adult education and qualitative research methods, and supervising graduate student research. Her doctorate is in adult education from Rutgers University. Dr. Merriam's research and writing activities have focused on the foundations of adult education, adult development, adult learning, and qualitative research methods. For five years she was coeditor of *Adult Education Quarterly*, the major research and theory journal in adult education. She is a three-time winner of the prestigious Cyril O. Houle World Award for Literature in Adult Education for books published in 1982, 1997, and 1999. She regularly presents seminars on adult learning and qualitative research throughout North America, southern Africa, Southeast Asia, and Europe. She has been a Fulbright Scholar to Malaysia and a Distinguished Visiting Scholar at Soongsil University in South Korea.

Ralph G. Brockett is professor in the Department of Educational Psychology and Counseling at the University of Tennessee, Knoxville, where he is coordinator of the adult education concentration. He received his B.A. in psychology and his M.Ed. in guidance and counseling from the University of Toledo, and he also holds a Ph.D.

in adult education from Syracuse University. Previously, he held faculty positions at Montana State University (1984–1988) and Syracuse University (1982–1984) and has worked in continuing education program development for health and human services professionals. He is past chair of the Commission of Professors of Adult Education and has served on the board of the American Association for Adult and Continuing Education. In addition, he is a past editor-in-chief of *New Directions for Adult and Continuing Education* and co-editor of *Adult Learning,* and has served on the editorial boards of four adult education journals. He received the Malcolm Knowles Memorial Self-Directed Learning Award in 2004 and was inducted into the International Adult and Continuing Education Hall of Fame in 2005.

Among Brockett's previous books are *Toward Ethical Practice* (2004, with R. Hiemstra), *The Power and Potential of Collaborative Learning Partnerships* (1998, co-edited with I.M. Saltiel and A. Sgroi), *Overcoming Resistance to Self-Direction in Adult Learning* (1994, co-edited with R. Hiemstra), *Self-Direction in Adult Learning: Perspectives on Theory, Research, and Practice* (1991, with R. Hiemstra), and *Ethical Issues in Adult Education* (1988, edited).

Brockett's major scholarly interests are in the areas of professional ethics for adult education, self-direction in adult learning, and the study of the adult education field.

Part I

Foundations of Adult Education

In the four chapters that constitute Part One of *The Profession and Practice of Adult Education: An Introduction*, we trace the development of adult education through its evolving purposes and definitions, its philosophical underpinnings, and its historical perspectives. We also explore several of the ongoing issues related to the field's foundation and evolution.

In Chapter One, "What Counts as Adult Education?" we begin by pointing out that the context of adult education in North America has shaped the definitions, concepts, goals, and purposes of the field. What has "counted" as adult education has changed over the years; furthermore, where one stands in relation to the field—as practitioner, academician, policymaker, or interested spectator—leads to particular understandings of what constitutes adult education.

The values and beliefs held by individuals and society as a whole shape which goals and purposes are considered important in the practice of adult education. Hence, Chapter Two outlines a number of philosophical frameworks that have influenced how the practice of adult education is perceived. In particular, we discuss the various schools—liberal and progressive, behavioral and humanist, and critical philosophical—and their manifestations in adult education. We also present a rationale for engaging in philosophical inquiry and offer suggestions for taking responsibility for articulating a personal philosophy.

Every field has its history. Rather than attempt to cover the history of adult education in a single chapter, we have instead chosen in Chapter Three to examine how history has been presented by various writers. We address the questions of who and what has been studied, how history is a historian's interpretation, and how we might benefit from studying our field's past.

In the fourth and final chapter of Part One, we grapple with three key issues related to the foundations of the field. The perennial question of whether adult education should work toward unity or toward preserving the diversity of the field is explored first. The second issue—whether adult education should align itself more closely with the rest of education—is, of course, related to the notions of identity and professionalism inherent in the first issue. The third issue centers on what the primary focus of adult education should be. Finally, all three issues are linked together in a discussion of their implications for public policy in adult education.

1

What Counts as Adult Education?

W hat is adult education? What are the boundaries of the field that help distinguish it from other educational and social endeavors? What does it mean to be an adult? What "counts" as adult education, and what doesn't? Who is or is not an adult educator? These are some of the questions that underlie this first chapter on the scope of the field. We begin by asking how you, the reader, connect with the field of adult education: how do you work with adults in an educational capacity? We then explore the concepts of "adult" and "education," which leads us to defining "adult education" and related terms.

In the second section of the chapter, we review what people have written about the aims, goals, or purposes of adult education, and how the emphasis on various purposes has shifted over the years. Again, we ask that you consider the goals and purposes of what you do as an educator of adults. In the final section, we explore how this theme of what counts as adult education structures the field's relationship to the larger world of education.

Defining Adult Education

Defining adult education is akin to the proverbial elephant being described by five blind men: it depends on where you are standing and how you experience the phenomenon. Perhaps you teach an aerobics class several mornings a week at your local YMCA or community center. Maybe your background is in nursing, and you plan continuing education programs for the hospital staff. You may have organized a group of citizens in your community to protest rent gouging or environmental pollution. You might administer a literacy or job-skills training program, or perhaps you work as a private consultant conducting management-training seminars for companies.

These are just a few examples of people's experiences with adult education. You, and many others like you, have probably not considered how you might be a part of a field larger than the particular arena in which you work. Yet the field of adult education encompasses all of these components. What your individual experience in adult education has in common with others' experiences is that you are working with adults in some organized, educational activity.

The Meaning of "Adult"

One key to defining adult education lies with the notion of "adult." But who is an adult? In North America, adulthood as a stage of life is a relatively new concept. According to Jordan (1978), the psychological sense of adulthood, "as we ordinarily think of it today, is largely an artifact of twentieth-century American culture [that] emerged by a process of exclusion, as the final product resulting from prior definitions of other stages in the human life cycle" (p. 189). The concept "did not appear in America at all until after the Civil War and not really until the early twentieth century" (p. 192).

Today, adulthood is considered to be a sociocultural construction; that is, the answer to the question of who is an adult is constructed by a particular society and culture at a particular time. For example, in Colonial America the notion of adulthood was based on English common law wherein males reached the "age of discretion" at fourteen and females at twelve (Jordan, 1978). In a monograph on adult education in Colonial America, Long (1976) considered "the formal and informal learning activities of individuals above twelve [to] fourteen years of age in Colonial America as adult education" (p. 4).

If biologically defined, many cultures consider puberty to be the entry into adulthood. Legal definitions of adulthood are generally anchored in chronological age, which varies within the same culture. In the United States, for example, men and women can vote at age eighteen, drink at twenty-one, leave compulsory schooling at sixteen, and in some states be tried in court as an adult at fourteen.

Other definitions of adulthood hinge upon psychological maturity or social roles. Knowles (1980b) uses both of these criteria, stating that "individuals should be treated as adults educationally" if they behave as adults by performing adult roles and if their self-concept is that of an adult—that is, the extent that an "individual perceives herself or himself to be essentially responsible for her or his own life" (p. 24). Knowles's definition of adult presents some problems. What about the teenage parent living on welfare? The married, full-time college student? The adults in prison or in a mental hospital?

In considering all of the ways in which the term can be defined, Paterson (1979) offers a way out of the quagmire. At the heart of the concept is the notion that adults are older than children, and as a result there is a set of expectations about their behavior: "Those people (in most societies, the large majority) to whom we ascribe the status of adults may and do evince the widest possible variety of intellectual gifts, physical powers, character traits, beliefs, tastes, and habits. But we correctly deem them to be adults because, by virtue of their age, we are justified in requiring them to evince the basic qualities of maturity. Adults are not necessarily mature. But they are supposed to be mature, and it is on this necessary supposition that their adulthood justifiably rests" (p. 13).

Education Versus Learning

Adult *education* can be distinguished from adult *learning,* and indeed it is important to do so when trying to arrive at a comprehensive understanding of adult education. Adult learning is a cognitive process internal to the learner; it is what the learner does in a teaching-learning transaction, as opposed to what the educator does. Learning also includes the unplanned, incidental learning that is part of everyday life. As Thomas (1991a) explains: "Clearly education must be concerned with specific learning outcomes and with the processes of learning needed for students to achieve those outcomes. Thus education cannot exist without learning. Learning, however, not only can exist outside the context of education but probably is most frequently found there" (p. 17).

Playing golf is thus differentiated from golf *lessons*, just as reading a mystery novel is different from participating in a Great Books Program. The golf lessons and the Great Books Program are designed to bring about learning and are examples of adult education. Still, playing golf and reading a book may involve learning, and herein lies a source of confusion for those trying to grasp the nature of adult education. Although one may have learned something while playing golf or reading a mystery novel, these activities would not be considered adult education, because they were not designed to bring about learning.

Using another example, a person who becomes ill may learn a lot about dealing with the illness through reading articles in magazines, talking with friends, or seeing a television show; this is adult learning embedded in life experience. If the same person were to participate in a patient-education program or a self-help group focusing on the illness, he or she would be involved in adult education. The difference is that the patient-education program and the self-help group are systematic, organized events intended to bring about learning.

So while learning can occur both incidentally and in planned educational activities, it is only the planned activities that we call adult *education*. And while we include references to adult learning as an integral part of the enterprise, our focus in this book is to describe the field of adult *education*.

Some Definitions of Adult Education

A definition of adult education, then, usually includes some referent (1) to the adult status of students, and (2) to the notion of the activity being purposeful or planned. An early, often-quoted definition by Bryson (1936) captures these elements. Bryson proposed that adult education consists of "all the activities with an educational purpose that are carried on by people, engaged in the ordinary business of life" (p. 3).

More than fifty years later, Courtney (1989) offers a definition— "for practitioners, . . . those preparing to enter the profession, and . . . curious others who have connections with the field"—that echoes Bryson's: "Adult education is an intervention into the ordinary business of life—an intervention whose immediate goal is change, in knowledge or in competence" (p. 24). Darkenwald and Merriam (1982) are even more specific with regard to the two criteria cited above: "Adult education is a process whereby persons whose major social roles are characteristic of adult status undertake systematic and sustained learning activities for the purpose of bringing about changes in knowledge, attitudes, values, or skills" (p. 9).

Some definitions emphasize the learner, some the planning, and others the process. Long (1987) believes that adult education "includes all systematic and purposive efforts by the adult to become an educated person" (p. viii). Although critiqued for its emphasis on formal education that seems to exclude self-directed efforts, Verner's often-cited definition (1964) focuses on planning: "Adult education is a relationship between an educational agent and a learner in which the agent selects, arranges, and continuously directs a sequence of progressive tasks that provide systematic experiences to achieve learning for people whose participation in such activities is subsidiary and supplemental to a primary productive role in society" (p. 32).

Probably the best-known definition emphasizing the process of adult education is that of Houle (1972). He argues that it is a process involving planning by individuals or agencies by which adults "alone, in groups, or in institutional settings . . . improve themselves or their society" (p. 32). Finally, Knowles (1980b) also identifies adult education "in its broadest sense" as "the process of adults learning." In its more technical sense, adult education is "a set of organized activities carried on by a wide variety of institutions for the accomplishment of specific educational objectives" (p. 25). Knowles also proposes a third meaning that "combines all these processes and activities into the idea of a movement or field of social practice" (p. 25).

Defining adult education, then, depends to some extent upon where one stands or, in keeping with the theme of this chapter, what counts. Experiences as an adult learner, and experiences with planning, organizing, and perhaps teaching in an adult educational setting lead to varying understandings of the field. What is common to all notions of adult education is that some concept of adult undergirds the definition, and that the activity is intentional. Likewise, the adult educator is one who has "an educational role in working with adults" (Usher and Bryant, 1989, p. 2). Therefore, we define adult education as *activities intentionally designed for the purpose of bringing about learning among those whose age, social roles, or self-perception define them as adults.*

Clearly, our definition and several of the others included above reflect a broad-based perspective on what counts as adult education: it is virtually any activity for adults designed to bring about learning. Thus, all of the examples at the beginning of this section would be considered adult education. Furthermore, we would consider the aerobics instructor, nurse, private consultant, literacy worker, and community activist all to be engaged in adult education.

Historically, the term *adult education* was preceded by several other terms designed to capture what was seen as a new educational phenomenon (Stubblefield and Rachal, 1992). In the nineteenth century, the term *university extension* was imported from England, but its meaning was too narrow to capture what was evolving in North America. "Popular education" was promoted by some in the late 1800s not only to include university extension but also to reflect a concern with appealing to the masses. The term *home education* was promoted by Melvil Dewey, inventor of the book-cataloguing system, to reflect general self-improvement for adults.

Sporadic use of the term *adult education* began to appear in the last decade or two of the nineteenth century, becoming more popular by about 1900. Stubblefield and Rachal (1992) write that "the period from 1891 to 1916 can be regarded as the gestational period in the evolution of the phrase that would both encompass and to a significant degree displace most of its competitors" (p. 114).

Three events occurred after World War I that served to cement the usage of *adult education* as the preferred term: a British publication reviewing the status of adult education was published, the World Association for Adult Education was formed, and the Carnegie Corporation became actively involved in establishing the field of adult education (Stubblefield and Rachal, 1992).

The scope of activities that the term *adult education* covers has evolved over the years. Knowles (1977), who documented the broad history of the field, observed that adult education has typically emerged in response to specific needs, and that its growth has been episodic rather than steady. In the Colonial period, for example, adult education had a moral and religious imperative, whereas after the colonies became a nation, adult education was more focused on developing leaders and good citizens.

The modern era of adult education has been concerned with educating and retraining adults to keep the United States competitive in a global economic market. In addition, population trends such as growing ethnic diversity and the "graying" of North America; the shift from an industrial to a service- and information-based economy, which is displacing workers and creating a need for retraining and new careers; and technological advances are forces shaping adult education today.

Various responses to these challenges have contributed to defining the meaning and scope of adult education. For example, the term *human resource development* (HRD) has sprung into use in North America in reference to the training, education, and development of employees in the workplace. Likewise, *distance education* reflects many of the technological advances that allow instruction to take place between geographically separated teachers and adult students.

Currently, there are multiple and sometimes competing conceptions of what adult education encompasses. Rubenson (1989), for example, points out that North American adult education is most often defined in terms of learners and learning, thus giving it a particularly psychological orientation in which "the context of education is largely ignored" (p. 59). Others see the context mainly in terms of technical and economic imperatives and thus are most comfortable with a human resource development orientation. Still others, such as Cunningham (1989), want a social action and community focus to have more prominence.

How we position ourselves to view the field is crucial to what is included in adult education. "If we ask different questions, seek different information, or allow different boundaries," Cunningham writes, "we might define the education of adults broadly as a human activity, not a profession or a field seeking 'scientific' verification. We might look beyond institutions to the popular social movements, grass roots education, voluntary associations, and communities producing and disseminating knowledge as a human activity" (pp. 33–34).

Related Terms and Concepts

A number of terms and concepts are used by some people interchangeably with the term *adult education*. Some terms are being promoted as preferred substitutes for adult education, while others refer to specific forms of adult education; and some are more popular outside North America.

Considered an equivalent of the broadest definition of adult education, the term *continuing education* is growing in usage in North

America. Apps, in his book *Problems in Continuing Education* (1979), makes the case for adopting the term rather than *adult education* because "for many people, 'adult education' connotes 'catching up'" and is thus associated exclusively with adult basic education (p. 73); this association is underscored by much national and state legislation. Furthermore, the use of the term *continuing education* gets around the problem of defining "adult" and the use of the term *adult educator* (as opposed to *child educator*? Apps asks). Finally, adult education is seen in a restricted way by some as an extension of the public school system (Apps, 1979).

Perhaps because institutions of higher education have also used the term *continuing education* to mean evening and weekend degree-credit offerings for adults, and because the word *continuing* is associated with professionals staying updated and credentialed (continuing professional education), the term by itself has not caught on as a replacement for *adult education*. Rather, *adult and continuing education* seems to be the preferred usage. For example, an encyclopedia-type overview of the field of adult education has been published approximately every ten years since the 1930s. The titles of these "handbooks" have all contained the term *adult education*, until one was published in 1989 with the title *Handbook of Adult and Continuing Education*.

It was also in the 1980s that the major professional association for adult educators added the word *continuing* to its name. Similarly, the popular *New Directions* monograph series, originally titled *New Directions for Continuing Education*, underwent a name change in 1990 to become *New Directions for Adult and Continuing Education*; this was done in an effort to broaden the target audience for the publication. Finally, a 1990 reference book defining terms in the field is titled *An International Dictionary of Adult and Continuing Education* (Jarvis, 1990).

Other common terms in use in North America refer to specific forms or content areas of adult education and reflect specific purposes and goals. *Adult basic education* refers to instructional programs for adults whose basic skills (reading, writing, and computation) are assessed below the ninth-grade level. Adult basic education usually includes *adult literacy education,* which focuses on adults whose basic skills are fourth-grade level or below.

For those adults whose skills are above the eighth-grade level but who have not graduated from high school, the term *adult secondary education* is used. Adult secondary education includes the general education development, or GED, diploma (a high school diploma through examination), high school credit programs for adults, and external diploma programs. Finally, "English as a second language" (ESL) programs are for adults who are not native speakers of English.

Postsecondary institutions, including vocational-technical schools, community colleges, and four-year colleges and universities, use a variety of terms to refer to credit and noncredit activities that extend beyond the daytime programs serving students of traditional college age. *Continuing education,* mentioned above, is one such term; *general extension* and *university extension* are others; while *community services* (which usually refers to noncredit leisure courses and cultural activities, particularly in the community college setting) is yet another.

The term *extension* is also used by the Cooperative Extension Service (CES), a program funded at federal, state, and local levels with offices in most counties of each state. CES offers information and educational programs to all residents on topics such as homemaking, agriculture, youth, the environment, public policy, and so on (Blackburn, 1988; Forest, 1989).

Two other terms, *nontraditional education* (or *nontraditional study*) and *community education,* are commonly used in North America. Invented in North America and popularized by the Commission on Non-Traditional Study, *nontraditional education* refers to the variety of ways in which adults can receive credit toward a degree in higher education. These ways include transfer credit, credit for experiential learning, and credit by examination. External degree programs and completion programs for bachelor's degrees make use of these nontraditional credit options. *Community education* may refer to any formal or informal action-oriented or problem-solving education that takes place in the community, or it may refer to a specific movement "supported for many years by the Mott Foundation and dedicated to making neighborhood public schools centers for educational, cultural, and recreational activity for people of all ages" (Darkenwald and Merriam, 1982, p. 13).

International Terms

A number of terms referring to adult education are more commonly used outside of North America. *Lifelong learning* and *lifelong education* actually refer to a concept of education broader than adult education; both terms cast learning or education as a cradle-to-grave activity in which public schooling as well as adult and continuing education are important but not exclusive players. This concept requires a rethinking of a society's educational structure, the timing of compulsory education, and so on.

The United Nations Educational, Scientific and Cultural Organization (UNESCO) has taken the lead in promoting lifelong learning as a kind of master concept "denoting an overall scheme aimed both at restructuring the existing education system and at developing the entire educational potential outside the education system; [it] should extend throughout life, include all skills and branches of knowledge, use all possible means, and give the opportunity to all people for full development of the personality" (UNESCO, 1977, p. 2).

In the United States, the terms can be found in the literature and rhetoric of both general education and adult education, but not much in practice. The U.S. Congress actually passed the Lifelong Learning Act in 1976 but never appropriated funds to implement it. Worldwide, "lifelong learning" is beginning to take precedence over "lifelong education." This probably represents a general shift from thinking in terms of education to thinking in terms of learning—a shift reflected in 1985 in UNESCO's focusing "not on the right to be educated but on the right to learn" (Thomas, 1991a, p. 18).

In a recent analysis of the terms *lifelong education* and *adult education,* Wain (1993) points out that "the common identification of lifelong education with adult education" has had "detrimental consequences . . . for both" (p. 85). According to Wain, UNESCO's withdrawal of support for the lifelong education movement, coupled with the movement's lack of substantive theoretical contributions since 1979, have resulted in the movement apparently being "on its way out" (p. 93).

Education permanente is the French term for lifelong education and is sometimes used in Europe, as is *recurrent education,* which again refers to lifelong learning and education. Recurrent education, though, has the additional connotation of alternating periods of work, leisure, and education or study throughout a lifetime, as life events and changing circumstances dictate (Organization for Economic Co-operation and Development, 1973).

Three terms very popular internationally and growing in use in North America are *formal education, informal education,* and *nonformal education.* This tripartite classification of educational activities, most often associated with adult education, is accredited to Coombs (Coombs, with Prosser and Ahmed, 1973). *Formal education* refers to educational institutions including all levels of schools both private and public, as well as specialized programs offering technical and professional training. *Informal education* is generally unplanned, experience-based, incidental learning that occurs in the process of people's daily lives—learning something, for example, by perusing a magazine in a doctor's office, from casual conversation with friends, from watching television, and so forth.

Coombs defines *nonformal education* as "any organized educational activity outside the established formal system . . . that is intended to serve identifiable learning clienteles and learning objectives" (p. 11). A Bible-study class offered by a local church, or a first aid program given by the Red Cross, are examples of nonformal education, which has become an accepted category for international and community development activities (Ewert, 1989); it is also a rubric for community-based or community development efforts in North America (Hamilton and Cunningham, 1989).

Finally, some but not all writers align "popular education" with nonformal education. Jarvis (1990) defines *popular education* as follows: "A term widely used in Latin America, having the following connotations: education is a right of all people, even the masses who were excluded from the school system's benefits; education which is designed for the people by the people; an instrument in the ideological class struggle, radical and often revolutionary; and education which involves *praxis* inasmuch as the education learned is then put into practice in the class struggle" (p. 269). However, Jarvis notes that the term *popular education* can also refer to traditional adult education in Denmark, Greece, and elsewhere in Europe.

Practice-Related Terms

Our tour of the landscape of adult education in North America would not be complete if we did not point out some of the concepts and terms that have come to be associated with our field of practice. Two major concepts are *andragogy* and *self-directed learning*. *Andragogy* is a term imported by Knowles (1980b) from Europe; he defines it as "the art and science of helping adults learn"—in contrast to *pedagogy*, which refers to children's learning (p. 43).

The assumptions underlying andragogy characterize adult learners and have formed the basis for structuring learning activities with adults. The concept is continually debated in the literature (see, for example, Pratt, 1993); nevertheless, it underpins much of the writing about the practice of adult education. In Europe, and especially in Eastern Europe, andragogy not only encompasses adult education but also refers to social work and community organization or university departments of study (Jarvis, 1990).

Self-directed learning, another major concept in our field, can be traced back to early research and writing by Houle (1961), Tough

(1967 and 1979), and Knowles (1975). This body of work refers to that learning in which *"the learner chooses to assume the primary responsibility for planning, carrying out, and evaluating those learning experiences"* (Caffarella, 1993, p. 28, emphasis in original). Closely related is the notion of *learner self-direction*, which refers to personal characteristics that predispose adults toward self-directed learning. Both andragogy and self-directed learning are discussed in more detail in Chapter Seven.

Other terms commonly in use in the practice of adult education are *program*, *facilitator*, and *practitioner*. While schools and postsecondary institutions usually speak of "curriculum" to mean the content—usually in a particular sequence—that is envisioned for a group of students to learn, the preferred term in adult education is *program*. What is meant by this term is the total educational offerings of an institution or agency (an evening-school program, for example), activities designed for a particular clientele (an older-adult program), or a specific topical activity (an environmental-waste program). A program can consist of activities of varying time lengths, ranging from ongoing programs to semester-length offerings to one-hour workshops.

Rather than "teacher" or "instructor," adult educators prefer to use the word *facilitator*, which denotes a more collaborative, student-centered mode of interaction. Finally, *practitioner* refers to anyone involved at whatever level in the planning and implementation of learning activities for adults; the term is generally interchangeable with *adult educator*. Usher and Bryant (1989) suggest that a spectrum exists in terms of practitioners' "consciousness of having an educational role in working with adults." This continuum ranges from "the full-time 'professional' educator of adults [to] the individual whose vocational and non-vocational activities have repercussions for adult learning" (p. 2).

Therefore, the answer to the question "Who is an adult educator?" is quite broad and again reflects what "counts" to the person doing the defining. Whether or not one *identifies* oneself as an adult educator—or is even aware of the role—varies with the setting and level of professional preparation. (See Chapter Nine for a more thorough discussion of professional roles.)

Goals and Purposes

Most practitioners in adult education are so caught up in the every-day concerns of getting the job done that they rarely consider what they ultimately hope to accomplish. And many have not identified themselves as adult educators, even though they may be working with adults in an educative capacity. The goals and purposes of the activity thus tend to become aligned with specific content. The aerobics instructor, for example, probably thinks of physical fitness as the goal; the nurse educator, of increased medical knowledge; and the consultant, of training employees to be better managers.

However, if we consider the purpose or goal of our work from the broader perspective of adult education, we get some different answers. Looking at the overall goals and purposes of one's practice is one way of situating oneself in the field; it is also another way of asking what counts as adult education. In Colonial America, for example, the primary purpose of adult education was salvation; learning to read the Bible was the means. After the Revolutionary War, the need for an informed and enlightened citizenry to sustain and lead the new democratic republic became crucial. Thus, the moral and religious emphasis of the seventeenth and eighteenth centuries was eclipsed by civic education by the late 1800s.

Modern-day goals and purposes of adult education have been catalogued in various ways, from general and sweeping categorization to detailed typologies. Two general purposes of adult education identified by Lindeman ([1926] 1989) have remained central to the field. "Adult education," Lindeman wrote, "will become an agency of progress if its short-time goal of self-improvement can be made compatible with a long-time, experimental but resolute policy of changing the social order. Changing individuals in continuing adjustment to changing social functions—this is the bilateral though unified purpose of adult learning" (p. 104).

Whether individual development or social change should be the primary purpose of adult education is a source of tension and debate even today (Galbraith and Sisco, 1992). We'll revisit this issue in subsequent chapters of this book.

From a slightly different perspective, Knowles (1980b) speaks of the "mission" of adult education as satisfying the needs of individuals, institutions, and society. It is an adult educator's responsibility to "help individuals satisfy their needs and achieve their goals," the ultimate goal being "human fulfillment" (p. 27). An institution's needs, on the other hand, are to develop its constituency, improve its operational effectiveness, and establish "public understanding and involvement" (p. 35). Finally, the maintenance and progress of society requires "a crash program to retool . . . adults with the competencies required to function adequately in a condition of perpetual change" (p. 36).

A number of writers have presented what Rachal (1988) calls "content-purpose" typologies. These typologies suggest the type of content in each category, as well as "the purpose of that form of adult education" (p. 21). Interestingly, content-purpose typologies have changed little since Bryson (1936) published his typology more than sixty years ago. Table 1.1 displays seven typologies, each having four or five categories.

While Bryson's five purposes will be used as references for discussion, note that there is considerable overlap between and among typologies, regardless of any particular category's label.

"Liberal," the first purpose of adult education in Bryson's list, appears by the same label in Grattan's and Rachal's typologies, and in Darkenwald and Merriam's as "cultivation of intellect." This purpose refers to the study of the humanities and of the social and natural sciences. Knowledge is valued for its own sake, and the goal is to be an educated person. The Great Books discussion program we mentioned above would be an example of liberal adult education,

Table 1.1. Goals and Purposes of Adult Education.

Bryson (1936)	Grattan (1955)	Liveright (1968)	Darkenwald and Merriam (1982)	Apps (1985)	Rachal (1988)	Beder (1989)
Liberal	Liberal	—	Cultivation	—	Liberal	—
Occupational	Vocational	Vocational/ Occupational/ Professional	Personal and social improvement	Career development	Occupational	Facilitate change
Relational	Informational and Recreational	Self-Realization and Personal and Family	Individual self-acutalization	Personal development	Self-Help	Enhance personal growth
Remedial	—	—	—	Remedial	Compensatory	—
Political	—	Civic and social responsibility	Social transformation	Cultural criticism and social action	—	Support and maintain the good social order
—	—	—	Organizational effectiveness	—	—	Promote productivity
—	—	—	—	—	Scholastic	—

as would be courses of study in higher education or other settings that focus on humanities, social science, and the natural sciences. For example, Elderhostel and Learning-in-Retirement Institutes, both programs for older adults, include liberal arts courses as part of their curricula.

Work-related adult education, long a major thrust of the field, can be found explicitly as "occupational" (Bryson, Rachal), "vocational" (Grattan, Liveright), "career development" (Apps), or implicitly in Beder's "facilitate change" and the "personal improvement" component of Darkenwald and Merriam's scheme. This purpose of adult education is exemplified in job-preparation and skills-development courses, in on-the-job and workplace training, and in management training. Much of adult education in this arena goes by the "human resource development" (HRD) label. HRD or training is also a component of "organizational effectiveness" (Darkenwald and Merriam) and "promote productivity" (Beder).

Although not labeled as such, a third purpose in Bryson's typology also finds expression in all the others. "Relational" refers to programs in which personal growth is a priority, such as those that help develop effective relationships, provide leadership training, improve self-esteem or foster self-actualization efforts, and offer other learning related to home, family, and leisure. This is captured under Grattan's "informational" and "recreational," Liveright's "self-realization" and "personal and family," Darkenwald and Merriam's "individual self-actualization," Apps's "personal development," Rachal's "self-help," and Beder's "enhance personal growth."

Apps lists "remedial" and Rachal uses "compensatory" as functions of adult education, but this function, too, is inferred by categories in the other typologies. Examples of practice in which this purpose is inherent are adult basic education programs that help adults learn to read, high school completion programs, and some basic skills-development programs. In addition to the traditional literacy-related elements of the remedial category, Rachal includes special education for the developmentally disabled adult.

Bryson's fifth category, "political," refers to adult education activities related to citizenship responsibilities in a democracy. "In the political realm," wrote Bryson (1936), "educational activities are, first, providing for discussion of public questions; and second, adapting public documents and technical writings to help the ordinary citizen to understand" the "country's business" (p. 46). Recently, P. A. Miller (1995) proposed guidelines for adult educators to "recover" the field's civic mission. Examples of this include citizenship classes for immigrants, local public and community-based forums on issues of concern, and the National Issues Forum sponsored by the Kettering Foundation. Liveright calls this category "civic and social responsibility," and Beder means something similar with "support and maintain the good social order."

Apps and Darkenwald and Merriam present the civic function in its more radical version as "cultural criticism and social action" and "social transformation," respectively. This emphasis would include educational efforts that have a more radical agenda of empowering adults to bring about change, rather than fitting into the status quo. Highlander Research and Education Center in Tennessee, for example, has a long history of training community activists. Beder points out, however, that "mainstream" adult educators are generally supportive of the American system, and that unlike in many developing countries, "there has not been an extensive radical tradition that has sought to eliminate the current system and to replace it with another" (1989, p. 41).

Echoing Knowles's thinking (1980b) that part of the mission of adult education is to meet institutional needs, Beder's and Darkenwald and Merriam's typologies list "promote productivity" and "organizational effectiveness," respectively, as a goal of adult education. As Darkenwald and Merriam (1982) observe: "Adults employed by public and private agencies and organizations are involved in educational programs designed to achieve the organization's goals. In the private sector, organizational and employee development programs are ultimately aimed at realizing greater profit; in the public sector the aim is enhancing service to the public" (p. 64). Staff and employee development and training programs are commonplace examples of this purpose. Prior to the 1996 Summer Olympics in Atlanta, for example, all 38,000 employees of the Atlanta airport were given fifteen hours of training in how to better serve the Olympic visitors and future travelers.

Finally, a purpose of adult education found only in Rachal's typology is what he calls "scholastic," defined as graduate study and research in adult education. Universities and professional associations are the primary providers of programs in this area.

Several interesting observations can be made by standing back from these typologies and considering the changing sociohistorical context. First, there is the absence of any explicit moral or religious purpose, although Apps (1985) does note that this was an aim of adult education in early America. Second, personal growth and development (including liberal education) and occupational and career-related education have been constant goals of modern adult education. Third, the stability of personal and occupational goals contrasts somewhat with the political and civic-related purposes. In other words, while preserving the democratic society is still a powerful rationale for much of adult education, a more recent perspective (as in the goal of "social transformation") sees adult education as a force for challenging and changing the social structure. A fourth observation is the recognition in the more recent typologies of the growing prominence of institutions, especially business and industry, and their focus on training and human resource development.

Circling back to the beginning of this section on goals and purposes, readers might now consider what they are trying to effect through the practice they are engaged in. What is your best "match" with the purposes listed in Table 1.1? Is there a purpose to your activity that is not represented in these typologies? Is your purpose congruent with your immediate employer's or with the type of institution for which you work? Such inquiry is part of developing your philosophy of adult education (see Chapter Two).

Adult Education's Relationship to Education

The effort to describe what counts as adult education is tied up with the desire to establish a separate identity from other education. Adult education has thus tended to distance itself from K–12 and higher education and historically has had to struggle for resources, recognition, and legitimacy. It has been viewed as a marginal enterprise, expendable in times of financial exigency, something that is nice but not necessary to society's well-being. The struggle to "professionalize" adult education has been one of establishing an identity separate from that of K–12 and higher education—an identity that is distinct and powerful enough to command attention in national educational policy formation, as well as find professional space both in academia and the workplace.

While these issues are still very much present in the discourse of the field (see Chapters Four, Nine, and Eleven), some common ground has emerged within the last decade where the formal educational system and the formal sector of adult education might meet. Certainly all educators are concerned about responding in meaningful ways to the challenges posed by the global economy, by the shift to an information- and service-based society, and by fast developments in technology.

In *Beyond Education,* Thomas (1991a) discusses four challenges that require the concerted efforts of all levels of education. The first is *entry,* by which he means "strangers" entering the society, the most obvious group being children born into the society. Other entry challenges are newcomers to the host society, including immigrants, guest workers, and refugees. The second challenge is presented in terms of the life cycle *passages* of society's members. A major passage, of course, is becoming an adult, but there are other family-related (marriage, parenthood) and work-related (first job, career change, retirement) passages as well. Third, Thomas identifies *societywide changes* such as wars, epidemics, social movements, and so on that "touch everyone in a society . to varying degrees" (p. 81). The fourth challenge is what Thomas calls *exceptions*. These are people with physical, mental, and emotional disabilities who are found in every society and whose behavior "differs from the societal norm and for whom special provision therefore must be made" (p. 85).

Another area of common ground is the current critique of formal education in both the schooling and adult education literatures. Questions are being raised in both fields as to the role of formal education in maintaining the status quo, in perpetuating a class society, and in reinforcing the present power structure that mitigates against social change (Apple, 1993; Hayes and Colin, 1994; Rubenson, 1989).

At the same time, society's *informal* and *nonformal* means of educating its youth and adults are being examined from a number of angles. Rubenson (1989) observes that nonformal education, often touted as liberatory, can also reinforce society's divisions, depending on its goals. The educative power of the family, the community, and the mass media has been critically considered by school-based writers and those with an adult perspective. Reed and Loughran (1984), in their study of learning "beyond schools," point out that "many groups of youth, as well as adults . learn more effectively in nonformal out-of-school settings" (p. 5). They identify vocational training, learning from experience, internships, and apprenticeships as common vehicles for such learning. In addition, and "perhaps more important," they write, "is the collective learning of entire groups of people as they become involved in the power structures of society" (p. 5).

The common ground that all of education shares is in figuring out the most effective way to prepare members of a society to accommodate change, and how best to realize the society's stated values and goals. That may mean learning to "fit in," or it may mean learning to challenge a social structure that does not reflect desired goals. These stances are discussed in more depth in the next chapter. Viewing learning—and indeed education—as a lifelong endeavor provides a basis for educators from all arenas to work together. At the same time, adult education need not forfeit its distinctive characteristics, many of which we have examined in this chapter.

Summary

Perhaps more than anything else, adult education in North America is characterized by its diversity of programs, clienteles, and purposes. Delineating the scope of the adult education field is thus a formidable undertaking of which this chapter is only a beginning. Here we concentrated on (1) defining adult education and related concepts, (2) identifying some of the goals and purposes of adult education, and (3) sketching out adult education's relationship to education in general. We hope that you the reader have considered where you fit in, what you think adult education is, and what the purposes of your practice are.

Implicit in the many definitions of adult education as a field of practice is a distinction between education and learning, and a recognition of what it means to be an adult. For our definitions, a focus on the *adult* learner is crucial, as is the notion that the activity is being *purposefully* educative. We discussed continuing education and lifelong learning as commonly used synonyms for adult education, and we also reviewed concepts and terminology related to its practice.

The purposes of adult education, often codified into typologies, reflect some notions of the field's aims that are held in common, as well as some that reflect changing interests and concerns. Adult education for liberal, vocational, personal growth, and remedial needs has remained constant, while its role vis-à-vis society and the press of organizations needing educated workers have shaped other purposes.

Finally, the field's relationship to education in general is historically grounded in adult education's efforts to professionalize and establish a separate identity for itself. Some people believe that adult education could benefit from being more integrally related to K–12 and higher education, and we considered areas of common interest that could lay the foundation for cooperation among K–12, higher, and adult education systems.

2

Philosophical Perspectives

For the second year in a row, the small town of New York Mills, Minnesota, held a public meeting in 1994 to debate the question "Does life have meaning, and if so, what is it?" A panel of judges selected four finalists from 650 essay entries to debate the issue. A commodities trader from St. Paul and a Zen Buddhist monk from Iowa argued against the proposition; a fisherman-turned-teacher insisted that meaning can be found in the rhythms of human experience, and an artist argued that meaning lies in the web of relationships (*Atlanta Journal/Atlanta Constitution*, June 9, 1994, p. D7). That an entire town showed enough interest in this age-old question to stage a public debate speaks not only to the relevance of the issue but also to the willingness of adults to set aside time for a seemingly impractical and even frivolous exercise.

While the public nature of such an undertaking may be unusual, the search for meaning—the desire to make sense of our world and our experiences in it—is a commonplace motivation in human beings that leads to critical examination, analysis, and philosophizing. Unfortunately, "philosophy," and what people associate with that term, usually translates into something too theoretical, too abstract, too dense, or too rarefied to be discussed by the "average" person. Many perceive philosophizing as a waste of time with no practical payoff. However, it is something that adults do on a regular basis, even though it may be known under different labels.

The aim of philosophy is, after all, to explain, to make sense of the world. The word *philosophy* literally means "love of wisdom or knowledge," and philosophy probes the nature of human beings, the mind, the physical universe, truth, and moral reasoning. When we set goals, negotiate life transitions or crises, or examine the beliefs and values that form the basis of our particular lifestyle, we are trying to make sense of our lives. Many of us have looked up at a star-filled sky and wondered about our personal significance. Or we've made statements about what we want out of life, about what's important to us; many of us have questioned why we are doing something the way we are, or why we do it at all. When we approach these questions and concerns *systematically,* we're philosophizing.

When we ask questions, examine assumptions, and delineate principles or laws about, say, art or history—we are dealing with the philosophy of art or the philosophy of history; and so, too, when the subject is education. A philosophy of education is a conceptual framework embodying certain values and principles that renders the educational process meaningful. A philosophy of education typically includes discussions of terms, aims and objectives, curricula, methods, the teaching-learning transaction, the role of society, and the roles of student and teacher.

This chapter is about philosophy and adult education. It is about how to think about philosophy and its relevance to our practice, and it is also about "philosophies" of adult education. In other words, proceeding somewhat chronologically, we review various adult education philosophies. We make a case for why we need philosophy and how it contributes to understanding adult education as a professional field of practice; philosophy, after all, enables us to articulate the grounds for our actions, and it imbues us with a sense of why we do what we do. In addition, we suggest ways to engage in philosophizing about adult education.

Why Philosophize?

Adult educators are very busy people. Programs must be planned, facilities checked out, budgets balanced, deadlines met, meetings attended. Most of us have little if any time to spend thinking about the "why" behind what we do. And unless the task is to form a mission statement or develop a strategic plan, even fewer institutions make space for issue-oriented, philosophical discussions as part of their regular staff meetings. But whether we do it individually or in groups, informally or formally, there are a number of good reasons for reflecting on what we do.

First, becoming aware of our underlying values and assumptions provides guidelines for making decisions and setting policy. Suppose, for example, that your program places a high value on adults from all socioeconomic classes having access to learning opportunities. A commitment to this value would involve policies reflecting funding and availability of support services such as transportation and child care. Or perhaps your organization values acknowledging learning with some form of certification or accreditation. Decisions then must be made about what form this credentialing might take, such as awarding diplomas or giving continuing education units.

A second and somewhat related reason for examining our philosophy of adult education is that what we assume and value can directly affect curriculum and instruction. What do you and your coworkers believe about the adult learner whom you serve? What assumptions do you as an educator, trainer, or consultant make about the adult students that you work with? What do you assume to be true about learning in adulthood? What do you believe about the learning process? About the role of the teacher? The student? Furthermore, what do you believe about the goal or end purpose of your work as an adult educator? The curriculum and nature of instruction will dramatically differ, depending on whether you feel that learners should gain a certain body of knowledge, or that personal development is the goal, or that learners should become empowered to effect social change.

Understanding the assumptions under which you and others are working leads to a third benefit: the facilitation of interpersonal communication. Practitioners who serve on planning committees, advisory boards, and steering committees may often wonder why they make so little progress at times in dealing with issues of mutual concern. A trainer from the business world who wants a more productive workforce may have little in common with a community educator interested in social action. Understanding which assumptions lie behind each position is a first step in confronting—and perhaps negotiating—differences.

A fourth outcome of articulating a philosophical stance in our practice is that in so doing, we as adult educators can make a contribution to our field. This happens in several ways. Apps (1985) suggests that philosophizing "serves as continuing education's conscience, raising questions of an ethical and moral nature about various practices and procedures" (p. 8). Such a stance also separates professional adult educators from others working in the field. Professionals are aware of what they are doing and why they do it; they have an end, a vision, in mind as well as the means. It is this vision that makes sense out of the means—the daily activities of our practice.

A philosophical stance also contributes to the field in that it serves to unite theory and practice. In observing what we are doing and asking why we are doing it, we expose the mismatches, the disjunctions, the tensions between what the rhetoric says we should be doing and what we actually do. A good example of the field's advancing as a result of theory and practice mutually informing each other is in the area of adult learning. Knowles (1980b) proposed that adult learners have independent self-concepts and hence like to be self-directed in planning and evaluating their learning. He also suggested that adults are, by and large, internally motivated.

In practice, *some* adults are self-directed, some are not, and some are self-directed only in certain situations. We also know from practice that many adults are *externally* motivated—for example, when professionals must take courses to maintain certification, when an employer insists that an employee be retrained, when courts order traffic violators to take a class. The examination of practice vis-à-vis Knowles's principles has, in essence, refined the knowledge base of adult learning. Such engagements lead to the development of better theory, and simultaneously to a more informed practice.

In summary, there are good reasons for philosophizing or for systematically examining the principles, values, and assumptions that underlie the practice of adult education. Such an activity provides guidelines for making decisions and setting policy, affects both curriculum and instruction, facilitates good interpersonal communication, and contributes to the development of adult education as a professional field of practice.

Major Philosophical Approaches

For those interested in examining the values and assumptions underlying the practice of adult education, there are a number of frameworks or systems from which to begin. Within the philosophy of education, a number of competing schools of thought have developed regarding basic questions about the aims of education, the nature of teaching and learning, and so on. Some of these orientations, such as Deweyan progressivism or Freirian radicalism are already familiar to most educators who have had some formal career preparation.

Frameworks that are applicable to adult education in particular have been proposed by Apps (1973), Elias and Merriam (1994), and Beder (1989). Apps suggests viewing adult education from the philosophies of essentialism, perennialism, progressivism, reconstructionism, and existentialism, while Elias and Merriam's framework consists of the six orientations of liberal education, progressivism, humanism, behaviorism, radicalism, and philosophical analysis. Phenomenology, critical theory, and feminist theory are included in their discussions of humanism and radicalism.

Beder collapses various schools of philosophical thought into what he calls three "traditions": liberal-progressive, countercritique, and personal growth.

In a manner similar to that of Beder (1989), several philosophical approaches have been combined into three categories for presentation in this chapter: liberal-progressive, behaviorist-humanist, and critical. Technically, several of these approaches are not exactly "philosophies" in themselves; rather, they draw from specific philosophies—hence, we talk about "approaches" or "perspectives." The progressive education movement is lodged in the philosophy of pragmatism, for example, and behaviorism reflects the logical positivist worldview. We thus first discuss the philosophy that has influenced a particular approach to education, explain its application to education, and then discuss its particular manifestation in adult education. The emergence and subsequent prominence of each of these perspectives is somewhat chronological, although there is overlap and all are currently represented in adult education practice.

That philosophy is a dynamic and changing discipline subject to the sociocultural—and indeed, the political—context of the times is underscored by Lawson (1991): "Philosophy and education are intertwined with each other and with the cultural values of our society. Each reciprocally influences and is in turn influenced by the others. [A]dult education is produced by the sum of forces operating within society, and educational thinking is influenced by political philosophy as well as by theories of knowledge, theories of existence, and so on" (p. 289). Even the vocabulary we use to express ideas about the philosophy of adult education reflects this exchange. According to Lawson, "The terms do not have fixed immutable meanings; therefore, terms such as *adult education* remain perpetually fluid and systematically ambiguous. We catch their meaning only as snapshots in time, yet they reflect their origins either by retaining some of the original ethos or by reacting radically against it" (p. 290).

The various philosophical perspectives on adult education we review in this chapter reflect the fluidity and change brought about by the interaction of adult education with the sociohistorical context in which it takes place.

Ideas and Experience: Liberal and Progressive Perspectives

The oldest educational philosophy in Western societies is *liberal education*, also called *classical humanism* and *perennialism*. This philosophy traces its roots back to the Greek philosophers, early and medieval Christian theologians, and Enlightenment scholars such as Locke, Kant, and Hegel. The aim of education was to produce an intelligent, informed, cultured, and moral citizenry. The first expression of this philosophy in North America was in the Colonial colleges, where the curricula consisted exclusively of liberal studies (philosophy, ancient languages, fine arts, and religion).

Liberal education values dominated educational practice in the United States until the mid-nineteenth century. Adult education, like other areas of education, reflected this tradition. Benjamin Franklin's Junto, a discussion group whose members wrote essays on politics, philosophy, and ethics, was one of the earliest forms, eventually merging with the American Philosophical Society (Merriam, 1979). Other examples of adult education reflecting liberal education philosophies were the establishment of Lowell Institute in Boston, Cooper Union and Bread Winner's College in New York, the national Lyceum Movement, and Chautauqua (Knowles, 1977). Other examples include the People's Institute in New York City, Meiklejohn's Experimental College at the University of Wisconsin, and the San Francisco School of Social Studies (Stubblefield and Keane, 1994). All of these involved reading books and participating in study groups, lectures, and courses in philosophy, religion, science, literature, the arts, and economics. Then and now, a liberal adult education perspective values the acquisition of knowledge, the development of a rational perspective, and the ability to analyze critically.

Today, the prominence of adult liberal education has been eclipsed by other orientations that are more congruent with contemporary issues and concerns. Nevertheless, there is still evidence of this tradition in the Great Books Programs, in college liberal arts curricula, in continuing education programs, and in community-based programs sponsored by libraries, museums, and institutes of higher education. For example, Elderhostel services and Learning-in-Retirement Institutes for older adults are sometimes held on college campuses.

There are also those who continue to espouse a liberal philosophy in education and adult education. Adler, who was instrumental in the establishment of the Great Books Program, in 1982 published a manifesto of sorts promoting the need for educating people in the liberal tradition, which Adler thought was the best preparation for lifelong learning. Bloom (1987), in his best-seller *The Closing of the American Mind,* argues for a liberal education that centers on reading the classics. Likewise, Hirsch, Kett, and Trefil's *Cultural Literacy* (1987) is concerned with what knowledge one needs from the Western cultural tradition to be deemed "literate" in today's world. While both of these books specifically address undergraduate curricula, their perspective and the subsequent debates over appropriate curricula have impacted the growing number of adults returning to higher education. The position the books take may also raise questions for adult educators in other settings. What is the appropriate curriculum for adults in formal or informal educational settings? How do adults best develop critical-thinking skills? Is familiarity with cultural classics necessary to being an educated adult?

A more direct contemporary influence on liberal adult education is from British philosophers Lawson (1975, 1982) and Paterson (1979, 1984). In analyzing the concepts of education, adult, and adult education, these philosophers come to the conclusion that education is inherently neutral and that the aim of education is to transmit knowledge that is "educationally worthwhile" (Paterson, 1979, p. 94). According to Paterson, what is educationally worthwhile is, for the most part, traditional liberal studies. The role of the teacher is to decide what is worthwhile and to transmit it to students. These views are more accepted in Great Britain—where adult education is defined more narrowly as liberal education—than in the United States.

Beginning in the mid-nineteenth century, the emergence of science and the scientific method, industrialization, and urbanization mandated a new approach to education—one that was more responsive to a growing industrial society. The new approach, loosely referred to as the *progressive education movement,* drew from the philosophy of pragmatism, which placed more value in knowledge derived from observation and experience than from tradition and authority. The dimensions of pragmatism that were particularly appealing to educators and politicians were (1) the acceptance of empirical rationality for understanding and solving social problems; (2) the reliance on experience rather than authority for one's source of knowledge; and (3) the allowance of social action and social reform as a legitimate concern of politicians, educators, and philosophers. By the turn of the century, according to Elias and Merriam (1994), "with the emergence of science and the growth of the new industrial society after the Civil War, the debate between the defenders of liberal education and the advocates of a more progressive and pragmatic education grew more intense. Secondary education became more vocationally oriented as the curriculum was expanded to include vocational and life-related subjects. At the same time, progressive education began to dominate the national scene" (p. 19).

The most eloquent and widely known advocate for the application of pragmatism to education was John Dewey. He was able to translate these new perspectives into concrete educational goals and programs and also to "place education at the very heart of social reform" (Elias and Merriam, 1994, p. 49). From Dewey and others emerged a philosophy of education, the major principles of which found expression in adult education. Those principles are

- A broadened view of education that goes well beyond liberal education

- A focus on learners and their needs and experiences rather than on predetermined content

- The use of scientific methodology incorporating problem-solving, activity, and experience-based approaches to instruction

- A shift from teacher as authority figure to teacher as facilitator of learning

- Education as an instrument of social action and social change.

The progressive movement in the United States coincided with the development of the adult education field, and for this reason has had a pervasive impact on adult education. From the 1930s on, many of the architects of the field, such as Eduard Lindeman, Ruth Kotinsky, Dorothy Canfield Fisher, Harry and Bonaro Overstreet, Alain Locke, Malcolm Knowles, and Cyril Houle have been profoundly influenced by the ideals of progressivism.

Examples of progressive adult education can be found in many forms, including citizenship programs, community education, cooperative extension courses, many adult basic education approaches, civic education programs (such as public-issues forums), the New School for Social Research, and many programs of the American Association for Adult Education and the Adult Education Association of the United States of America. Indeed, many contemporary adult educators espouse the principles of progressive education outlined above, as do numerous adult education programs.

Lindeman, who was directly influenced by Dewey, is probably the most prominent proponent of progressive adult education. His book *The Meaning of Adult Education*, published in 1926—the same year that the American Association for Adult Education was founded—continues to be a standard resource for articulating the philosophy of contemporary adult education. For Lindeman, the aim of adult education was to improve the individual and society: "changing individuals in continuous adjustment to changing social functions—this is the bilateral though unified purpose of adult learning" (p. 105).

Life experiences play a significant role in adult learning. Lindeman's "conception" of adult education "points toward a continuing process of evaluating experiences" (p. 85). He advocated a "situation" approach to learning and stated that "the best teaching method is one that emerges from situation experiences" (p. 115). "Every adult person finds himself in specific situations with respect to his work, his recreation, his family-life, et cetera—situations which call for adjustments. Adult education begins at this point" (p. 122). And like Dewey, Lindeman (Gessner, 1956) saw a new role for the teacher: "He is no longer the oracle who speaks from the platform of authority, but rather the guide, the pointer-out, who also participates in learning in proportion to the vitality and relevance of his facts and experiences" (p. 160).

Writers after Lindeman have reinforced the applicability of progressive education's principles to adult education. Bergevin (1967) called for a problem-centered approach to adult education, which was instrumental in the civilizing process and essential for preserving a democratic way of life. Knowles (1980b), who has had a tremendous influence on adult education, developed his theory of andragogy out of both humanistic and progressive philosophies. As Pratt (1993) observes, andragogy rests upon Knowles's belief in "the ideals of a democratic citizenship and the belief that civic and democratic virtue would arise out of natural self-fulfillment through adult education" (p. 20).

The linking of liberal and progressive philosophies of education in this section reflects their convergence in adult education. Lawson (1991) comments that contemporary adult education "emerged as individualistic, libertarian, egalitarian, and democratic in its main outlines. The picture that emerged did of course represent a whole series of ideas and values drawn from the tradition that gave it birth.

It was a picture uniquely suited to liberal democratic societies as they had then developed" (p. 292).

Liberal and progressive philosophies also share some similar goals. Both value the development of critical-thinking skills, as well as an informed and cultured citizenry who can provide leadership in maintaining and enhancing a democratic society. Where they differ is in the means they use to achieve these ends. Instructional methods, curriculum content, and the role of teacher and learner clearly differ in these two orientations.

Performance and Potential: Behaviorist and Humanist Perspectives

Behaviorism is a psychological theory that draws from a number of philosophical systems, most notably *logical positivism*, which is characterized by the view that reality exists external to the knower and can be known through the senses, and that this reality is observable and measurable. Founded by Watson in the 1920s and developed into a scientific system by Skinner between the 1930s and 1970s, behaviorism is concerned with the overt, observable behavior of animals and humans.

Behaviorists believe that human actions are the result of prior conditioning and the way in which a person's external environment is arranged. Emotions, feelings, intellect, and so on are the means by which humans rationalize their responses to environmental stimuli. Much of the early research on adult learning was conducted from a behaviorist perspective, the most notable being Thorndike's (1928) studies.

It was Skinner (1974), however, who brought behaviorism to the forefront of American education. The now familiar concepts of reinforcement and operant conditioning were readily applied by Skinner and others to learning and hence to the entire educational enterprise. Skinner also provided a philosophical base for his psychology of behaviorism. In *Beyond Freedom and Dignity* (1971), Skinner proposes that by arranging the environment to elicit desired responses, we can control human behavior and thereby develop a better society—and ultimately ensure the survival of the human species. Skinner's philosophy sees personal freedom as an illusion: the "struggle for freedom is not due to a will to be free, but to certain behavioral processes characteristic of the human organism, the chief effect of which is the avoidance of or escape from the so-called 'aversive' features of the environment" (1971, p. 42). In Skinner's philosophy, a carefully designed educational system is key to survival.

Many concepts and practices in education (including adult education)—such as behavioral objectives, accountability, competency-based curricula, instructional design models, and some program-planning and evaluation models—are behaviorist in nature. Tyler's *Basic Principles of Curriculum and Instruction*, first published in 1949 and still in print today, is a good example of a planning model from a behaviorist orientation. Most contemporary program-planning models have drawn heavily from Tyler (see Sork and Busky, 1986). Furthermore, at least two arenas in which adult education takes place—business and industry and the military—work largely out of a behaviorist model in the design, implementation, and evaluation of training. It is in fact telling that education in these settings is referred to as "training." Much of the burgeoning literature in human resource development is firmly rooted in a behaviorist philosophy (see, for example, Carnevale, Gainer, and Villet, 1990; Jacobs, 1987; Nadler and Nadler, 1989).

Like liberal philosophy, humanism as a philosophy draws from the same Greco-Roman thinkers, from the Italian Renaissance, and from the Enlightenment scholars of the eighteenth century. Unlike liberal philosophy, however, humanism is a very broad philosophy that has been able to incorporate a number of expressions and themes over the years, including scientific humanism, Christian humanism, Marxist humanism, and existentialism. This ability to absorb several emphases has led to the popularity of humanism as a philosophy for formulating educational practice.

Drawing heavily from the philosophy of humanism, humanistic psychology emerged as a challenge to behaviorism's reign in the early decades of the twentieth century. Known generally as the "third force," humanistic psychology objected to the deterministic perspective of human behavior favored by behaviorism and Freudian psychoanalytic theory. By the mid-1950s, writings by Maslow, Rogers, Buhler, and Bugental—all prominent psychologists—had established humanistic psychology's view of human nature and learning. Philosophy and psychology from a humanist perspective came together midcentury with the codification of basic principles and tenets in the *Humanist Manifesto I and II*, and in the principles delineated by the Association for Humanistic Psychology (Elias and Merriam, 1994).

Assumptions common to both humanistic philosophy and psychology are as follows. First, human nature is intrinsically good. Human beings are free and autonomous creatures who exercise choice in determining their behavior. Humanism also emphasizes the notion of the *self*—a self that has the potential for growth and development, for self-actualization. Finally, the focus on self does not mean self-centeredness; a person has the responsibility to develop to the fullest, which in turn contributes to the good of humanity in general.

These tenets mesh particularly well with American democratic values, which emphasize independence, individualism, and self-fulfillment. The translation of these humanistic assumptions into education, primarily by Rogers (1969, 1983), has resulted in the shaping of contemporary adult education into a humanism-based practice.

When applied to education, and to adult education in particular, humanistic assumptions lead to a focus on developing the potential of the learner; indeed, the development of persons is an oft-expressed goal of the entire enterprise of adult education. Further, humanistic education is learner-centered because the view assumes that learners are internally motivated, can identify their own needs, and can make decisions about content, instructional method, and evaluation. The teacher is a *facilitator* of students' learning, not an authoritative dispenser of information. The learning transaction necessitates affective as well as cognitive involvement; consequently, learning has an impact not just on the behavior but also on the attitudes and personality of the learner. To effect this involvement, instructional techniques that are experiential, nonthreatening, and collaborative work best.

Many adult educators research and write from a humanist perspective. Probably the most prominent writer in the field is Malcolm Knowles, whose work on self-directed learning, groups, and andragogy are clear expressions of humanistic psychology. Andragogy is Knowles's charter for adult learning. It consists of assumptions about the learner and explains how those assumptions translate into practice.

In an essay titled "Andragogy After Twenty-Five Years," Pratt (1993) finds that andragogy is based on the humanistic values of placing the individual at the heart of the learning transaction, of believing in the goodness of human nature and the potential for growth and fulfillment, and of valuing autonomy and self-direction. "Clearly," Pratt concludes, "andragogy is saturated with the ideals of individualism and entrepreneurial democracy" (p. 21).

Andragogy and self-direction in learning have come to define much of what is considered unique to adult education. Self-directed learning has, in and of itself, evolved into a major thrust of research and theory-building in adult education, and its predominant orientation is humanistic (Brockett and Hiemstra, 1991; Caffarella, 1993).

With its broad philosophical and psychological base, humanistic adult education has seen several other recent expressions in the literature. McKenzie, drawing from humanism, liberal education, and existentialism, wrote two books presenting a philosophical framework for adult education (1978, 1991). In the earlier work, McKenzie suggests that adult education can effect a courageous, Promethean spirit in individual learners. He offers seven mostly humanistic principles about the goals of adult education. In his 1991 book, McKenzie proposes that the ultimate goal of adult education is for adults to construct a worldview that is personally meaningful. Adults can do this on their own, "but insofar as any educational experience contributes to a person's interpretive understanding of the world, education is involved in worldview construction" (p. 109).

Sometimes considered a separate school of philosophy, *phenomenology* has emerged as another perspective on adult education. Like McKenzie, Stanage (1987) offers the field a way of thinking about adult education—in this case, from the perspective of investigating various phenomena central to the field using the "tools" of phenomenological analysis. It is in his focus on feelings, consciousness, and experiences of the adult learner that Stanage expresses a humanistic orientation.

Finally, Jarvis's writing on types of learning and paradoxes of learning can be seen to draw from humanism as well as from existentialism and critical social theory. He writes, for example that "teaching and reflective learning and human growth and development are all facilitated in the process of genuine human interaction. Teaching is a humanistic enterprise, and only in human relationships is it possible to establish the best conditions for human growth" (1992, p. 245).

In the previous section of this chapter, we grouped together liberal and progressive educational philosophies because of their similarities and their emergence in the earlier periods of adult education. By contrast, the contemporary philosophies of behaviorism and humanism are more sharply differentiated from each other in their views of reality, human nature, and learning. Consequently, their manifestation in education and in adult education practice is quite different.

Critical Philosophy

The emergence of a critical or radical philosophical framework in American adult education can be dated to the late 1960s and early 1970s in the writings of Paulo Freire and Ivan Illich. Their work is considered "radical in the political sense of utilizing education to bring about social, political, and economic changes in society" (Elias and Merriam, 1994, p. 139).

A radical perspective draws heavily from the views of Karl Marx, who maintained that capitalism produces a class structure wherein the ruling class owns the means of production and thus has control over—and in fact exploits—the working class. To bring about a more egalitarian (what Marx called "classless") society, revolutionary change in social, political, and economic structure must occur.

Most societies use institutionalized education to reinforce and perpetuate the status quo—that is, the power arrangements and class structure in place. This line of thinking led Illich (1970) to call for the deschooling of society, and prompted Ohliger to mount an attack against mandatory adult education (Elias and Merriam, 1994).

Critical philosophies share with progressivism a commitment to social change. However, unlike progressives, who base their view on the assumption that the system of democracy is basically good and that change can be brought about by modifying the system, those with critical views tend to see capitalistic and democratic perspectives as fundamentally flawed. The critical perspective, then, holds that change can best occur when the existing system is abandoned and replaced with a different perspective.

The most eloquent proponent of the radical position was, and still is, the Brazilian educator Paulo Freire. Maintaining that education can be used to effect radical social change and liberate (as well as domesticate and oppress), Freire has had a profound influence on adult education worldwide. Freire's educational philosophy can be found in a number of publications (1970, 1973, 1985; see also Freire and Faundez, 1989; Shor and Freire, 1987), and is summarized by Beder: "Freire (1970) believes that the oppressed lack critical consciousness of the forces that control their lives, and lacking that consciousness, they are powerless to redress the oppression that dominates their lives. The role of adult education is, through dialogue with learners, to facilitate acquisition of critical consciousness. Once learners become conscious of the forces that control their lives, they become empowered, and empowerment leads to action" (p. 47).

Two recent works drawing from a Marxist base are by Inkster (1985) and Youngman (1986). Inkster's work has a historical focus on mechanics' institutes, while Youngman looks at restructuring contemporary adult education. Youngman finds Freire's philosophy and pedagogy too broad-based and eclectic to guide adult education practice; he instead proposes a socialist pedagogy based on an explicit Marxist framework wherein "general knowledge and technical expertise" are acquired to "reorganise production and society in a fully democratic way" (p. 197).

A critical philosophical stance also draws from critical theory and feminist theory, both of which acknowledge their linkages to Freirian concepts of oppression, liberation, and empowerment. In addition, both look to society and how it is structured to understand how certain individuals come to be in more powerful positions than others. Both are interested in finding ways to empower individuals and groups to change the oppressive conditions of their lives. While critical theory focuses more on economics and the institutions of society, feminist theory emphasizes interlocking systems of sex, race, and class in analyzing assumptions and power relationships that serve to oppress and control women.

When applied to adult education, critical theory's main thrust has been to critique the field's growing preoccupation with technical competence at the expense of social action. For example, C. Griffin (1983, 1987) suggests that instead of defining itself in terms of needs, designs, strategies, and structures, adult education should define itself in terms of the philosophical and political ideals that commit workers to the field in the first place.

Collins (1991) also laments the field's being sidetracked into the "ideology of technique," and he calls for adult educators to be politically involved: "A critical practice of adult education provides a context where shared commitments towards a socially more free, just, and rational society will coalesce. If these shared concerns are to drive a transformative pedagogy, . . . conventional notions of professionalization will have to be set aside in favour of a vocation that seeks to work directly with . . . popular constituencies" (p. 119). Pietrykowski (1996) argues that adult educators must be "attuned to the various ways in which power is deployed through their own discourse about particular discipline-specific knowledge" (p. 82).

A practical illustration of critical theory in the context of adult literacy can be found in deMarrais (1991). Using the case study of "John," she explains how John's socioeconomic background and his early experiences with schooling resulted in his being functionally illiterate at age thirty-five. "Critical theory," she writes, "takes the burden of school failure from individual students and looks to other reasons for these failures" (p. 17).

Feminist theory, which includes a diverse range of views, is also influencing philosophical thinking in adult education. Indeed, elements of humanistic psychology, radical thought, and critical theory can be found in various feminist writings. Some writers, such as Hart (1992), focus on the structured nature of power relations in society that results in women being marginalized; others emphasize the individual woman and how women come to be empowered. Whether the analysis is from a societal or an individual frame, the key is a critical stance toward women's experience.

Feminist pedagogy explores these issues from the context of education. In adult education, a number of writers have examined curricula and instructional practices in light of women's experiences and have suggested ways to enhance women's learning (Blundell, 1992; Hayes, 1989; Hayes and Colin, 1994; Tisdell, 1993a, 1995).

Critical theory and feminist theory as parts of the critical philosophical perspective represent the most recent thinking and writing in adult education. They present the field with provocative analyses of our practice and call attention to some of the assumptions under which the growing enterprise of adult education operates. In a sense they stretch and extend, yet underscore Freire's notions of oppression and empowerment.

Yet another perspective beginning to have an impact on adult education—and one that draws from a number of philosophical frameworks, including critical theory and feminist epistemology—is *constructivism*. Sharing the reaction of Gestalt psychologists against behaviorists who reduce a phenomenon to its parts *(reductionism)*, constructivists believe that the whole is greater than the sum of its parts. Rather than being a single unified theory, though, constructivism is "a cluster of related perspectives that are united in their underlying view of the world" (Candy, 1991, p. 254).

Phillips (1995), for example, sketches contributions to constructivism from science and math education, cognitive science, feminist writings, Kuhn's work on scientific revolutions and paradigms, Piaget's theory of cognitive development, and Dewey's and James's ideas on knowledge construction. He compares constructivism with "a secular religion," and states that "as in all living religions, constructivism has many sects" (p. 5).

What all these strains of constructivism have in common is the notion that reality can be known only subjectively (a moderate constructivist view) or that reality apart from the knower does not exist (a more radical view). Knowledge is the meaning that people make out of their experiences. Individuals construct meaning, but cultures are also socially constructed realities. Some constructivists are more concerned with perception and cognitive activity, others with affective domains, and still others with sociopolitical constructions of knowledge.

Constructivism has recently captured the interest of K–12 educators, and we are beginning to see it framing some of the thinking in adult education. As Phillips (1995) observes, "[T]he educational literature on constructivism is enormous, and growing rapidly" (p. 5). Candy's book (1991) on self-directed learning is also from a constructivist perspective. "Learning," Candy writes, is "an active process of *constructing* a system of meanings and then using these to *construe* or interpret events, ideas, or circumstances. As such, the constructivist view of learning is particularly compatible with the notion of self-direction, since it emphasizes the combined characteristics of active inquiry, independence, and individuality in a learning task" (p. 278, emphasis in original).

Mezirow's theory (1991a) of perspective transformation, with its focus on meaning-making and individual growth and development, also draws from both constructivism and humanistic psychology (see Chapter Six).

To summarize, constructivism and the critical perspective are challenging our thinking about what we know and how we know it. They have not yet had a major impact on practice in the field— at least in North America, where the actual practice of adult education is characterized more by the other philosophies we reviewed in this chapter. Examples of liberal-progressive and behaviorist-humanist philosophies are readily identifiable. This is not at all surprising, given the value that our society places on an educated citizenry, a democratic way of life, individualism and personal development, and efficiency and accountability.

Engaging in Philosophical Thinking

So far in this chapter, we have presented (1) a rationale for the importance of engaging in philosophical thinking and (2) a review of several existing philosophical frameworks, any one of which a practitioner might adopt as a personal philosophy of adult education. More commonly, one might operate from an eclectic position, choosing compatible aspects of different theories to explain and guide practice. There are even inventories available to assist adults in this process (O'Neil, 1981; Zinn, 1990). Particularly helpful is Zinn's Philosophy of Adult Education Inventory (PAEI) (Zinn, 1990). Based on the schools of philosophy outlined in Elias and Merriam (1994), PAEI is designed for adult education practitioners who want to identify their personal philosophy of education and compare it with prevailing philosophies.

Working from existing schools of thought has its drawbacks, however. As Apps (1985) has observed, this approach "can prevent analysis and original thought. Once one reads through a description of these various philosophies, the tendency is to try to fit one's own philosophy into one of these established philosophies. Once one has done so, the inclination is to become comfortable with this new-found intellectual home and stop questioning and challenging and constantly searching for new positions. We cannot retreat into someone else's philosophy as a kind of storm cellar that protects us from facing our practice head on" (pp. 72–73).

As an alternative, Apps suggests a process in which we first identify beliefs we hold about adult education; we then search for contradictions among our beliefs. The next step is to try to uncover the sources of our beliefs, such as personal experience or the authority of others. Finally, we evaluate our beliefs, considering which ones to maintain and which ones we might want to change. This "belief analysis process" puts us in touch with our own implicit philosophy of adult education.

Apps (1985) provides some additional concrete activities for engaging in a philosophical analysis. We can examine the assumptions that underlie our own or someone else's practice, clarify definitions, search for metaphors, or examine slogans. Hiemstra (1988b) suggests a similar process using a "Personal Philosophy Worksheet." This worksheet asks you to identify, for example, your beliefs about reality and the nature of being human, as well your views about professional practice, including its aims, method, and content.

Once we are comfortable with articulating some of the beliefs and values we hold about our practice, we might go a step further and *critically* reflect on the origin of these beliefs and how we have come to adopt them. The critical school of philosophy offers us a model of some of the questions and issues we might raise. How have our positions in organizations and social structures defined our values? What part do power and oppression play in how we define the world? How has adult education's historically marginalized status affected our stance vis-à-vis national educational policy? How has the drive to professionalize colored our values? Connecting our personal views to the larger sociohistorical context may lead to a richer and deeper understanding of why we do what we do in our practice.

A final suggestion for engaging in philosophical inquiry is to examine some of the ethical dilemmas that arise in practice settings. Ethics is in fact a branch of philosophy that deals with moral reasoning and moral behavior. Since ethical behavior is based on values, a discussion of ethical issues can serve to uncover personal values and beliefs. Articulating one's values provides a starting point for formulating a philosophy.

There are any number of ethical issues in adult education that could stimulate this kind of inquiry. Singarella and Sork (1983) and Brockett (1988a) have identified the areas of program planning, marketing, administration, evaluation, the teaching-learning transaction, and research as fraught with questions of ethical conduct. In a study of adult education practitioners and their ethical concerns, McDonald and Wood (1993) conclude that "the ethical dilemmas cited by practitioners in the study as examples of what they encounter are dramatic testimony to the profound and varied ethical issues that they face" (p. 256). The authors call for "more dialogue (and more urgent dialogue) among practitioners locally and in the professional organizations about ethical problems, ethical practice, and the roles that codes of ethics can play" (p. 256).

Our experiences in working with learners attempting to sort out their philosophy of adult education suggest that the best place to begin is with situations, incidents, or issues from everyday practice. What tensions have you felt with colleagues, for example? What policies have been difficult to formulate? When have you needed to make a choice between several courses of action? What has been the point beyond which you refuse to compromise in a given situation?

Any such incident can be examined for the underlying assumptions, the hidden agendas, the beliefs that may have structured your and others' responses. Bringing these to the forefront and reflecting on them begins the process of articulating individual philosophies. It is the premise of this chapter that reflecting on what we do ultimately leads to more informed and perhaps better practice.

Summary

The practice of adult education does not happen in a vacuum. It occurs in a context that manifests certain beliefs and that values certain behaviors over others. Understanding what those beliefs and values are can only lead to more informed and reflective practice. In this chapter, we have presented a rationale for engaging in philosophical thinking, reviewed a number of philosophical frameworks already in use, and suggested strategies for thinking philosophically.

Attending to the assumptions, beliefs, and values that we hold can lead to more informed decision making, to improved design of curricula and instruction, to better communication with fellow educators, and to the development of the field itself through offering a vision of where adult education as a field is going.

In this chapter, we outlined several perspectives on, or approaches to, adult education derived from various philosophies and grouped them together in a loosely chronological order. Liberal-progressive adult education emerged first, followed by behaviorist-humanist. Then came the critical perspective, which is receiving growing attention today.

Finally, we presented two general strategies for engaging in philosophical thinking: practitioners can work from existing schools of philosophy, or they can inductively identify or develop a uniquely personal philosophy of adult education.

3

Perspectives on the Past

As we discussed in the previous chapter, philosophy can be an invaluable tool for understanding the diversity of adult education and helping each of us to better understand where we fit into the field. In a similar way, an understanding of the past can help us gain a perspective on how adult education has reached its current state and consider its possibilities for the future.

The history of adult education is filled with rich stories. Sometimes these stories are about situations in which the human spirit is able to overcome great obstacles because of individuals or organizations committed to the education of adults. Other tales document shortcomings of society—and often of adult education itself—in addressing inequities and injustices that are a very real part of the American experience.

Collectively, these stories give us perspectives on our past, which can help us understand that adult education has not developed in a vacuum. Instead, its history has unfolded over four centuries and is inextricably linked to the history of our society at large. As such, the story is laden simultaneously with joy, pain, victory, defeat, glory, and struggle.

What value does an understanding of history hold for contemporary adult education? As Whipple (1964) has stated, "History deals with the past—it is an attempt to describe, organize, and analyze the experience of mankind in a way which will make it meaningful to the present" (p. 201). Whipple goes on to suggest that two major purposes for making history a part of the study of adult education are that (1) historical research has contributed to the knowledge base of adult education, and (2) history can be used as a tool to improve practice. We believe that while the first use has value for enriching the field's body of knowledge, the second use is relevant to anyone who wishes to seriously engage in the practice of adult education. Whipple states that history can provide the adult educator with "a useful supplementary discipline or tool" that can contribute to more effective practice.

More recently, Long (1990) argues that a knowledge of history has two kinds of pragmatic value for adult education. One type of value relates to experience; here, "a sense of history helps in the development of principles that extend beyond mere impressions of current facts," and it enhances practice "by suggesting what has worked, or not worked, in practice before, why it did or did not work and options or alternatives for consideration" (p. 7). Another pragmatic value is that history can be useful in understanding trends in adult education by helping educators "recognize [the] past in the present form" (p. 8).

Stubblefield (1991b) takes the discussion further by suggesting that the value of history becomes clear when it is viewed as a way of learning. He goes on to describe history's unique tasks as follows: "(1) [T]o explicate why the present arrangements, structures, and provisions exist, (2) to probe into the social and ideological movements of the past that are expressed in present activities, and (3) to seek to understand the origins, processes, and dynamics of educational change" (p. 325).

Perhaps the most compelling case for understanding our past is presented by Allison (1995) in this observation: "The point is that who we are as humans, our very concept of reality, is determined by our histories, by what the past has handed down to us. And those who are most ignorant of their history are the most controlled by it because they are the least likely to understand the sources of their beliefs. They are the most likely to confuse their inherited prejudices with Truth" (p. xiv).

To have a historical perspective on the development of adult education is to have a perspective that will facilitate understanding of who we are and where we fit into the mosaic that is contemporary adult education. As Welton (1993) notes, "Those of us who think and write about the history of adult education are swept up like everybody else in a maelstrom of contestation, questioning, doubt and revisionism. We are literally being forced to be self-reflective and self-critical. What are historians of adult education actually doing? What are we choosing to write about? What kinds of stories are we telling? To what use are we putting our stories?" (p. 135)

The overall purpose of this chapter, then, is to examine the value of history as a way to critically reflect on who we have been and where we have come from in order to better understand the possibilities of what we can become (Wilson and Melichar, 1994). Similarly, history can be used to reflect on the meaning of current practices. While it would be tempting to review the historical development of adult education in the United States, it would be difficult to do justice to such a broad topic in a single chapter. Those readers who seek a comprehensive history of the field should examine other sources (see, for example, Knowles, 1977, 1980a; Stubblefield and Keane, 1994; Kett, 1994).

In this chapter, we have instead opted to highlight *aspects* of the past that can lead to greater understanding of and appreciation for the history of the field. To accomplish this, we will explore several questions relative to the scope of adult education history, and we will follow this with an examination of three potential benefits that can be derived from an understanding of the field's historical development. Throughout the chapter, we will refer to a wide range of historical sources. In this way, readers should gain an appreciation for the value of adult education's history.

Understanding the Scope of Adult Education's History

The history of adult education is very rich, yet it is often difficult to understand. Most people who enter the field come with a limited background in history. Because of its complexity, and because scholars and students have often overlooked the potential of history for informing the contemporary field, the topic is often minimized or neglected in the study of adult education. It is our belief that history provides an invaluable source of ideas and insights. Exploring the following questions can help us gain a greater understanding of the past:

- What is the object of study?

- How does interpretation shape historical understanding?

- What are some different types of historical interpretation?

What Is the Object of Study?

This question addresses who or what is being studied. In other words, who or what is the history *about*? It is possible, for example, to have a history that centers on the life of an individual, a particular institution or program, or the development of an idea that has influenced the field in some way. To the top of this list we would also include the category of "comprehensive history," which is designed to provide a broad outline of adult education's history. Here it is important to add a caveat: The object of the field's history is largely determined by the interests of specific historians relative to their particular interest in adult learning (Welton, 1993).

With this point in mind, let's take a closer look at these categories and some relevant examples of each.

Comprehensive Histories

Perhaps the broadest way of looking at the object of history is through what we refer to as comprehensive histories. These are efforts to present a general history of adult education, rather than focusing on specific elements of history. Comprehensive histories strive to offer a broad look at the individuals, institutions, and ideas that have defined adult education's past and present.

To date, there have been five such comprehensive histories of adult education (J. T. Adams, 1944; Grattan, 1955; Knowles, 1962, 1977; Kett, 1994; Stubblefield and Keane, 1994). Each of these books strives to tell the story of adult education from a different vantage point. Thus, while there is considerable overlap in the content covered in each book, the meanings ascribed to this content by the various authors differs considerably. We will discuss these histories later in the chapter as an illustration of how interpretation influences the different ways in which writers can construct the story of the past.

History of Individuals

One of the most valuable historical resources can be found in the life stories of others. Biography and autobiography can focus on the entire life of an individual or on a particular episode in a person's life. One of the most notable examples of the former is the life of Eduard Lindeman, who has been the object of three major biographies (Konopka, 1958; Stewart, 1987; Leonard, 1991) and two anthologies (Gessner, 1956; Brookfield, 1987b). Each of the three biographies addresses major aspects of Lindeman's life and career, but they do so from different perspectives. Konopka's book focuses on Lindeman's contributions to social work, while Stewart concentrates on Lindeman's ideas about adult education.

There are many other examples of the history of individuals. The story of Dorothy Canfield Fisher (Yates, 1958) is another example. Fisher's contributions to adult education make up only a small portion of this book; however, as was true for most of the early leaders in the field, Fisher's interest in adult education was an outgrowth of a primary interest in another area (writing and literature, in Fisher's case).

Still another example is Booker T. Washington. While numerous biographies of Washington's life have been published, Denton (1993) concentrates specifically on Washington's contributions to the adult education movement. Autobiographies include the personal accounts of leaders such as Alvin Johnson (1952), Hilda Worthington Smith (1978), and Malcolm Knowles (1989). There are also collections of essays about and by adult educators; besides the two volumes on Lindeman mentioned earlier are studies of Alexander Meiklejohn (Brown, 1981) and J. R. Kidd (Cochrane and others, 1986).

In addition, at least two books provide chapter-length profiles of a wide range of contributors to the field (Moreland and Goldenstein, 1985; Jarvis, 1987b). And in recent years, two volumes have been published on adult education of African Americans (Neufeldt and McGee, 1990; E. A. Peterson, 1996), the latter of which explores contributions of such leaders as Alain Locke, Marcus Garvey, Septima Clark, W.E.B. DuBois, and Booker T. Washington.

Many biographical works take the form of an article-length treatment of a particular aspect of a person's life. A few selected accounts include works about Alain Locke (Guy, 1994), James Harvey Robinson (Rohfeld, 1990a), and Everett Dean Martin (Day and Seckinger, 1989).

History of Institutions

Some of the most compelling historical accounts have been of specific institutions or programs. The examples presented in this section serve to demonstrate the breadth of institutional histories that exist. Cartwright (1935) documented the first decade of the American Association for Adult Education (AAAE), one of the earliest national associations dedicated to the field. More recently, Rose (1989a) went to such sources as the archives of the Carnegie Corporation to present a different perspective on the motives behind the AAAE's founding.

T. Morrison (1974) wrote a history of Chautauqua Institution, a center for liberal adult education located in western New York

State that started as a training school for Sunday-school teachers. Rutkoff and Scott (1986) have chronicled the history of the New School for Social Research, an institution established by an early group of adult education leaders that has continued to provide innovative approaches to serving adult learners. Rohfeld (1990b) has documented the first seventy-five years of the National University Continuing Education Association (NUCEA), an organization focusing on continuing higher education, through an anthology of previously published articles and her own analysis of the NUCEA. Counter (1992b) tells the story of the Montana Study, a program aimed at providing education to rural communities throughout that state during the late 1940s. And there have been several histories of the Highlander Center for Research and Education, a center located in east Tennessee dedicated to promoting education for social change and community action (see, for example, F. Adams, 1975; J. M. Glen, 1988; A. I. Horton, 1989; M. Horton, J. Kohl, and H. Kohl, 1990). These few examples demonstrate the range of histories designed to tell the story of specific institutions and programs.

When considering the history of institutions, it is crucial to look beyond the boundaries of school-based programs for adults. Welton (1993) cites the work of Lawrence Cremin (in, for example, 1970, 1977, and 1988) to illustrate how "institutions like museums, households, farm movements, or the workplace could be understood as educative, forming and shaping outlook and character" (p. 139). The point here is that limiting a discussion of "institutions" only to efforts found within the more traditional confines of "schooling" misses much of the richness and vitality that is to be found in education for adults.

History of Ideas

A final object of history is an emphasis on a particular type of program (as opposed to a specific institution) or on a particular theme. We use the term *history of ideas* to describe these kinds of studies.

The following five examples capture some of the flavor of this type of historical work.

Cotton (1964, 1968) examined the literature of adult education to argue that the field has evolved out of two perspectives: social reform and professional traditions. Using historical evidence, Cotton wrote that the challenge confronting the contemporary field is to draw upon *both* of these traditions. This, he argued, could be accomplished through a blending of the idealism, social concern, and missionary zeal of social reformism with the realistic perspective of the professional tradition. According to Cotton, the dilemma facing the field is that "[w]e have a great tradition, but not enough of our co-workers are inspired by it" (1964, p. 86).

A second example of the history of ideas can be found in the work of Stubblefield (1988), who writes that three themes characterize the development of adult education: (1) diffusion of knowledge, (2) liberal education, and (3) social education. Stubblefield argues that these unifying themes, which are reflected largely in people and practices from the 1920s through the 1950s, are important because they helped to define for the first time what makes adult education a unique element of American society.

Some of the most enlightening perspectives on adult education have come from discussions of ideas that have often been marginalized. Kornbluh and Frederickson (1984), for example, have compiled an anthology related to women's and workers' education. Their volume addresses the lives of such leaders as Hilda Worthington Smith and programs like the Bryn Mawr Summer School for Women Workers, the Southern School for Women Workers, and the "She-She-She Camps"—a derogatory term used to describe a New Deal program for jobless women that is often compared with the Civilian Conservation Corps.

Another illustration of the history of ideas can be found in an article by Hugo (1990), who identified the problem of sex bias in the study of adult education history. Hugo refers to many of the women who have played key leadership and scholarship roles throughout the adult education movement. One such example is Ruth Kotinsky, who in 1933 published *Adult Education and the Social Scene*, one of the first books to address the importance of the social context in which adult education occurs.

A final example involves efforts to recognize the contributions of African Americans to the adult education field. With a few exceptions, this history has been largely ignored. Morgan (1982) discussed the development of adult education in Harlem during the Great Depression; and Neufeldt and McGee (1990) and E. A. Peterson (1996), both mentioned earlier, edited volumes on the contributions of African Americans to adult education.

How Does Interpretation Shape Historical Understanding?

Like other forms of scholarship, history is not neutral. Every historian has a purpose in writing a particular history. Some historians have a clear political or philosophical orientation in their analysis and writing, while others are less overt in their orientation. It is important to remember, however, that no history is neutral, for even those historians who do not actively advocate a particular stance are indeed expressing their own values by the way in which they frame their questions and by the information they have chosen to include or not include in their analysis. As Wilson (1995) puts it, "[W]henever we read history, we have to ask whose story is being told and whose is not. Why is this voice being heard and why not another? Whose interests are being served by this tale and whose silenced? And, perhaps most importantly, whose present are we trying to justify by crafting the stories to come out a certain way?" (p. 240).

History involves interpretation of the past. According to Stanford (1994), "[H]istorical knowledge rests upon the interpretation of evidence" and is often "no more than a balance of probabilities" (pp. 111–112). Thus, the essence of historical research is to discover and *give meaning to* information about people, places, and events.

Baritz (1962) has provided a useful metaphor for understanding historical interpretation by comparing the work of the historian to that of the playwright. The historian cannot re-create the lives and events of the past; therefore, like the playwright, the historian must be able to both explain and narrate as well as show how and why characters move from the opening to the final scene. The historian is, according to Baritz, "a teller of stories . . . that were once acted out. . . . In a basic sense, the historian is a playwright after the fact" (p. 340).

In the context of adult education, this means that when reading history it is crucial to understand the values, experiences, and theoretical frameworks that have influenced the historian. Examples of interpretation abound in the histories of individuals, institutions, and ideas in adult education, as well as in comprehensive histories of the field.

To illustrate this point, we will look at five books that have offered comprehensive histories of adult education over a half-century period (1944 to 1994); they include works by J. T. Adams (1944), Grattan (1955), Knowles (1962, 1977), Kett (1994), and Stubblefield and Keane (1994). In looking at these five books, it is clear that there is considerable similarity in topics covered: each book, for example, examines such themes as the Lyceum, Chautauqua, the Americanization movement, agricultural extension, and forums. However, each author has attempted to interpret the adult education field from a different vantage point. This is reflected in such factors as the authors' backgrounds, the reasons for writing the books, and the actual content of each volume.

In 1982, Stubblefield made a comparison of the books by J. T. Adams, Grattan, and Knowles. He observed that Adams, a professional historian who did not have knowledge of or experience in the field of adult education, was commissioned by the Carnegie Corporation to write *Frontiers of American Culture* (1944) using data primarily from materials provided by the American Association for Adult Education. In the book, Adams stressed adult education as a means of diffusing knowledge and promoting democracy. This approach is consistent with the orientation of the AAAE.

Similarly, C. Harley Grattan's *In Quest of Knowledge* (1955) was commissioned by a foundation-supported program—the Fund for Adult Education, sponsored during the 1950s by the Ford Foundation to promote liberal adult education. Here Grattan (who, like Adams, was a professional historian) stressed the contributions of liberal adult education, which was consistent with the aims of the Fund for Adult Education.

The third comprehensive history was Malcolm Knowles's *The Adult Education Movement in the United States* (1962, 1977). Unlike the two earlier authors, who were professional historians with an interest in adult education, Knowles wrote as an experienced adult educator with an interest in history, having previously served as executive director of the Adult Education Association of the U.S.A. during most of the 1950s. Knowles's study, which grew out of his doctoral dissertation at the University of Chicago, differs from the other two works in that it stressed the development of a coordinated adult education movement and gave considerable attention to the formation and evolution of professional associations and institutions in the field.

Like the authors of these previous comprehensive histories, Kett (1994) and Stubblefield and Keane (1994) have covered major milestones in the history of adult education. However, their two books look at adult education through very different lenses. Like Adams and Grattan several decades earlier, Joseph Kett comes from the discipline of history. He is perhaps best known for his collaboration with E. D. Hirsch on books such as *Cultural Literacy* (1987). In his 1994 book *The Pursuit of Knowledge Under Difficulties: From Self-Improvement to Adult Education in America, 1750–1990*, Kett writes from the perspective of a historian whose interest in adult education evolved from a more specific interest in self-education and mutual improvement in antebellum America. In a review of Kett's book, Schied (1995) states that it "combines a breadth and depth rarely seen in works on American adult educational history" (p. 232)—a claim based on the strength of an author who is familiar with mainstream directions of

American history and who has developed his study from an extensive base of research.

Like Knowles, Harold Stubblefield and Patrick Keane developed their 1994 history, *Adult Education in the American Experience*, from the perspective of experienced adult educators with an interest in the history of the field. They have responded to criticisms of the first three comprehensive histories by seeking to provide a more inclusive picture of the field than the previous works provide. In the book's preface, Stubblefield and Keane state that a "description of the evolution of institutional settings, programs, and clienteles reveals adult education's holistic nature, and an analysis of factors that have affected public access to adult education provides a critical perspective of the field" (p. xii). Thus, the book includes chapters devoted to the influence of women and minorities and to the importance of adult education programs designed to promote social change.

It is quite likely that the Kett and Stubblefield and Keane books will be recognized for some time as the major comprehensive histories of adult education. Inevitably, there will be efforts to analyze both works side by side, and energy will be invested in trying to determine which is the "better" book. Perhaps a more useful approach is to recognize that each book attempts a different *interpretation* of adult education history and that, taken together, the two will ultimately advance our understanding of our past in a way that was not possible prior to their publication in 1994.

To further illustrate the role of interpretation in historical writing, we can turn briefly to the example of the Americanization movement, which had its roots in the late 1800s and early 1900s. The traditional view of Americanization—one that has often been passed down to successive generations as folklore—emphasizes immigration as the development of the "melting pot" in which contributions from diverse cultures are valued and incorporated into the total amalgam of American culture.

However, Robert Carlson (1970, 1987) uses historical evidence to construct a very different picture. Carlson has argued that most of these Americanization efforts involved indoctrination, stressed conformity, and discouraged diversity. By presenting evidence culled from sources ranging from archival documents and popular literature of the time to a host of secondary sources about the Americanization movement, Carlson was able to "build his case" and thus provide a critical reconsideration of a perspective long taken for granted by many.

Interpretation is vital to history, for it reveals the true interests and intentions of the historian and allows those who seek to understand a field's history to see how the same set of events can look very different when seen through different eyes. As we pointed out earlier, history is not neutral; interpretation allows us to understand the perspectives, emphases, and biases of the historian.

What Are Some Different Types of Historical Interpretation?

As we noted above, interpretation is a central feature of history. The *Dictionary of Concepts in History* (Ritter, 1986) has identified thirty-one types of history—including such categories as biography, cultural history, intellectual history, new history, popular history, and social history—each of which represents a different way of interpreting the past. Although a detailed analysis of these various approaches is clearly beyond the intent of this chapter, it can be helpful to make some general distinctions. Therefore, we will differentiate among three types of history: celebrationist, narrative, and critical.

Celebrationist History

We use the term *celebrationist* to refer to historical work that tells a story from the past to pay tribute to an individual, institution, or idea or to fulfill a "public relations" agenda on the effectiveness of a program. Celebrationist history is valuable in terms of illustrating an individual's major milestones and accomplishments. Examples might include an obituary, or an article honoring a person who has made a lifetime of contributions to the field.

An early example of celebrationist history is found in Morse Cartwright's *Ten Years of Adult Education* (1935). In the book, Cartwright reflects on the first decade of the American Association for Adult Education from his perspective as its executive director. Other examples include two volumes of biographical sketches about contributors to the adult education movement (Moreland and Goldenstein, 1985; Jarvis, 1987b), an article by Hiemstra (1980) that paid tribute to the lifetime contributions made by Howard McClusky, and a book of autobiographical reflections by Malcolm Knowles (1989).

Celebrationist history can offer informative, insightful, and even moving testimony about its subject. When reading such history, it is especially important to understand the relationship of the author to the object, as well as the author's purpose for writing the history.

Narrative History

At its most basic, history involves the telling of stories. According to D. H. Fischer (1970), "Good historians tell true stories. Great historians, from time to time, tell the best true stories [that] their topics and problems permit" (p. 131). Narrative history, according to Fischer, attempts to explain how and what but does not specifically address why. This does not mean that the author of a narrative history is not providing interpretation or analysis, nor does it mean that other types of history do not necessarily involve narration. What it does mean is that the writer is more concerned with providing a chronicle of events designed to inform the reader rather than persuade the reader why such events occurred.

The recent comprehensive history by Stubblefield and Keane (1994) is an example of narrative history. In this work, the authors tell a story about adult education in the United States from early America to the present. While they do not tie their discussion overtly to a specific philosophical framework, it is clear that by virtue of the topics they have chosen to address they make a statement about how they interpret the adult education field. For example, previous historical works have often been criticized because they have failed to include the voices of women and minorities; Stubblefield and Keane are quick to acknowledge this earlier omission and actively seek to include such voices in their volume. Their efforts to be more inclusive of people and events places them in a progressive-democratic tradition. In essence, their book attempts to chronicle the adult education movement without trying directly to persuade the reader of the reasons such events took place, or critiquing earlier portrayals of the field's history.

Critical History

While narration is a key element of historical work, some histories go beyond narration to try to explain the past. In the history of education, for example, writers such as Bernard Bailyn and Lawrence Cremin have argued that educational history needs to encompass an understanding of the entire cultural milieu rather than focus merely on the history of schools and schooling (Stubblefield and Keane, 1994). Other critical perspectives are considered more radical because they work from the assumption that education has been a mechanism to promote the status quo or the perpetuation of white middle-class cultural values. Such perspectives are often grounded in Marxism, feminism, or Afrocentrism.

Critical history, therefore, involves telling the story of the past, but it does so from an orientation that does not merely "add on" diverse perspectives. Rather, critical history looks at the past through a very different lens than that of more traditional history. Welton (1993) captures the spirit of this point when he states that such history "speaks to us with eloquent fierceness and anger about oppression, suffering, and exclusion" (p. 134).

In her discussion of gender and the history of adult education, Hugo (1990) presents a useful way to distinguish between narrative and critical history. She suggests that there are two ways to develop a more inclusive history. A "compensatory" approach involves "writing women back into the history of adult education" (p. 11).

Because it involves reappraisal of and additions to existing history, a compensatory approach exemplifies the narrative perspective. A "critical" approach, on the other hand, raises new questions about relationships between gender, power, and such aspects of adult education as program development, leadership, professionalization, and theory development (Hugo, 1990).

Some of the most important historical work being done today in adult education is from a critical perspective. Examples include the work of Michael Welton on politics and adult education in Canada (1986, 1987); Fred Schied on workers' education (1993, 1994); Amy Rose on the founding of the American Association for Adult Education (1989a) and on the politics of post–World War II veterans returning to higher education (1991); Kathleen Rockhill on university adult education in the United States (Taylor, Rockhill, and Fieldhouse, 1985); Arthur Wilson on controlling the professionalization of adult education (1993a); and Robert Carlson's work on Americanization (1970, 1987).

In essence, celebrationist history strives to honor the accomplishments of a person or program. Narrative history involves telling a story by focusing on questions of "how" and "what." And critical history seeks to *retell* a story from a particular perspective—usually one that challenges the limitations of previous interpretations. Thus, celebrationist history attempts to honor the past, narrative history to interpret the past, and critical history to reinterpret the past's meaning.

Benefits of History: Information, Insight, Inspiration

Clearly, the rich tradition out of which the adult education movement has grown is a valuable resource. However, questions often arise about how this history can benefit the contemporary field. More than three decades ago, Cotton (1964) noted that while adult education has a great tradition, "not enough of [us] are inspired by it" (p. 86). How, then, can a historical foundation be beneficial to all who engage in the education of adults? One way to address this dilemma is through an understanding of three benefits of history: information, insight, and inspiration.

Information

For many people, what comes to mind when we think of history are names, dates, places, and events—or what are often referred to as "facts." According to D. H. Fischer (1970), a *fact* is a "true, descriptive statement about past events," and an *event* is "any past happening" (p. xv). The term *information,* used in this context, consists of two elements: fact and chronology. Here the intent is to be able to describe events in the order in which they have taken place. Such information can be helpful in understanding the sequence of events through which a particular development has transpired. For instance, while it may not be important to be able to recall that Chautauqua Institution was founded in 1874, the *idea* of Chautauqua—that a program with its humble beginnings as a camp for Sunday-school teachers evolved over more than a century into a major center for liberal adult education—is the stuff of which a rich and insightful story might be (and, indeed, has been) constructed (see, for example, T. Morrison, 1974).

Stanford (1994) points out three reasons for being concerned with chronology: plot, causation, and influence. Telling a story according to how events have occurred helps to clarify the *plot.* In addition, chronology can provide insight into *causation* by showing how later events are the result of past happenings. Finally, according to Stanford, chronology can sometimes show how earlier events have had *influence* on later ones, thus offering "not so much a cause as a reason for those actions" (p. 176). Therefore, while it may not be necessary to memorize and later recall names and dates in order to benefit from history, it is important to understand *where* different pieces fit into the puzzle.

In addition, an understanding of fact and chronology makes it possible to place events into the larger social context of the times. Hilton (1981, 1982) provides an examination of adult education during the decade of the 1930s, with discussions focusing on such developments as public forums, New Deal programs, university extension, and the role of women as "co-architects" of the adult education movement (1982, p. 12). In describing the process through which he constructed his history, Hilton writes about how he spent a period of time "seeking out the journalism, history, criticism, and even films and autobiographies [of the period] *before* pursuing the literature of adult education" (1982, p. 2). Thus, when he discusses developments in adult education during the 1930s, he does so with an understanding of the larger context in which these stories unfolded.

To summarize, the main benefit of history as "information" is that it provides a chronological perspective, which makes it possible to understand how various events occur in relation to one another. By doing so, we can identify and understand potential links between events and how they relate to the larger picture of the society at that particular time.

Insight

A second benefit of history is that it can help us gain *insight* into current problems of practice. Those who have come before us have dealt with many of the same problems or issues that we face in the field today. For example, the question of whether professionalization of adult education is desirable has been debated for decades, and many writers have offered perspectives that remain relevant today. (This issue is discussed more fully in Chapters Ten and Eleven.)

To ignore history is to neglect a valuable source of insight. However, while the past can help us gain insight into the present, it is important to avoid merely transplanting ideas from the past into another period of time. It is an error of historical work to read present-day values into past events (D. H. Fischer, 1970). The social milieu of an earlier time that produced particular programs and practices will almost certainly differ greatly from present conditions. Thus, it would be both naive and erroneous to advocate, for instance, applying programs that were successful as parts of the New Deal legislation of the 1930s to solve today's economic situation simply because they were effective in the past.

Writing from the perspective of government and public policy, Neustadt and May (1986) suggest that "thinking in time" can prove invaluable in decision making. For example, the authors show how the Kennedy administration used history in making decisions regarding the Cuban missile crisis of October 1962. To Neustadt and May, the value of historical insight can be expressed as follows: "Better decision-making involves drawing on history to frame sharper questions" in a systematic and routine way (p. 32).

Educators of adults can likewise use history to "frame sharper questions." Let us consider, as an example, an ethical dilemma that adult educators often face when trying to recruit new learners. While most of us in the field consider it appropriate and even desirable to respond to learners' needs, there are situations in which an educator may be faced with the need to "create" a market; that is, to help learners "discover" a need that they did not previously recognize. The impact and implications of creating a market did not go unnoticed by Amidon (1933), who told a story about four acquaintances who shared a love of chamber music and met regularly to play together. Amidon related what transpired when they met up with a "professional educator"

> who pointed out to them how little they really knew, how sketchy were their results, how silly it was to saw away by themselves in a city where the best of musical instructions could be obtained at reasonable cost, and so on. . . . They decided to give up their "chamber music evenings" in favor of "really learning something." They enrolled in evening classes . . . and arranged for weekly

lessons on their chosen instruments. They overlooked
the fact that what they had been doing was recreation in
a real sense, and that what they were undertaking was,
from the point of view of people with full-time jobs and
home responsibilities, "serious work." . None of them
continued it for more than three months. And, unfortunately, in the rigid routine of "lessons" and "classes" and
"systematic practice" they lost their old enthusiasm for
making music. They have not resumed their chamber
music evenings [p. 385].

Although Amidon told this story more than six decades ago, it can
help us today, in times of tight budgets and demands for recruiting
new learners, to reflect on how we how develop and market our programs effectively and ethically.

A second example of how history can provide insight is found
in the story of the Montana Study, a community education undertaking of the University of Montana in the late 1940s. Through a
combination of historical document analysis and interviews with
former participants, Counter (1992b) was able to provide new
insights into a program designed to present a unique approach to
adult and community education in several rural communities
throughout Montana. By telling the story in a way that brought out
both the political struggles surrounding the program and the success of many of the community study groups, Counter concludes
that the Montana Study was simultaneously an idealistic institutional failure and an innovative program success. The lessons
learned from this study have clear implications for contemporary
educators seeking insight into the politics of program development.

Graduate study in adult education provides the backdrop for a
final illustration of insight from the past. Restructuring and "down-
sizing" have become common realities throughout higher education
in the 1990s, and adult education graduate programs seem to be particularly vulnerable. As adult education considers future directions

for preparing its leaders, seeking insight from the past might be beneficial. During the decades of the 1920s and 1930s, as the first efforts to prepare leaders for adult education were undertaken, questions emerged about (1) whether the emphasis should be on "lay" versus "professional" leaders, and (2) whether such training should focus on developing expertise in the subject being taught or in the techniques of teaching adults. Regarding the first concern, Dorothy Canfield Fisher (1930) argued on behalf of a lay emphasis, because she believed that professional educators had rejected the opportunity to step forward and consider "the marvelous possibilities of continuing the process of education during the years of maturity" (p. 10).

On the other hand, Fansler (1931) presented a case on behalf of the professional educator. He stated that the amateur can be a philosopher and friend, "but not a guide" (p. 58), and he went on to argue that "the specialty of an educational institution should be education and not entertainment" (p. 60).

In terms of whether the preparation of leaders should emphasize content expertise or techniques of teaching, MacKaye (1931) argued that training "should deal with the subject matter of living and not with the techniques of teaching" (p. 294). Taking more of a middle position, however, Brunner (1936) noted that since adult education is not a "single subject" that exists in an "intellectual vacuum," institutions involved in preparing adult education leaders "should not fall into the error of teaching them techniques *alone*" (pp. 457–458; emphasis added).

The point relative to the present discussion is that these concerns, which were important several decades ago, are still raised today. As graduate programs and, indeed, the entire adult education field consider future directions for the preparation of leaders, questions such as those we have raised above will merit further consideration. And while merely attempting to "apply" past perspectives to the present is erroneous, we would be equally short-sighted to ignore the questions of the past and how they might lead us to insight and, therefore, to framing our questions more sharply.

Inspiration

A third potential benefit of history is what we have labeled *inspiration*. It is important to note that inspiration, as we used the term here, is quite different from the celebrationist approach, in which ideas are typically presented in an uncritical or even evangelical way. Here, the term rests on the belief that the past can inspire those of us who practice in the adult education field today, as we realize we are a link in the chain of a rich heritage.

One source of inspiration to many is the story of the Highlander Center for Research and Education. In 1932, in the mountains of east Tennessee, Myles Horton established a school to bring adults together to learn strategies for solving community problems. During its early years, Highlander worked primarily with organizing labor unions. In the 1950s and 1960s, its emphasis shifted to playing a key role in supporting the civil rights movement in the South through an array of literacy programs, voter-registration activities, and community-organizing workshops.

Highlander was actually one of the few places in the South that blacks and whites could meet, live, and learn together as equals. Rosa Parks, Martin Luther King Jr., Septima Clark, and Bernice Robinson are a few of the movement's leaders who visited Highlander to learn strategies for community action. Indeed, it was not long after one such workshop that Rosa Parks returned to Montgomery, Alabama, and refused to vacate her seat at the front of a bus—an action that is often viewed as a symbolic turning point in the civil rights struggle.

Eventually, the Highlander Folk School (as it was originally known) was closed by the State of Tennessee and relocated to Knoxville, where it operated for several years before moving to its current location in New Market, Tennessee, about twenty-five miles from Knoxville. Today Highlander's primary emphasis is on programs addressing economic development problems and environmental issues in Appalachia.

Over the years, the story of Highlander has been told by many different writers from many perspectives. These range from personal narratives (F. Adams, 1975; Brown, 1990; Horton, Kohl, and Kohl, 1990) to more scholarly treatments of Highlander's history (Glen, 1988; Horton, 1989). While it is important to avoid virtually deifying any institution or program, there is much in the story of Highlander that warrants a sense of pride and affinity in those adult educators who value its ideals.

Oral history often provides stories that can inspire. For his study of adult education in the 1930s, Hilton (1982) interviewed several leaders from the period, including Bonaro Overstreet, who told the following story of a community-based adult education program:

> There was a woman in New York, Rachel DuBois, a Quaker girl, who was asked by the public school system to invent some method of keeping immigrants from countries that had been hostile to each other in the Old World, keeping them from infecting their children in our public schools with the antagonisms that they had brought with them. . . .
>
> Rachel DuBois, who was enormously inventive, planned a program [that] she called Neighbors in Action. She would gather together clusters of parents, usually she could get the mothers more easily than the men, to just come in and sit around and talk. We attended a few of these. She asked us to come and see how they did it, what she was thinking of, and give her an estimate of what we thought it was worth.
>
> We thought it was marvelous! One evening, for example, there was a cluster of these parents from mutually antagonistic backgrounds. She asked them to recall their first memories of bread and share them. You see, here was something that undercut the differences. Here

is the bread of life; here is that which they all had to have in one form or another.

It was simply miraculous the way the hostilities faded as they compared notes on the kinds of bread that their mothers had made when they were children. As simple a thing as that. But the hostilities faded.

At the end of it, a young black man who was there suddenly rose and started singing, "Let Us Break Bread Together on Our Knees." And the whole crowd began singing. A lot of them did not know it, but he taught it to us.

It was a miraculous experience. That's adult education too: adult education of the spirit. It isn't just facts; it's sharing [pp. 14–15].

This story is almost self-explanatory in terms of its inspirational value. At a time when adult education is struggling with issues of professionalization and social responsibility, it is enlightening and inspirational to recognize that Rachel DuBois is part of a chain that leads to the contemporary field. And while it would be naive to try to recapture or re-create her specific innovative effort, we can use her example as a vision of what is possible for each of us to strive toward.

As the examples of the Highlander Center and Rachel DuBois demonstrate, adult education has a proud and rich heritage. This, of course, does not negate the inequities and injustices that have often silenced some voices or reinforced the influence of some groups in society over others. But it does reaffirm that being an adult educator is and should be something of which to be proud.

Summary

The history of adult education is a rich resource that can help us understand our past and how we each fit into the mosaic of the field. It can help us frame sharper questions about our own practice. At the same time, it can be trivialized and misused, particularly when we justify current practice simply because "it was done in the past" or when we celebrate our past while ignoring important perspectives that could contribute to new ways of looking at the past. Each of us has a responsibility to develop some understanding of our past so that we can avoid being controlled by it.

In this chapter, we have examined the value of studying the history of individuals, institutions, and ideas, as well as the broad history of the field. We have suggested that celebrationist, narrative, and critical histories can each provide useful though different perspectives. Finally, we suggest that three potential benefits of history are information about people, places, and events in the past; insight into how the same historical events can be viewed through very different lenses; and inspiration that comes from recognizing the richness of adult education's past. The professional literature of adult education abounds with illustrations of each example.

Often, the preparation or professional development of adult educators ignores or downplays the history of the field. This is unfortunate, because history can be an invaluable tool in the development of reflective practitioners and scholars.

4

Adult Education in Contemporary Society

Like any other field, adult education has its share of issues that are debated off and on in the literature, at conferences, and in informal discussions in practice settings. Galbraith and Sisco (1992), for example, chose seven "controversies" for debate from numerous ones "begging for reasoned judgment and action" (p. 12). And as with other fields, rarely is there a resolution to a particular issue in adult education. By debate and discussion, we hope for more informed and reflective practice—central to which is a knowing not just how something is done but also *why* it is being done in the first place. These discussions can and do have an impact on public policy in adult education.

As we stated in the Preface, one of the goals of this book—in addition to describing the field of adult education—is to raise awareness of and encourage reflection on critical issues. This chapter deals with several issues related to the foundations of the field (that is, material covered in the preceding three chapters on the scope of the field and on its philosophy and history.

We intend to illuminate several issues by presenting various points of view, and we see our discussion as an entry point for you, the practitioner, to begin grappling with the issues regarding your own beliefs, values, and attitudes. Where do you stand on each of these issues? How does the tension manifest itself in your particular setting? Which course of action, if any, would you recommend?

A number of issues or tensions in the field are directly related to how adult education has come to be defined and what people see as its purpose or goal. Philosophy and history are fundamental to this discussion, as no issue is bereft of values, beliefs, or historical context. Thus, the tensions explored in this chapter are derived from—and at the same time are influenced by—the field's philosophical and historical foundations.

We have selected three such tensions for discussion:

- Should adult education work toward unifying the field or toward preserving its diversity?

- To what extent, if any, should adult education align itself with the rest of education?

- Should the primary focus of adult education be the individual or society?

For each of these issues, we discuss its relationship to the foundations of adult education, why it is of concern to the field, and how it has been conceptualized from various points of view.

Unity Versus Diversity

Many of us have had the experience of trying to explain to an outsider what adult education is or what we do as adult educators. The general public has formed its own vague image of the field from personal encounters with adult education or from mass-media portrayals that most often focus on literacy. As a result, adult education is usually perceived as something related to basic skills, leisure activities, or perhaps job training. Rarely does anyone outside the field—or even practitioners from one corner of it—have a sense of the scope of activities, purposes, or clienteles that make up the broad range of adult education.

This diversity is viewed as a strength by many, but it has also led to no small frustration on the part of those adult educators in positions to influence policy. Being able to define the field and convey what adult educators are trying to accomplish has an impact on one's ability to secure funding and other forms of support that ultimately affects those whom the field is trying to serve. The issue of preserving this diversity, as opposed to seeking a more unified identity, is integrally related to how adult education has evolved over the years, its past and present goals and purposes, and the extent to which the field has become professionalized.

Adult education has not always been so diverse in scope or mission. As we mentioned in earlier chapters, adult education in Colonial America was predominantly characterized by moral and religious goals; learning to read was important so that one could study the Bible. After the Revolutionary War, the new nation needed leaders and an informed citizenry, so civic education—which included learning about reason, science, and politics—became more prominent than the religious aspect.

The focus shifted once again with the growing industrialization of the late nineteenth and early twentieth centuries. "Americanization" and citizenship programs were established to acculturate the massive influx of immigrants to the United States. Finally, the "official" founding of the adult education field in 1926 was accompanied by a distinct social agenda that has since been subsumed (some would say co-opted) by the emphases on technical, job-training, and human resource development orientation in the late twentieth century.

While a major thrust of adult education at any particular time reflects the historical context, various other purposes and orientations are also carried along. So at the brink of the twenty-first century, adult education appears more diverse and more fragmented than ever before. Examples of adult education out of liberal, progressive, behaviorist, humanist, and radical perspectives are alive and well—even thriving—today. From Great Books clubs to national-issues forums to literacy instruction to job training to community-based social-action initiatives, adult education reflects the range of philosophical orientations we discussed in Chapter Two.

Many practitioners feel as Von Pittman (1989) does—that "the diversity of interests, constituencies, and institutions demanding and providing programs has been one of [the field's] strengths. However, this diversity has also worked against the evolution of a common sense of identity and self-interest" (p. 21). While no one suggests that we eliminate this diversity (even if it were possible to do so), there is concern with how to go about achieving a clearer sense of identity amid such diversity.

Some have suggested that what the field needs for a clearer focus is a comprehensive policy—an umbrella definition or concept—or a set of principles that various elements will support and promote. A real problem inherent in this quest, one that we touched on in Chapter One, is the fact that thousands of educators who work with adult learners are unaware of being *adult educators*, or choose not to identify themselves as such. High school math teachers who also teach in evening programs are most likely to see themselves as math instructors; trainers in a business setting will probably identify with the field of human resource management or development. For those who advocate some sort of unifying mechanism, the question remains as to whether there is a compelling need to bring these educators of adults into the picture—and if so, how it can be facilitated.

Also involved in the issue of a unified perspective is how this perspective should be defined. Should we define what we do as a "field of practice," an "occupation," "a discipline," a "profession"? Throughout this book, we talk about adult education as a field of practice rather than a discipline or a fully developed profession. In fact, the extent to which our field of practice should become professionalized is a major issue in and of itself (see Chapters Nine, Ten, and Eleven).

The question here is the extent to which we should either celebrate our diversity or strive for a more unified field of practice. In this struggle, adult education is not unlike other fields, such as social work or even medicine. As Cervero (1992) points out, "The assumption that professions are best understood as communities united by common interests is simply a myth" (p. 47); those working in any occupation, profession, or field practice out of "different (and to some extent competing) purposes, knowledge, and ideologies" (p. 48).

What allows social work and medicine to *seem* more unified is that these fields have a credentialing mechanism that restricts who can practice. Adult education, for the most part, does not have such regulations and is thus more like the field of administration, which in most situations requires no credential or certification to practice. The MBA degree, like a degree in adult education, does not guarantee entry into the field, nor does *not* having one prevent someone from being an administrator.

This situation presents a dilemma for those who see diversity and nonrestricted entry as strengths but at the same time realize that they can be something of a liability when lobbying for resources or setting policy. Several writers suggest that we should decide on a set of principles, an overriding purpose, or a set of strategies that we can agree on as a means of conceptually bringing our practice together.

In a discussion of purposes and philosophies of adult education, Beder (1989), for example, acknowledges the "currents and crosscurrents, critiques and countercritiques [that] abound in the thought of adult education," and then goes on to propose five "core principles that form the basic foundation of the field" (p. 48):

1. Whether society is basically good or inherently flawed, it can and should be improved. In this, adult education can and should play a major role.

2. If individuals, and ultimately society, are to prosper, learning must continue throughout life.

3. Adults are capable of learning and should be treated with dignity and respect.

4. All adults should have access to learning the things required for basic functioning in society.

5. Although adults may or may not differ from preadults with respect to the basic cognitive processes of learning, the context of adult education differs substantially from the context of preadult education. Therefore, adults should be educated differently from preadults.

Rather than establishing a set of principles, Apps (1979) would have us settle on one clear overriding purpose of continuing education: "to enhance the quality of human life in all its personal and social dimensions" (p. 91). This purpose, according to Apps, is broad enough to encompass developmental and rationalist (liberal) aims, individual and societal emphases, and vocational (versus liberal) goals. In a later publication, Apps (1989b) speculates that the tasks of the practitioner and the structures and delivery systems of adult education will continue to change and proliferate. In light of this *increasing* diversity, he suggests that we "rediscover" a focus on societal problems as well as individual need.

For Apps, the future requires a "deeper and broader vision" (p. 29) of adult education's place in society, and development of relationships with other fields and areas of education. It also requires that we "get off the defensive hobbyhorse . and take the offense" (p. 30) in explaining who we are and what we do. "We must quit worrying about what adult and continuing education is and what it is not, about who is and who is not an adult educator. Such chest beating will only use up our energy and divert our attention" (p. 29).

Other "solutions" to the lack of a clear identity in adult education call for a reflection of the realities of postindustrial society. In a document assessing national economic trends, Perelman (1984) proposes a new kind of learning enterprise for the postindustrial economy, one "focused on adults rather than children, on learning rather than education, on technology rather than institutions, and on private competition rather than public administration" (abstract).

However, writes Perelman, "the major barrier" to creating this new adult-focused enterprise "is an appalling lack of timely and accurate information about the entire system of adult learning in the United States. This information must be gathered, education must be made learning centered rather than degree centered, and new technology must be used, in order to meet the economy's growing need for flexible human capital" (abstract).

Perelman's call for "timely and accurate information" is echoed by Koloski (1989), who explains her frustration in representing the national association of adult and continuing educators. In dealing with the lay public, "it seems that the avenues of adult learning are so broadly based and construed that it might be impossible to deliver demographic information about the field in any qualitative or quantitative manner. Anybody and everybody may be in the business of delivering some form of adult education in any number of locations and institutions and for any number of purposes. We are unable, as a field, to provide solid data to identify our colleagues" (p. 73).

To bring some clarity to the field, Koloski recommends that we do several things. First, a major database needs to be constructed in which we "count, categorize, and characterize individuals, programs, and professional affiliations for our field" (p. 74). Second, we must agree on "the professional competencies necessary for the privilege of being called an adult educator," followed by "delineat[ing] standards of practice for each endeavor in the field, from literacy through continuing professional education, from training to civic empowerment" (p. 75). In Koloski's view, these pragmatic steps are necessary to create a distinctive image for adult education, one that will allow us to be better advocates in the important arenas of public policy and funding.

Certainly, in a pluralistic society such as ours, achieving a single purpose, a comprehensive definition, or a particular philosophical stance is not likely to happen. Yet while we can recognize the value of diversity—and even encourage it—the downside is an image of the field that is vague, fragmented, and perhaps to some extent dysfunctional. How can we allow for diversity, yet be able to convey to others what adult education is? The basis on which the field can present a unified image has yet to be worked out.

Should Adult Education Align with the Broad Field of Education?

Defining adult education as a field of practice involves considering its goals and purposes and the clientele it serves. These foundational issues shape the debate about whether or not the field should align itself more closely with the rest of education. Those in favor of a closer relationship often advocate a lifelong-learning model of education that focuses on the needs of individuals to function in society regardless of age. As Darkenwald and Merriam (1982) state, "Adult education is, after all, *education*. The fact that its clientele is made up of mature people and that its purposes, methods, and settings are often distinctive does not negate this fundamental reality. Turning back from separatism does not mean denying adult education's distinct attributes, but rather developing them more fully within an education profession that has been reconceptualized to acknowledge the reality of lifelong learning" (p. 23, emphasis in original).

In this philosophy, the overriding goal of educational institutions at any level would be to learn how to learn, since specific content becomes obsolete in a fast-changing society (Smith, 1987). Furthermore, such a concept mandates a much more flexible educational structure and timetable for learning. In the more utopian models of lifelong learning, creative approaches to the delivery of education, as well as the timing of education, free up learning at any age from the rigidity of current practice. That is, the K–12 progression of schooling followed by higher or adult education would be revised so that children and adults would step in and out of formal education as the need arose. In addition, nonformal and informal education would be equal options as mechanisms for learning.

Such a radical restructuring of the total educational system is, of course, probably not going to happen. There are too many vested interests, and this model hands over too much power and control to the learner. As many writers have noted, educators are a conservative lot, not prone to radical change. Further inhibiting such a move is the wane in interest among educators themselves in this model— hastened, some think, by its too-close association in this country with adult education alone. In any case, while this is a much more viable concept internationally (see Chapter Seven), in North America it is little more than occasional rhetoric.

Historically, adult education has attempted to forge a separate identity by distancing itself from preadult education. Probably the most graphic example of this is Knowles's promotion of andragogy. Imported from Eastern Europe in the late 1960s, *andragogy* is defined as the art and science of helping adults learn, as opposed to *pedagogy*, the art and science of helping children learn (1970, 1980b). From assumptions that underlie andragogy, Knowles developed a "technology" of teaching adults that contrasted with teaching children. It was not until the 1980 version of his book *The Modern Practice of Adult Education* that Knowles softened the dichotomy, turning it into a continuum ranging from pedagogical to andragogical techniques suitable for learners of all ages, depending on the situation. (We discuss andragogy more fully in Chapter Six.)

The separation of adult education from the rest of education was also based on the perception of very different missions. The primary focus of preadult education is to develop productive, contributing adult members of society. Hence, child education has been recognized as heavily value-laden, in which the inculcation and development of acceptable morals and attitudes is acknowledged. Adults, on the other hand, come to an educational setting with already-formed values and attitudes.

What, then, is the mission of adult education? Quite clearly, it has to be something other than learning how to be an adult. Hence, a number of "purposes" or goals—such as remedial skills, work-related training, civic education, personal development, and the like (see Chapter One)—have evolved, along with a service orientation focusing on meeting the needs of individual learners.

However, while adult education may not overtly profess to socializing its learners in the same way that preadult education does, it is hardly a value-neutral enterprise. As a number of writers have pointed out, adult education operates in a context in which issues of power and privilege, race, class, and sex shape the very nature of the activity (Cunningham, 1990, 1991; Hayes and Colin, 1994; Welton, 1993). Furthermore, work-related learning, for example, whether it is undertaken to enter the job market, upgrade skills, or change careers, functions to socialize people into the "system" overall and into the culture of the occupation in particular. Thus, on this account our field is not so different from preadult education after all.

This drive to establish an identity separate from other areas of education has, some have argued, resulted in a view of adult education as a marginal or even expendable activity. Usher and Bryant (1989) write that "the emphasis on uniqueness has not served adult education well. On the contrary, one could say that an essentialist defence of adult education has, in fact, contributed to its marginalization" (p. 3). Usher and Bryant argue that because of this marginalization, which they see as detrimental to adult education, "it is even more important for adult education to both *see itself* and *be seen as* part of the world of education" (p. 3, emphasis in original). Yet others make a case for preserving the field's marginality, for the reason that it allows adult education to be entrepreneurial and highly responsive to changing learning needs (Burnham, 1989). (For more on marginality, see Chapter Five.)

Somewhat related to the marginality issue is the argument that aligning too closely with the broad field of education will lead to adult education's becoming too much like schooling, too "institutionalized"—and in so doing lose its responsiveness, its nonformal and voluntary nature, and its social agenda. However, as

Cunningham (1991) points out, the institutionalization of adult education has already happened:

> With institutionalization, the field has become *more and more like schooling* in practice while claiming in theory to be more and more distinct from schooling. In other words, adult education as a field of practice in the United States and most developed countries has increasingly been used by the state and professionals to reproduce the existing social, cultural, and economic relationships. Accordingly, discourse in adult education has been dominated by theories of individualism; market-oriented promotional strategies; deficit models for defining the adult learner; devaluation of volunteerism and voluntarism; exhortations to professionalism; and increasing concern with a close relationship of adult education, work, and the workplace [p. 351, emphasis added].

Deshler (1991) underscores this point with his analysis of the "proliferation of instrumental adult education in North America, in service of the state and of business and industry"; this close linkage with government, business, and industry "has injected values and interests into adult education that are external to its historical interests" (p. 395).

Both Cunningham and Deshler see the institutionalization of adult education as responsible for the growing invisibility and perhaps devaluation of informal, community-based forms of adult education based on social action. Cunningham (1989) pushes us to see the adult education that lies beyond schooling: "popular social movements, grass roots education, voluntary associations, and communities producing and disseminating knowledge as a human activity" (p. 34). She and others also make the case that what we know of our field's history has been dominated by institutional forms and structures; we know little about, for example, African American or

Native American contributions, workers' education, adult education in social movements (civil rights, peace, and the environment), labor colleges, nonformal immigrant education, or women's contributions (Courtney, 1989; Deshler, 1991; Hugo, 1990).

However, the institutionalization of adult education can be employed as a partial argument *in favor of* more closely aligning with other areas of education. For example, the growing numbers of adults in higher education has "blurred" the lines between adult and higher education (Apps, 1989a); and there is a further blurring of boundaries between content and delivery. Many institutions of higher education (most notably community colleges) have business centers or institutes that offer training to the business community; conversely, a number of corporations provide accredited degrees (Eurich, 1985). Finally, the split between learning and living is no longer clear-cut. Formal educational institutions offer credits and degrees, but they also offer noncredit, personal-enrichment, and leisure activities; at the same time, informal life experiences can be accredited by various institutions, boards, and agencies.

Peters (1991a) offers yet another rationale for more closely aligning adult education with general education. To continue to develop as a profession, our field must maintain academic departments in institutions of higher education, because that is where we train adult educators and contribute to the growing knowledge base. To maintain the study of adult education, writes Peters, "[first] the field should locate itself in the broader field of educational practice. Second, it should locate itself in the professional school of education. Third, it should locate itself next to the social science disciplines, not in them" (p. 432). Recent closings of departments of adult education or mergers into other departments serve to underscore Peters's concern.

Thus, a case can be made for adult education aligning itself more closely to education in general. Like other forms of education, our field is already highly institutionalized, with considerable overlap between our constituencies. Apps (1987) makes the point that it is important for adult educators to know what happens in school, in the family, and in the mass media, for these arenas all have their learning agendas. "Unless we begin to be more concerned about the rest of education," Apps writes, "the field of adult/continuing education will increasingly be concerned with remedial education" (p. 17). Apps also notes that it would benefit the field "to develop policies that relate continuing education to other facets of education" (1985, p. 203). To promote the differences rather than seeing what we can learn from one another is, in Apps's opinion, a "shortsighted position" (p. 203). Apps outlines two politically expedient reasons for adult education to forge closer ties with elementary, secondary, and higher education: "By virtue of having the word *education* in the title of our field, when various facets of education are criticized, we by association are also criticized. It matters not that we wish to disclaim any ties to these forms of education known, usually pejoratively, as schooling. And . . . those of us who work as practitioners in continuing education will eventually see the results of schooling in our workshops and classes. We must be concerned about these students' preparation" (p. 206).

Thus, the range of debate on the alignment issue is embedded in the historical and philosophical development of the adult education field. Historically, it was easier to be separate when there was less merging of institutional forms and delivery systems than exists today. At one time, in fact, adult education was known as the *fourth level* of education—after elementary, secondary, and higher education. However, we could argue that in some ways aligning ourselves with general education is *philosophically* more difficult today, due to education's growing technical marketplace orientation; that is, such an alignment may make it harder for our field to preserve any sort of social agenda.

The Individual or Society?

One of the most frequently discussed tensions in the field has to do with the proper focus of adult education activities. Should we be responding to the individual learner or to the issues and concerns of society? Or do we somehow try to do both? Furthermore, if we consolidate our efforts to address the needs of society, is our task to support the status quo or to challenge it? How adult education has been defined and conceptualized, how its aims and purposes have been framed, and how the historical context has shaped the field are all part of the discussion of what should constitute the overriding raison d'être of adult education.

A number of writers have pointed out that the American cultural values of individualism, independence, and a Protestant-capitalist work ethic underpin the philosophy of individualism that is characteristic of adult education (Beder, 1987, 1989; Brookfield, 1989; Rubenson, 1989). While some minor variations may exist depending on political-party affiliation, "both American parties operate within a consensus framework in which the capitalist free enterprise ethic is, essentially, unchallenged"; the capitalist economic system "reflect[s] the values of individuality and entrepreneurial freedom which lie at the culture's core" (Brookfield, 1989, p. 150). Out of this ethic comes adult education's focus on individual learners, the technology of the learning transaction, the self-directed-learning phenomenon, and a meet-the-needs service orientation.

Most who support the individual focus argue that our primary mission is to facilitate individual *change*. Beatty (1992) reviews many of the arguments for "the individual and change within the individual [being] "the starting, focal, and ending points of adult education" (p. 23). In support of this position, Beatty explores the "commitment to the individual and the individual change process" underpinning most definitions of adult education, as well as the individual orientation of psychological learning theories, philosophical stances, and ethical principles in the field (p. 19). Beatty also presents what she calls "arguments from the societal perspective" in support of the individual ethos (p. 21). From an economic position, writes Beatty, education is a commodity possessed by individuals; from a political perspective, educated individuals "will ultimately form an educated citizenry for an improved society" (p. 22). Finally, from a social stance, adult educators "shape experiences and environments for individuals to foster change" (p. 23). Although not articulated in this way, the individual focus is also clearly predominant in Knowles's (1980a) work and in many of the studies on self-directed learning (for example, Brockett and Hiemstra, 1991; Candy, 1991; Tough, 1979).

Yet another position in the individual-versus-society debate promotes what Lindeman called the "bilateral" purpose of adult education—that of "changing individuals in continuous adjustment to changing social functions" ([1926] 1989, p. 106). This position, originating from a liberal-progressive tradition (see Chapter Two), maintains a focus on the individual but at the same time posits that changed individuals will have the *collective* effect of changing society.

Indeed, in a review of the philosophical roots of adult education for social change, Heaney (1996) argues that "action to change and sculpt social conditions was the point—the redeeming social purpose that inspired the fledgling, newly identified field of adult education." In building democracy, adult education aimed not only "to *inspire* individual learners . . . but also to enable those learners to *conspire*—to unite, melding their individual agendas in collaborative planning and collective action" (p. 13, emphasis in original).

Mezirow's transformative theory of learning (1990, 1991a) provides a recent example of this viewpoint. Perspective transformation is presented as a comprehensive theory of adult learning in which autonomous, individual adults who undergo changes in their perspectives of the world can, in turn, bring about social change. "We must begin with individual perspective transformations," Mezirow argues, "before social transformations can succeed" (1990, p. 363).

Some have argued, however, that the relationship between the individual and society is much more complex than the notion of society consisting of "the sum of the individuals who compose it" (C. Griffin, 1991, p. 260). Rather than a real focus on social transformation, Griffin argues, what we are seeing is a "reformulation of what may loosely be called [adult education's] liberal tradition, focusing upon individual learning in conditions of social change" (p. 268). He and others (Jarvis, 1987a; Rubenson, 1989) feel that we need a sociological rather than psychological base for understanding the connection between the individual and society. What is currently lacking, according to Griffin, is "any sense of the irreducibly 'social' in human life—a sense of historical, economic, and cultural forces that shape the possibilities for and the meaning of individual growth and transformation" (1991, p. 268). He goes on to point out that while we may have an individual-focused ideology, in today's world the "state and business and industry play the major role in determining the ultimate shape of much adult learning" (p. 273).

Indeed, something of a continuum can be laid out with regard to the individual-versus-societal tension. On one end of the continuum are those like Beatty and Knowles, who promote individual change as the overall purpose of adult education. A middle position is that individual change and social change go hand in hand. At the other end are those who feel that the primary purpose of adult education should be to address social concerns and problems. And at the far end of this position are those who believe that adult education should promote radical social transformation.

In addressing social concerns, adult education in North America has been most timid and not nearly as "political" as in other parts of the world (A. M. Thomas, 1991b). Beder (1989) points out that "generally speaking, mainstream adult educators have considered the American system to be basically good, albeit capable of improvement through adult education. Given this general perspective, in this country there has not been an extensive radical tradition that has sought to eliminate the current system and to replace it with another" (p. 41). More often than not, adult education in North America serves to socialize adults into changing circumstances, allowing them to "fit" into a changing but basically democratic-capitalist social structure. In an analysis of one focus of adult education—immigration and citizenship—A. M. Thomas (1991b) points out the political and ideological dimensions of the problem:

> Recently, governments have become concerned with issues adjacent to citizenship, such as multiculturalism and literacy. Large numbers of people now move throughout the world as immigrants, refugees, and guest workers, carrying their languages and cultural habits with them. The movements have stimulated interest in the practicability if not the inescapability of "hyphenated" citizenship, resulting in complex educational and political responses. Governments are therefore concerned about "resocialization." This concern has shifted the preoccupation with citizenship onto a lifelong spectrum, making citizenship a problem of continuous renewal rather than a one-time effort [pp. 306–307].

A further exploration of the politics of immigration and education can be found in Carlson (1987) and Stewart (1993). Carlson's view is that historically, immigrant education has been used as a means to promote conformity to "mainstream" society. Stewart argues that meeting immigrants' educational needs is in the nation's best interest for a democratic future.

A number of writers have called for an active social agenda in adult education, one that addresses the inequities in society. Ilsley (1992), for example, has little patience with those who focus on individuals, and calls meeting individual needs "the mission by default in adult education"; individualism "by itself . is not enough to change the inequities and societal misalignments that threaten our future" (p. 30).

Nor is it enough to adopt a "social welfare" model wherein educational programs for the unemployed, the functionally illiterate, the homeless, and so on are instituted to preserve the status quo (Cunningham, 1991; C. Griffin, 1991; Rubenson, 1989). Rather, an active social agenda from this perspective is one that *challenges* the status quo and seeks to make radical changes in the present social organization.

As Beder (1989) accurately points out, this is not a popular stance of adult educators in North America. However, it is a major orientation of the field in other parts of the world, and there is a growing awareness of this position in North America. Cunningham (1991) delineates several forces from within and outside North America that are challenging "the former narrowly conceived ideology [of adult education] based on positivism" (p. 353). First are "North Americans with worldviews" who have introduced the rest of us to international issues, sociological rather than psychological perspectives, critical theory, and feminist critiques. A more powerful force, according to Cunningham, has been "challenges from the Third World," such as Freire's liberatory pedagogy and participatory research. "The legitimation in North America of critical pedagogy, liberatory education, and participatory research, concepts flowing from the Third World, was assisted by links between the architects of the concepts and social critics in the United States" (p. 361). Cunningham argues that liberatory forms of adult education—such as the Highlander Research and Education Center, the Transformative Research Network, critical literacy programs, and international exchanges and publications—have done much to bring this perspective into the discourse on the proper mission of adult education.

Foundation Issues and Public Policy

It is probably clear that while the preceding three tensions have been identified and treated separately for discussion, they are in reality quite interwoven. The question of whether adult education should revel in its diversity or seek unity and thus achieve a clearer sense of identity is not unrelated to whether the field should align itself more closely with education in general. This issue is, in turn, related to what we see as the primary focus or mission of our practice. That is, the institutionalization or "schooling" of adult education is seen by most critics as solidifying the interests of the power elites at the expense of the powerless, the marginalized, and the underrepresented in our society. From this perspective, an agenda of social action or social transformation is what should guide our practice.

The debate over what adult education public policy is, what it could be, and what it should be reflects the ideological and historically contextualized tensions discussed above. First, while public policy covers all of a government's interventions in people's lives, social policy generally focuses on health, education, and social welfare.

In an analysis of social policy in adult education, Quigley (1993) has proposed that there are three social policy models, each of which reflects specific philosophical orientations. First is the "market model . supported by vocational behaviorist philosophies of practice" (p. 120). This is the dominant model in North America. Concerned with "economic vitality through education policy," the market model "can be seen in numerous educational policies which . . . support and foster adult education vocationalism—from professional education to work-place literacy. Individualism and minimal governmental intervention are championed. . . . The call for accountability based on measurable criteria in basic, higher and vocational education programmes is one clear example, the demand for 'systems that produce large gains in basic skills and hold them accountable for achieving those gains' (Chisman 1989: 17) in literacy education is another" (p. 122).

Underlying the market model is the capitalistic socioeconomic system in which economic productivity "becomes the predominant rationale for all publicly funded social interventions including adult education" (Beder, 1987, p. 107). In addition to the rationale of economic productivity driving public policy, Beder notes two other ways in which the capitalist paradigm affects adult education. Social justice becomes equated with providing "opportunity for members of the underclasses to amass more income and material goods," and a social position is "equated with economic position" (p. 109). The third effect is that since adult education "is largely financed through learner fees," the enterprise becomes entrepreneurial, technical, and market driven (p. 109).

Quigley (1993) labels the second model "progressive-liberal-welfare," in which "active and direct government intervention is here advocated to enhance societal and individual conditions" (p. 123). While New Deal legislation of the 1930s and Great Society programs of the mid-1960s exemplify this model, it has come under challenge in the 1980s and 1990s.

The third model, which Quigley calls "social redistribution," reflects a more liberatory, social-reconstruction philosophy that advocates social change. More prevalent outside North America, this model reflects practice that "has tended to range from reformist, frequently Freirian-influenced, community-based ideologies seeing a need for counter-hegemonic action, to classic socio-economic reconstruction which adopts a class struggle approach to societal issues" (p. 124).

Quigley (1993) argues that adult educators in North America have contributed little to social-policy formation. This point echoes the frustration of Koloski (1989) in trying to represent a field whose sense of identity is so amorphous that its ability to have an impact on policy is almost impossible. The field's fragmentation was also a motivating force behind Knowles's documenting the institutional history of the field (1962, 1977). A history and an identity, it was hoped, would allow adult education to command a place in the formation of public policy. Unfortunately, Quigley (1993) argues, the field "is becoming—some say has already become—an instrument of the state without the advisement, consent or even the full awareness of the field" (p. 118).

Social policy, of course, is intricately related to the philosophical issue of the extent to which adult education reinforces the status quo, promotes social equity, or advocates radical social change. Two writers have conceptualized these issues from policy and programmatic stances. Nordhaug (1986) offers a classification scheme that organizes social issues according to collective versus individual efforts to either support or oppose the existing social order. In Table 4.1, the first of four cells is collective opposition, in which there is open class struggle involving political education and radical protests. The individual dimension of opposition—the second cell in Nordhaug's scheme—can be manifest through religious movements. In the third cell, social policy with a collective focus that preserves the social order might be addressed to illiterates, immigrants, and prisoners. These are "public efforts to compensate for social, ethnic, generational, gender, and regional inequities in society" (p. 47). The fourth possibility is an individual focus that preserves the social order. Here, profit is the ultimate goal, and courses are offered on a purely commercial basis.

Somewhat similar to Nordhaug's scheme is Cunningham's adaptation (1989) of Paulston and Altenbaugh's typology (1988); see Table 4.2. This typology is built on the two axes of goals for social change (low, middle, and high) and on individual-versus-system-level control of learning. For example, the types of adult education with the least devotion to social reform in their agenda are consumer-oriented adult education, with its focus on self-actualization and leisure activities, and conventional adult education from formal systems such as business, government, and the military. An

Table 4.1. A Classification Scheme for Adult Education and Related Degrees of Social Commitment.

	Opposing the social order	Not opposing the social order
Collectively Oriented	I	III
Individually oriented	II	IV

Source: Nordhaug, O. (1986). Adult education in the welfare state: Institutionalization of social commitment. *International Journal of Lifelong Education*, 5(1), 45–57. Reprinted by permission of Taylor and Francis, publishers, and the author.

example of adult education with a high social-reconstruction agenda would be a radical humanist approach that supports struggles for human liberation. At the formal-systems level would be radical structuralist education found in revolutionary societies such as China and Iran. The middle ground is exemplified by co-ops, peace movements, and women's movements.

In a recent analysis of U.S. educational policy and adult education since 1964, Cunningham (1995) writes that the field has "lost the vision of building a strong inclusive participative democracy" (p. 88). Rather, adult education as it is reflected in policy at the federal level "is about professionalism and reproducing the society as is" (p. 87).

These analyses of public policy highlight how the nature of the enterprise of adult education reflects certain definitional, philo-

Table 4.2. A Typology of Adult Education Programs.

	Program Control	
Goals	Individuals	Formal systems
High	Type 4 Radical humanist (struggles for human liberation: Black Panthers, Weathermen)	Type 5 Radical structuralist (in new revolutionary societies: China, Nicaragua, Iran)
Middle	Type 3 Reformist adult education (co-ops, peace movements, women's movements)	
Low	Type 2 Consumer adult education (self-actualization, leisure)	Type 1 Conventional adult education (business, government, military)

Source: Cunningham (adapted from Paulston and Altenbaugh, 1988), 1989, p. 41.

sophical, and sociohistorical factors. As we pointed out in Chapters Two and Three, examining our history and philosophy is not a useless undertaking; both of these foundational disciplines very much shape the scope and nature of the field and dramatically affect what has become public policy. Perhaps such an examination can lead to a more proactive influence on public policy.

Summary

Out of the historical and philosophical foundations of adult education have come a number of interlocking issues or tensions that characterize the field. Adult education's wide diversity of activities and purposes is considered simultaneously a strength and a weakness; with diversity comes fragmentation and little sense of a common identity. How to preserve our diversity while promoting a unified enterprise to puzzled outsiders has been a major concern in the field since the 1930s.

Closely linked with the diversity-versus-unity issue is whether or not it would be in our best interests to more closely align ourselves with the rest of education. This could be easily done if our society were inclined to adopt a true lifelong-learning perspective; however, such a perspective requires a rethinking and restructuring of schooling—an undertaking that most educators consider too radical. Those wanting to remain apart point to the separate mission of adult education and the problems of becoming too institutionalized. Others use the same factors—mission and institutionalization—to argue for closer alignment.

The third issue we discussed in this chapter is the ongoing debate about whether the individual or society should be the focus of adult education. The discourse around this issue can be plotted on a continuum, with the individual at one end and the mission of changing society at the other. Between these two opposites are those who advocate a *dual* mission of changing individuals and society and those who emphasize adult education's role in maintaining and improving our democratic society as it is.

These foundation-related issues have implications for public policy in adult education. We reviewed several models that help us think about public policy: Quigley's tripartite model representing a market orientation, a progressive-liberal-welfare approach, and social redistribution; and Nordhaug's and Cunningham's models—both of which are anchored in the debate around the mission of adult education.

Part II

The Organization and Delivery of Adult Education

Part One of this book dealt with the foundations of the adult education field in terms of definition, philosophy, history, and related issues. In Part Two, we cover several dimensions related to the organization and delivery of adult education. In particular, we describe the formal delivery system in the United States (Chapter Five); the participants in adult education programs and important concepts of adult learning (Chapter Six); adult education from an international perspective (Chapter Seven); and the troublesome issues of opportunity and access (Chapter Eight).

Chapter Five addresses the thousands of organizations in the United States that plan and implement educational programs for adults. The easiest way to describe this practice is through various typologies that encompass all or some of the field's dimensions. In addition, we "map" the field by content area and personnel and explore the considerable overlap that exists among institutions, content, and personnel. We also address the process involved in delivering programs, including planning, administration, and financing.

Wherever in the world adult education takes place, learners are involved. Chapter Six reviews the participation patterns of men and women involved in organized adult education. In this chapter, we also discuss some of the theories and concepts related to adult learning, including andragogy, self-directed learning, and transformational learning. Finally, we review some of the newer developments in understanding the phenomenon of adult learning.

Shifting to a global context, in Chapter Seven we explore adult education worldwide from several perspectives. First, we examine adult education in other countries, including similarities and differences across cultures. International adult education can also be seen as a forum for the exchange of ideas and information, as well as an academic field of comparative studies.

As with Part One, the last chapter in this section addresses key issues related to the organization and delivery of adult education from a global perspective. These issues center on who has access to adult education and the reasons that participation is so skewed toward one segment of the world's population. We also analyze three responses— political, educational, and technological—to the inequities of access and participation.

5

Providers of Formal Adult Education

Most people's familiarity with adult education is based on first-hand experience with one or more of the agencies or institutions that offer programs for adults. For instance, the county extension office can give you advice on how to freeze strawberries or plant a container garden, the local adult school offers an exercise class that you enroll in, your church sponsors a Bible study class, or you participate in company-sponsored training programs. These examples represent a range of adult education providers. Some agencies are more educational in their mission, and they more easily come to mind as providers of adult education; others (unions, social movement groups, prisons, and the like) are not so readily identified with providing learning opportunities for adults.

In this chapter, our mapping of the field begins with the institutions and agencies that provide formal, organized adult education. Next, we outline the field from the perspectives of content areas and clienteles—both dimensions of which intersect with the institutional map. In the second half of the chapter, we discuss the functions of program planning, administration, and financing and their relevancy to the delivery of formal adult education.

Maps to Organize the Field

In a sense, we have already advanced several maps or frameworks for organizing the adult education field through the first four chapters of this book. Definitions and purposes—what "counts" as adult education (Chapter One)—give us one template, as do different philosophical perspectives (Chapter Two), history (Chapter Three), and some of the issues that frame the field (Chapter Four). In this chapter, we concentrate on the institutions, programs, people, and tasks involved in the delivery of adult education.

There are a number of schemes, models, and typologies that purport to capture the adult education "enterprise." Some, such as those proposed by Boyd and Apps (1980) and Schroeder (1980), are complex schemes that try to encompass all dimensions of the field—processes as well as structures, clients as well as delivery systems. This chapter's tripartite model of institutions, content, and clienteles was inspired by Knowles's basic scheme (1964) introduced more than three decades ago. He suggested that there were five dimensions to the "field of operations in adult education" (p. 41): institutional, content, geographical, personnel, and morphological (for example, various forms of activities such as conferences, workshops, and lectures). Over the years, the terms *institution*, *content area*, and *personnel*—the latter of which includes providers and clients—have been most frequently used to describe the field's structure and delivery systems (Darkenwald and Merriam, 1982; Merriam and Cunningham, 1989; Smith, Aker, and Kidd, 1970). This section on the field's organization focuses on institutions, content areas, and personnel.

Institutions and Agencies

The most visible dimension of the adult education enterprise is its institutions. Not only do the individuals who are working with adults commonly identify themselves in reference to the *institution* for which they work (rather than with the general field of adult education), but learners themselves also talk in terms of the institutional sponsor of their learning activities. Furthermore, while much of adult learning goes on in informal settings and by individuals on their own, forms of adult education that have become institutionalized or that are components of preexisting institutions have received the most attention in the literature.

The comprehensive histories discussed in Chapter Three (J. T. Adams, 1944; Grattan, 1955; Kett, 1994; Knowles, 1962, 1977; Stubblefield and Keane, 1994) are largely efforts to document the emergence of institutional forms of adult education from Colonial to modern times.

Institutional Typologies

One mechanism for capturing the diversity and prevalence of the institutional dimension of adult education is through typologies— which, Kowalski (1988) argues, "allow organizations to be grouped according to characteristics cogent to the practice of adult education" (p. 23). They reveal how types of organizations differ, and how differing organizational contexts play "a major role in shaping the behaviors of the programmer and other administrators responsible for formulating key decisions."

Indeed, the centrality of the adult education program vis-à-vis the parent or host institution is crucial to the amount of power and authority the program has relative to its administrative, planning, and financial matters—even to its very survival. Most classification schemes reflect a range with regard to the centrality of the adult education mission. At one end are institutions exclusively devoted to adult education, and at the other end are institutions in which adult education may be used to underscore another (unrelated) mission entirely. Reflecting this range, for example, is Verner and Booth's simple typology (1964) consisting of (1) institutions of which adult education is the primary function, such as Ben Franklin's Junto or Canada's Frontier College; (2) institutions for which adult education is an extension of the primary function, such as school systems and libraries; and (3) institutions for which adult education is a means of achieving another primary function, such as in business and industry, the armed forces, and health and welfare agencies.

Two better-known typologies are adaptations by Schroeder (1970) and Darkenwald and Merriam (1982) of Knowles's typology (1964) of organizations. Schroeder divides institutions and agencies into the four following types:

- *Type I agencies.* Established to serve the educational needs of adults, they include proprietary schools and independent residential centers.
- *Type II agencies.* Established to serve the educational needs of youth but also serve adults as a secondary function, these agencies include institutions of higher education and public schools with adult evening or day programs.
- *Type III agencies.* Established to serve both educational and noneducational needs of the community, they include libraries, museums, and health and welfare agencies.
- *Type IV agencies.* These were established to serve the needs of special groups, often using adult education as the primary method of service. Examples of this type of agency include adult education that takes place in religious institutions, in correctional facilities, and in government, business, and industry.

Darkenwald and Merriam's typology is essentially the same as Schroeder's, except that their names for the four agency types are clearer and more precise. They are:

- *Independent adult education organizations.* These organizations exist for the primary purpose of providing learning opportunities specifically for adults. They can be community-based—for example, learning exchanges and grassroots organizations—or they can be private, such as literacy groups (Literacy Volunteers of America, Laubach Literacy International, and the like) and proprietary schools or residential centers such as the Highlander Center for Research and Education.

- *Educational institutions.* This category includes educational institutions, including public schools and postsecondary institutions of all sorts, that have the primary mission of serving youth. As we in the field are aware, the numbers of adults attending postsecondary institutions, especially community colleges, have increased dramatically over the years. It is even projected that by the year 2000 more students on college campuses will be over the age of twenty-five than under (Lawler, 1991). Also included in this category is the Cooperative Extension Service (CES), whose primary mission is "to disseminate, and encourage the application of, research generated knowledge and leadership techniques to individuals, families and communities" (Forest, 1989, p. 336).

- *Quasieducational organizations.* Whether public or private, these organizations consider the education of the public to be an integral part of their mission, and they view education as an allied or corollary function of their primary mission. This category includes cultural organizations (libraries, museums, and the mass media) and community organizations such as service clubs, religious and civic organizations, and the like.

- *Noneducational organizations.* These are similar to quasieducational organizations in that their primary mission is not educational; the difference is that rather than viewing education clearly as an allied function, noneducational organizations consider it a means to some other end. Furthermore, educational opportunities are mostly geared to the organization's employees instead of to the public. For example, business and industry exist to make a profit. To the extent to which education (more often called "training" in this setting) can increase profits, these institutions support it. Government agencies at the local, state, and federal level are also engaged in extensive training and education, as are the armed forces, unions, and correctional institutions.

Kowalski (1988) makes the point that the Darkenwald and Merriam typology, while easy to comprehend, results in too many wildly divergent sponsors of adult education being placed in the fourth category. Prisons and health agencies, for example, represent such different contexts that few implications for planning can be drawn. Kowalski suggests a six-part typology that reduces this diversity while at the same time effecting a more equal distribution of sponsoring organizations. His typology is as follows (p. 27):

- *Type* A institutions provide adult education as an exclusive function.
- *Type* B institutions are schools and other educational institutions that offer adult education as a secondary function.
- *Type* C institutions are community service agencies that provide adult education as a secondary function.
- *Type* D institutions are private organizations that offer adult education as a secondary function.
- *Type* E institutions are voluntary organizations and groups that provide adult education as a secondary function.
- *Type* F institutions are government agencies that offer adult education as a secondary function.

The first two types are identical to those in the Darkenwald and Merriam typology, while types C through F break out sponsoring agencies according to purpose, function, and climate. Under Type C, for example, Kowalski includes museums, libraries, clinics and hospitals, and media such as public television. Type D, private organizations, includes business and industry and private foundations. Type E, voluntary organizations, includes service clubs, YMCAs and YWCAs, churches, professional organizations, and unions (which are theoretically voluntary). Finally, Type F stresses adult education that takes place through governmental agencies.

These institutional typologies help us get a sense of adult education's pervasiveness in our society. The money spent on training in business and industry alone amounts to billions of dollars each year, surpassing what is spent on K–12 and higher education combined (U.S. Department of Education, 1994). When we also con-sider the numbers of adults employed in local, state, and federal gov-ernmental agencies who receive training—as well as the numbers of adults returning to school for credit and noncredit courses—it becomes clear why the field's institutional base is the most visible aspect of adult education.

Characteristics of the Institutional Dimension

In tracing the institutional history of the field, Knowles (1977) identified six characteristics of the growth of adult education insti-tutions that also illuminate the nature of the field today. First, he noted that institutions "typically emerge in response to specific needs, rather than as part of a general design" (p. 257). For exam-ple, when a need presents itself—for example, training for a cultur-ally diverse workforce, or meeting literacy requirements in an increasingly technological society—organizations such as consult-ing firms and literacy agencies form to address the need. Related to this first characteristic is the second, which states that the field's development tends to be episodic rather than consistent. "In a sense," Knowles writes, "adult education has thrived on crises, since needs are greatest and clearest then. Similarly, it has tended to retrench in periods of placidity" (p. 258).

Knowles's next three principles have to do with the relationship of adult education institutions to other institutions. According to Knowles, institutional forms of adult education "tend to survive to the extent that they become attached to agencies established for other purposes" (p. 258). While some independent adult education agencies exist at any point in time, "the great bulk . . . that have survived have become attached to some host institution" (p. 259).

While such a linkage tends to ensure survival, Knowles's fourth observation is that the adult education program "tend[s] to emerge with a secondary status in the institutional hierarchy" (p. 259). Many adult educators can relate to this phenomenon. Continuing education programs in higher education, public education programs sponsored by social agencies, and even training departments in business and industry are often not understood by central administrators; they sometimes must pay their own way and are often the first to be cut in times of retrenchment. These programs "gain stability and permanence," Knowles points out in his fifth principle, "as they become increasingly differentiated in administration, finance, curriculum, and methodology" (p. 259).

Finally, Knowles observes that even if institutional forms of adult education "crystallize into organized substructures" (p. 260), it is usually done without awareness of being part of a larger field of adult education. These substructures tend to identify more readily with the host institution, with a particular content area (such as literacy or health education), or with a particular clientele (for example, women or older adults).

Several of Knowles's observations reflect aspects of marginality—an important concept characterizing the institutional structure of the field. Uncovered in B. R. Clark's study (1956, 1958) of Los Angeles public school adult education in the 1950s, marginality refers to the status of many such programs in relation to their host or parent institution. That is, with the exception of independent adult education institutions, all other formal adult education is connected to other institutions whose primary mission is something other than adult education.

Clark identified several problems with the field's marginal status. One is goal diffusion, wherein the adult education unit does not have a clear purpose or aim, which in turn leads to a cafeteria-style approach to programming. Furthermore, the financial health of the adult education unit within the larger organization is often driven by an enrollment economy—that is, funding is tied to the number of adults enrolled. These factors combine into problems of identity and integrity. "Identity," writes Clark, "depends upon a sense of limits, and personnel in a service organization must make at least some careful projections about what kinds of 'service' they are going to render to what kinds of people, and with what purpose" (1958, p. 11).

Subsequent research and writing on marginality has generally underscored the detrimental nature of this status (see Chapman, 1990, for a review). Gilley and Galbraith (1986), for example, link marginality to the development of the field as a profession. Because of marginality, many in the field do not identify themselves as adult educators, nor do they understand that a body of knowledge exists that can unite practitioners. They recommend some type of certification to legitimize the field. (We discuss the link between marginality and professionalism in more detail in Chapters Nine and Ten.)

Not everyone sees adult education's marginal status vis-à-vis the parent institution as negative. Marginality allows for creativity and responsiveness to changing needs; indeed, the entrepreneurial quality of much of adult education would not be possible if it were encumbered with large bureaucratic structures. Furthermore, as summarized by Chapman (1990, p. 27) in her review of the literature, "marginality allows the provider to maintain organizational distance and avoid being co-opted, seduced or forced to collude with the client system's self-serving objectives. Also, the marginal practitioner's interventions are not ridden with hidden agendas. Finally, marginality allows the practitioner to be in contact with the outside professional world and fresh approaches to old organizational problems, and it allows the practitioner to take risks."

The institutional dimension is thus one major means of bringing some organization to the field of adult education. The typologies we present here act as templates that can be placed on a field of practice that includes a staggering number of sponsors of educational programs for adults. If we consider the provision of adult education from an institutional perspective, in conjunction with Knowles's characteristics and the notion of marginality, we get a context from which to better understand practice.

Content Areas

The institutional dimension offers us one map of the field; another can be drawn by content areas reflected in the realm of adult education.

Just what do adults learn about in programs sponsored by various institutions? At first glance, it would seem to be clear what the content of a program offered by certain institutions would be: religious organizations would offer programs related to religious beliefs, health agencies would offer programs related to health, and so on.

However, upon closer scrutiny it becomes obvious that content areas tend to cut across institutional lines. Some religious organizations hold workshops or classes in interpersonal skills and relationships (coping with divorce, for example); and many hospitals offer their employees training and development activities that have little to do with health concerns. Furthermore, a great deal of adult education is not sponsored by institutions but is *noninstitutional*—structured by particular interests and needs. To get a fuller picture of the scope of adult education, it is thus worth looking at the field from the perspective of content areas.

Content areas generally reflect the goals and purposes of adult education. A number of these frameworks were presented in Chapter One (see Table 1.1). For example, one enduring purpose of adult education is preparing for or enhancing one's work life. As Rachal (1989) states, "[W]ithout question, the workplace is the engine that is changing the nature of adult education, and technology is its fuel" (p. 7). Whether they label it "occupational," "vocational," "career development," or something else, adults preparing for employment or wanting to make changes in their work life seek out learning opportunities from any number of sponsors. Vocational-technical schools, community colleges, four-year colleges and universities, proprietary schools, and professional schools—as well as most employers—offer work-related educational and training opportunities. Studies have shown that employment needs are in fact the primary motivation for participating in adult education (see Chapter Six).

The single biggest work-related content area is *human resource development* (HRD), the term given to adult education that occurs in business and industry. HRD as a specialized field of practice is newer than adult education and thus is still defining itself and its scope of activities. Today, it is widely assumed to refer to both organizational and group levels of learning, as well as individual employee learning (Pace, Smith, and Mills, 1991; Rothwell and Sredl, 1992).

A corollary of work-related adult education is the area of continuing professional education. Professional groups of all sorts permeate our daily lives—from educators who decide what people should learn to doctors who decide who is healthy to accountants who decide what taxes we need to pay. Most professional groups have come to recognize that they need continuing education to stay abreast of changes in their field and ultimately to better serve their clients. For many professions, continuing education is mandatory (L. Phillips and Associates, 1994)—an issue that has been a point of debate within adult education (see, for example, Brockett, 1992; LeGrand, 1992). Just as with work-related programs, continuing education can be offered by a variety of sponsors, including the profession itself, the institutional employer (such as a hospital or an accounting firm), continuing education divisions of institutions of higher education, and private consulting firms (Cervero, 1988; Houle, 1980).

A content area that is sometimes linked to work-related needs and is sometimes considered "remedial" or "compensatory" is basic skills education. Adults in our society who are functionally illiterate, who did not complete high school, or whose first language is not English can take advantage of learning opportunities sponsored by the government, employers, and any number of private, public, and community-based groups.

While remedial and work-related content areas (including training and continuing professional education) can be easily identified, those programs that address personal growth, family life, and recreational needs are sometimes more difficult to differentiate from each other or from remedial and work-related content areas. Much depends on the motivation of the adult participating in the activity. For example, a workshop on interpersonal communication skills could be taken for personal interest, to help in dealing with family members, or for getting along better at work. As with any other content area, learning opportunities such as these are offered by a wide range of organizations.

A broad content area addresses the adult's role as a citizen in society. Citizen education has been known by a number of names over the years. For example, the 1936 *Handbook of Adult Education in the United States* (Rowden) contains a chapter on "political education"; and the 1948 *Handbook* (Ely) has an entire section consisting of seven chapters on "civic participation and responsibility." The latest version of the handbook (Merriam and Cunningham, 1989) includes a chapter on "public affairs education" in which Jimmerson, Hastay, and Long (1989) point out that civic education is really "a praxis combining (1) public consideration of current issues, (2) programs to increase citizens' ability to act collectively on issues, and (3) efforts to create institutional frameworks to perpetuate this acquired ability" (p. 451). In a recent book on civic education, Boggs (1991) delineates a number of themes that characterize modern-day adult education's involvement in fostering good citizenship. Civic education can also encompass a variety of philosophical positions, from preserving the status quo to advancing more revolutionary ideologies (see Chapter Two).

Finally, a case can be made for an emerging content area unique to the turn of the twentieth century: technology. Some could argue, of course, that "technology" is what has accounted for many of humankind's advances over the centuries. Certainly the technology of the industrial revolution created major changes in society— changes to which adults had to adjust. What perhaps differentiates earlier technological changes from today's is the current emphasis on *educational* applications.

Interestingly, a chapter in the 1989 *Handbook* on new educational technologies was placed in a section on the future of adult education (Lewis, 1989). Now, less than a decade later, most would agree that educational technologies are here and are pervading our daily lives. They have quite literally created a learning need that is being addressed by a multitude of adult education providers, from employers to educational institutions to private consulting firms. Perhaps no other content area can boast the range of providers and delivery systems that technology can.

Technology as a content area is unique in that while people can learn *about* it, they can also learn other content areas *through* it. Although the Internet and especially the World Wide Web are the current technological rage in terms of educational access for individual learners, teleconferencing and other technologies developed for distance learning hold great promise for groups of learners. Much of continuing professional education, for example, is done via teleconferencing and telecomputing, or what some have labeled the *virtual classroom* (Porter, 1993). In addition, computer-assisted instructional packages are available on nearly any topic.

In summary, the field of adult education can be mapped by content area as well as by institutions and agencies. Content areas are reflective of adult education's goals and purposes, of which there are a number of typologies (see Chapter One). A strength of viewing the field from content areas is that learning encompasses a much wider range than just what formal institutions and agencies deliver. Any topic can be studied independent of formal institutions. There are many examples of groups forming spontaneously around a need or interest, of individuals designing their own learning projects, and of technology mediating instruction and learning outside of institutions.

Personnel

A third way to approach the diverse and somewhat amorphous field of adult education is to consider who is involved. This can be broken out into two major categories: those who deliver learning opportunities and the target audiences who benefit from these opportunities.

In considering the personnel involved in the delivery of adult education, one can get trapped in a debate about who is and who is not an adult educator, and about the extent to which practitioners may or may not identify themselves as adult educators (see Chapters One, Nine, and Ten). Sidestepping this debate for the moment allows us to focus on describing who is involved with providing adult education.

An often-cited analysis of this personnel issue is Houle's famous pyramid of leadership (1970). At the base of the pyramid are volunteers who lead groups or tutor other adults in a wide range of content areas. At the middle level of the pyramid are the hundreds of thousands of part-time workers who are paid on an hourly basis for their work. At the top and narrowest point of the pyramid are the full-time adult educators, including program administrators, professors of adult education, training directors, and staff of the Cooperative Extension Service. It is the people in this group at the pyramid's apex who most readily identify with being in an adult education career. Houle writes of the group: "One of the great challenges of the field is to create a sense of common identification and community among these leaders who will then influence the workers at the other levels of the pyramid" (p. 112).

This distribution of personnel in adult education impacts the development of the field as a profession. For example, only the smallest group of full-time adult educators have anything close to a "career ladder." Furthermore, such a large cadre of volunteers and part-time workers makes the consideration of certification problematic (see Chapter Nine). Perhaps a more basic issue is the extent to which seeing the field in terms of "levels," as in Houle's pyramid, leads to an elitism and pseudo-distinctions about who is and who is not a "legitimate" adult educator (Brockett, 1991b).

A more helpful model might be Usher and Bryant's continuum or spectrum of adult education practitioners (1989). Based on the extent of "consciousness of having an educational role in working with adults," the continuum spans from "the full-time professional" on one end to the individual whose "activities have repercussions for adult learning" on the other end (p. 2). Our view is that *adult educators* and *educators of adults* have different intentions in their work but represent parallel structures in the delivery of learning opportunities.

Turning to the second major category of personnel—those for whom programs are planned—it is common practice for providers of adult education to target their offerings to particular clienteles, especially when such clienteles are perceived as having special learning needs and interests. At the turn of the twentieth century, for example, massive programs to acculturate immigrants into the American way of life dominated the adult education scene (Knowles, 1977). Such "officially" sponsored Americanization education was not the only response to the influx of immigrants, however. Immigrant communities established their own adult education activities designed to help them both preserve their cultural heritage and adjust to their new life in North America (Seller, 1978). Similarly, working-class men and women established workers' schools and labor colleges that addressed their interests better than "outside" adult educators or employers could (Hellyer and Schulman, 1989). Today, workers' education "is designed by, with, and for workers to satisfy their own goals for daily survival, long-term security, and, if possible, empowerment" (Hellyer and Schulman, p. 575).

Besides being the recipients of adult education programs planned by outside agencies, immigrants and workers have originated their own educational programs. This pattern of provision from both within and outside the clientele is characteristic of most groups. However, we tend to know more about programs planned *for* particular groups, since these are typically institutionally based and more visible. (See Chapter Ten for a discussion on the "invisible" side of practice.)

There are as many clienteles for adult education as there are ways to define particular groups of people: programs for women, men, middle-aged people, parents, rural people, African Americans, alumni, older adults, veterans, handicapped individuals, and so on. The social climate of an era often defines particular groups of adults as targets for adult education. For example, the women's movement of the 1960s and 1970s gave more visibility to women's needs that could be addressed through education; likewise, many men's groups formed in response to women's empowerment. That is not to say that women weren't doing their own adult education all along: from the first *Handbook* (Rowden, 1936) on, women as a special clientele have been acknowledged.

Another example of how social context raises the visibility of particular client groups is adult education for older adults. With the aging of the population, the numbers of older adults in our society continue to increase. People are also living longer. The need to respond to large numbers of relatively healthy and continually better-educated older adults has even spawned a separate field of practice: educational gerontology (D. A. Peterson, 1983). Two special programs for older adults—Elderhostels and Learning-in-Retirement Institutes—are relatively new responses to the needs of this clientele.

Other groups are defined as society becomes aware of their presence and, in particular, of the potential threat to social stability; or perhaps becomes embarrassed by the group's challenge to society's ideals.

Hareven (1978) discusses how this process works with regard to the segmenting of different age groups: "The 'discovery' of a new stage of life is itself a complex process. First, individuals become aware of the specific characteristics of a given stage of life as a distinct condition. This discovery is then passed on to society in popularized versions. If it appears to be associated with a major social problem, it attracts the attention of agencies of welfare and social control. Finally, it is institutionalized: legislation is passed and agencies are created to deal with its special needs and problems" (p. 203). Groups that have been so defined in North America within recent years—and for whom federally financed programs have been established—include functionally illiterate adults, unemployed or underemployed workers, homeless people, displaced homemakers, Vietnam War veterans, AIDS patients, and disabled people.

In summary, the organization and delivery of adult education can be understood from a number of perspectives. We have chosen to describe the field from the institutions that offer educational programs, the content areas that these programs address, and the personnel involved. Treating these three perspectives as discrete organizing frameworks is a bit misleading, however. In reality, much overlap and many interrelationships exist among institutions, content areas, and personnel. For example, a community college offers credit programs to prepare adults for careers and career changes; it may also have a basic education program for adults in the community who want skills training; it may offer leisure and recreational activities for all community residents; and it may sponsor an Elderhostel program for older adults. Volunteers, as well as full-time and part-time teachers, may be involved in any of these programs.

Just as any institution may deliver a myriad of programs to diverse clienteles, any content area or clientele may be served by a variety of formal, nonformal, or informal delivery modes. For example, people can learn about computers by taking courses sponsored by institutions, in on-line and off-line computer users' groups, and on their own through self-help software packages.

Programming, Administration, and Financing

In addition to mapping the organization of the field and the delivery of programs according to institutions, content areas, and personnel, we might also consider some of the components crucial to the *process* of delivering learning opportunities to adults. As we noted earlier in this chapter, the organizational context shapes the actual practice of adult education. How a program is planned, administered, and financed at a military base training center, for example, differs significantly from how it is done through a community college evening program. Nevertheless, the *functions* of program planning, financing, and administration or management are common to all adult education settings.

Program Planning

Program planning, also referred to as program development, is often considered one of the functions of adult education practice. However, it is such a central feature in the provision of adult education that it is also treated as a discrete topic with its own research and knowledge base. Knox (1991) underscores this point: "[A]bout one-third of adult education research is on aspects of program development. It makes up the single largest part of scholarly and professional writing in the field, which is understandable because program development is applicable across all types of provider agencies" (p. 228).

As we discussed in Chapter One, using the term *program* instead of *curriculum* implies a range of activities related to and characteristic of an adult education program (of which the actual content or curriculum is one part). Delivering programs to adults typically involves making decisions about what to offer, how to offer it, and how to evaluate it. Numerous, well-known models are available to guide this process: no fewer than ninety-three publications containing explicit or implicit program-planning models were reviewed by Sork and Buskey in 1986. Most models are built upon Tyler's *Basic Principles of Curriculum and Instruction* (1949) and present program planning as a linear process of assessing needs, setting objectives, organizing learning experiences to meet the objectives, implementing the program, and evaluating results.

Few practitioners, however, follow a prescribed program-planning model. Sork and Caffarella (1989) speculate that "practitioners take shortcuts in planning in order to get the job done," and/or contextual factors that are unique to each situation shape the planning process (p. 243). Pennington and Green (1976), in a study of how planning actually occurs, drew attention to this gap between theory and practice. They found, for example, that few planners conducted formal needs assessments, and fewer still evaluated their programs in any systematic manner. Brookfield (1986) has also discussed how models fail to account for the "personality conflicts, political factors, and budgetary constraints [that] alter neatly conceived plans of action" (p. 202).

Accounting for the context of program planning can be traced back to Houle's classic *The Design of Education* (1972). His "fundamental system of practice" is set within educational situations in which "the design of an educational activity is usually in a constant state of reformulation" (p. 39). Houle's system consists of two parts: the category of educational design systems (individual, group, institution, or mass), and the components of the program development process. Caffarella's eleven-component "interactive model" (1994) is based on the assumption that "the development of educational programs is a complex interaction of institutional priorities, tasks, people, and events. [Furthermore,] program planners often work with a number of components and tasks at the same time and apply the model in different ways; and they rarely work alone" (p. 27).

An emphasis on context and politics distinguishes Cervero and Wilson's recent work (1994a, 1994b) on program planning. They maintain that planning is "a social process of negotiating personal and organizational interests in contexts of structured power relations" (1994b, p. 253). The world of the program planner is one of power relationships, of interests that are the "reasons, or ends to which action is directed" (p. 255), and the responsible negotiation of those interests. Their model offers a theoretical basis for understanding how program planners interact with the context of their practice in the planning and implementing of programs for adults.

In summary, much of the practice of adult education revolves around the planning of programs. Many models exist that delineate the various decision points in the process. However, practitioners rarely find these models a good fit with what actually occurs. Most planners must deal with the constraints of the institution or setting in which they work, with the resources available to them, and with people—from supervisors to potential learners—who have a vested interest in the process and outcomes.

Administration-Management

The delivery of adult education programs could not occur without people who are responsible for planning, implementing, and evaluating activities that carry out the group's or organization's mission. Administering adult education programs is one of the primary functions of the adult educators who form the top of Houle's pyramid of leadership that we presented earlier in the chapter. These individuals include deans and directors of continuing education, program managers and staff, and training directors. Knox (1991) makes the point that "the predominant reliance on part-time and short-term staff members and volunteers to plan and conduct programs makes educational leadership by full-time administrators essential for the success of an agency" (p. 223). We should point out that while many of us tend to think of administrators as being in institutional settings, community-based and nonformal modes of adult education also have individuals and even groups that are responsible for administrative activities.

There is a growing base of literature on the administration, management, and leadership of adult education programs. These terms are sometimes used interchangeably, although various writers make distinctions between them. Smith and Offerman (1989) define management as "the art and science of achieving goals through people," and they prefer its usage to the term *administration*—which, they claim, "is more concerned with carrying out tasks" (p. 246). However, within the field of adult education, *administration* seems to be the more commonly used term (Courtenay, 1990; Knox, 1991; Mulcrone, 1993).

Leadership, while certainly a desired attribute of an administrator or manager, is applicable to a broad range of people involved in the provision of adult education, not all of whom are administrators (Apps, 1994; Edelson, 1992; Knox, 1991). Indeed, we believe that leadership has more to do with how people function in their particular settings, rather than with the roles and titles they may hold. This overlap of terms is partly due to the knowledge base accumulating from several sources, including literature from outside the field (in management, for example) and context-specific research in such realms as higher education, adult basic education, and community-based adult education.

Depending on the source, various functions of adult education administration have been identified. Courtenay's review (1990) of the literature on administration uses nine functions: philosophy and mission; goals and objectives; planning; organization and structure; leadership; staffing; budgeting; marketing; and evaluation. Smith and Offerman (1989) identify planning, organizing, and evaluating as three major functions that form a matrix with the four "managerial tasks" of programming, staffing, financing, and marketing. Knox (1991) considers administrative functions to be leadership, developing programs, attracting participants, staffing, acquiring resources, coordinating, and fostering external relations. One function, decision making, cuts across these other functions and is the "unifying feature" (p. 221) of all that administrators do.

Several of Knox's functions are elaborated on in interesting ways by the authors of *Current Perspectives on Administration of Adult Education Programs* (Mulcrone, 1993). Heaney (1993), for example, suggests that strategic planning can be a more democratic and participatory activity; Vernon, Lo Parco, and Marsick (1993) propose thinking about learning in new ways, which in turn leads to alternative evaluation or accountability procedures that managers can employ.

This brief overview of administration gives us just a glimpse of an important component of delivering educational programs to adults. Some people in this role—a hospital's director of staff development, for example—may not even identify themselves as adult education administrators, while others consider themselves career professionals. What they all have in common is that in their roles as administrators or managers, they perform the tasks and functions that are crucial to providing learning opportunities to adults.

Financing Adult Education

In North America, the education of children is considered a public responsibility residing primarily within the jurisdiction of each state. State tax dollars, augmented by both federal money and private donations, support education; and schooling is compulsory until age sixteen. North American society is committed to educating its youth; no such consensus exists for teaching adults. Thus, a very different financial picture emerges for adult education: one that is complex and at the same time not clearly drawn.

The field can actually be mapped according to the financial category of institutions providing adult education. Apps's map (1989a), for instance, is structured around the notion of a marketplace where information is the commodity to be bought and sold. As we discussed in Chapter Four, many of us do indeed feel that adult education's social mission has been subsumed by a technical, instrumental, and marketplace orientation. While not necessarily agreeing with this thrust, Apps maintains that his framework accurately represents the state of affairs at this point in time. As shown in Figure 5.1, there are four types of learning opportunities for the adult learner who stands in the middle: tax-supported, nonprofit, for-profit, and nonorganized. Apps notes that while self-directed learning is not a separate category, a self-directed learner may choose to learn from among the four options.

Tax-supported sponsors include postsecondary institutions, cooperative extensions, libraries and museums, the armed forces, prisons, and so on—in other words, any agency that gets some or all of its funding from taxes. Nonprofit agencies are self-supporting and include religious institutions, community-based agencies like YMCAs and YWCAs, service clubs, and professional organizations. For-profit providers include proprietary schools, private consultants, and business and industrial firms that offer training designed to increase profits. Apps (1989a) maintains that the for-profit sector is the fastest-growing segment of adult education and often the most innovative—"taking the lead with new formats, new technology,

Figure 5.1. Provider Framework.

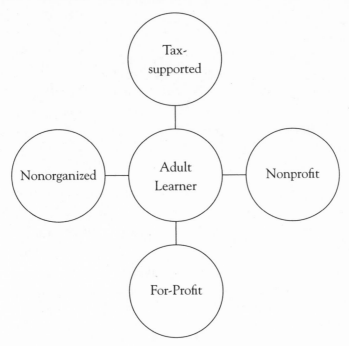

Source: Apps, 1989, p. 279.

and explorations into helping adults learn in a variety of settings" (p. 284).

Finally, Apps's fourth category—nonorganized adult education—encompasses the learning opportunities found in informal activities and environments such as the mass media, travel, work and family settings, and recreational pursuits.

The type of funding base—tax-supported, nonprofit, and for-profit—in Apps's model is represented by the three major funding sources for adult education: taxes (local, state, and federal), private gifts or grants, and participant fees. "In general, basic skills programs, adult secondary education, and vocational education are heavily supported in the United States by both state and federal funds, while recreational, personal enrichment, and professional development programs usually are supported with program fees" (Griffith with

Fujita-Starck, 1989, p. 171). Other than this generalization, it is nearly impossible to get a sense of how much of adult education is funded by specific sources. First, both public and private funding can be found under a variety of budgetary categories; and second, some institutions do not define some programs as adult education.

The funding picture is particularly complex and ill-defined at the federal level. In a study of federal support for adult education between 1964 and 1994, Cunningham (1995) divides legislation and funding into three categories depending on their goal: human capital formation, social equity, and support of popular movements. Not surprisingly, most legislation and funding has been granted to support human capital programs such as literacy, basic education, and job training. These programs are "littered throughout the federal bureaucracy (85 programs in 12 agencies studied by Alamprese and Sivilli with more than $247 million expended in 1992)" (p. 85). Much lower levels of funding have gone to social-equity programs like Volunteers in Service to America (VISTA) and to popular movements such as AIDS education and the National Institute for Peace.

Private funding of adult education is equally difficult to track. Probably the largest source of private funding is business and industry. Employer investment in workplace training is estimated to be approximately $210 billion annually (Carnevale, Gainer, and Villet, 1990). Of this amount, about $30 billion—or up to 2 percent—is spent on formal training, while the remaining $180 billion is allocated for informal or on-the-job training. In addition, other private sources such as foundations underwrite the costs of programs that are consistent with their goals and objectives. For example, the Kettering Foundation, which exists to improve the practice of democratic politics, supports the National Issues Forum, a civic education program in which local citizen groups study and debate current issues (Oliver, 1987).

Finally, many adult education programs are sustained by participant fees or tuition. This source of funding is, of course, also difficult to assess, since some participant costs are subsidized by other public

and private sources. For example, public institutions of higher education are supported by state tax money in addition to tuition paid
by each participant, who may in turn have received federally funded
grants or loans or a private scholarship. Further, some adult students
in higher education programs are subsidized by their employers.

The issues of who should pay and what the sources of these funds
might be are interlocked with how adult education is defined and
the value a society places on it. In countries where adult education
is a national priority, there is more centralization of resources (see
Chapter Seven). In North America, adult education is much more
fragmented, both in its mission and its delivery systems. This factor
is reflected in its diffuse pattern of funding.

Summary

The organization and delivery of adult education in North America is a decentralized phenomenon that can be viewed from a number of organizational frameworks. In this chapter, we chose three
dimensions of Knowles's model (1964) to organize our discussion of
the provision of adult education. While recognizing the existence
of nonformal, community-based modes of adult education, our discussion in this chapter largely (though not exclusively) refers to formal delivery systems.

The first dimension we discussed—and probably the most visible
aspect of the field—is adult education's institutions and agencies.
These fall into several categories: independent adult education organizations; educational institutions; quasieducational organizations
such as libraries, the mass media, and community organizations; and
noneducational organizations, such as prisons and trade unions, that
nonetheless often use education to achieve other ends.

Content area was the second dimension we presented. Content
areas reflect a variety of purposes of adult education and include work-
related programs, remedial education (especially adult basic education and high school completion programs), personal improvement

courses, civic education, and recreational and leisure pursuits. Content areas cut across the institutional base of adult education—that is, the same content can be and often is offered by all four types of organizations listed above.

The final dimension we discussed was personnel. This dimension includes the people who organize and deliver adult education programs, as well as the clienteles to whom the programs are targeted. Again, any number of agencies can serve the same clientele.

The last part of this chapter dealt with three important aspects of the delivery of adult education: planning, administration, and financing. We presented program planning as the most comprehensive function in delivering adult education, and we discussed the nature of program planning, including the more recent emphasis on the context and politics involved. Delivering adult education also involves administration and planning, and we reviewed the roles and functions in the administration of programs. Finally, we discussed how adult education programs are financed, including the three main sources of funding: participant fees, private funds, and local, state, and federal taxes.

6

The Adult Learner and Concepts of Learning

In Chapter Five, we examined the delivery of adult education specifically in terms of providers and functions. Program planning, administration, and financing are central to the provision of formal educational programs. In this chapter, we shift our focus to the participants in these programs—the adults themselves.

Just as knowledge of children and adolescents is necessary preparation for working in a K–12 setting, an understanding of adults and how they learn is vital to successful adult education practice. Knowing who is likely to participate in our programs, why adults choose to participate, and what barriers must be overcome before they can participate is knowledge that educators can put to good use in planning and delivering programs. Furthermore, the success of most programs is dependent on what actually takes place in the instructional setting. The teaching-learning transaction is at the heart of all adult education practice. It is thus imperative that we in the field know as much as we can about the sociocultural context of adulthood, how learning intersects with adult life, and how adults actually learn.

The intent of this chapter, then, is to review what we know about adult learners and the nature of adult learning. The chapter is divided into three sections. The first part examines the adult learner in terms of demographic characteristics, as well as reasons for participation and nonparticipation. In the second part, our emphasis will shift to a look at the adult learning process when we explore several major ideas and concepts that have influenced how educators work with adult learners. Finally, we will review several recent additions to understanding adult learning.

The Adult Learner

What do we know about the adult learner? Several decades of research have provided information about the demographic makeup of adult participants, their reasons for engaging in learning, and the kinds of concerns that serve as barriers to participation. In this section, we examine each of these areas.

Who Is the Adult Learner?

A starting point for understanding the adult learner is to look at who actually participates in adult learning and what they learn. Since the 1920s, literally hundreds of studies have been done on participation, ranging "from a local program wishing to augment its current offerings" to "the federal government collecting data to inform policy decisions" (Merriam and Caffarella, 1991, p. 61).

The first national study of participation in adult education, conducted by Johnstone and Rivera (1965), found that 22 percent of all American adults participated in some form of learning activity in the course of a year and that the majority of these activities were practical and skill-oriented rather than academic. Johnstone and Rivera offered a profile of the adult learner, which largely holds up today, after three decades: "The adult education participant is just as often a woman as a man, is typically under forty, has completed high school or more, enjoys an above-average income, works full-time and most often in a white-collar occupation, is married and has children, lives in an urbanized area but more likely in a suburb than a large city, and is found in all parts of the country, but more frequently in the West than in other regions" (p. 8).

Since 1969, the National Center for Educational Statistics has collected data about participation of adults in education. Seven surveys have provided data from 1969, 1972, 1975, 1978, 1981, 1984, 1991, and 1995 (Kim, Collins, Stowe, and Chandler, 1995; Kopka and Peng, 1993; Merriam and Caffarella, 1991). These surveys show that participation in organized adult education programs has increased slightly from 10 percent in 1969 to 14 percent in 1984 (S. T. Hill, n.d.). However, the 1991 survey reveals a participation rate of 32 percent, and the 1995 survey 40 percent. Kopka and Peng (1993) could identify no definitive reason for this increase, but they speculate that it may be linked to "a possible increase in the demand for adult education as a result of rapid changes in technology and the job market," as well as changes in definitions and methodology in this survey from previous efforts (p. 7). Kim, Collins, Stowe, and Chandler (1995) also point to differences in how the data were collected and analyzed.

In the most recent surveys, participation rates for males and females are equal. Individuals with children under the age of sixteen reported higher rates of participation than those with no children under this age. According to Kopka and Peng (1993), different participation rates were found among respondents who are white (33 percent), black (23 percent), and Hispanic (29 percent). By far the greatest discrepancies in participation are correlated with prior educational attainment. Rates of participation ranged from 16 percent for those with less than a high school diploma to 58 percent for those with a bachelor's degree or higher (Kim, Collins, Stowe, and Chandler, 1995). Of the 40 percent of respondents who reported participating, "the most common activities were work-related courses only (14 percent of adults) and personal development courses only (12 percent of adults). In addition, 5 percent of adults participated in both of these types of activities. Participation in these two activities, taken separately and in combination, accounts for 31 percent of adults, a large majority of the 40 percent overall participation rate" (p. 4). In the most recent survey, only 3 percent reported participating in adult education to earn some sort of credential such as a certificate, diploma, or degree.

Why Do Adults Participate in Learning?

Research on participation in adult education has been one of the most fully developed areas of inquiry in the field to date. Surveys such as those described above provide strong evidence that participation in formal adult education is most often tied to career or job motives. Studies on why adults participate have added further insights into this area.

A classic study of participation, *The Inquiring Mind* (Houle, 1988; originally published in 1961) served as the impetus for much of the current interest in research on both participation and self-directed learning. In 1960, Cyril Houle interviewed twenty-two individuals who were considered active, engaged learners. From these interviews, Houle concluded that the learners he interviewed fell into one of three "subgroups": (1) *goal-oriented* learners who participate to meet specific objectives; (2) *activity-oriented* learners, whose reasons for participation have little or no bearing on the content of the activity; and (3) *learning-oriented* learners who "seek knowledge for its own sake" (pp. 15–16). By identifying these distinctions, Houle set in motion the idea that the motives underlying adult learning can vary considerably.

Houle's study served as the stimulus for several other lines of inquiry. The most fully developed of these has been derived from the work of Roger Boshier and the Education Participation Scale (EPS) (Boshier, 1971; Boshier and Collins, 1985). The EPS is a forty-item scale that attempts to assess adults' reasons for participating in education. Morstain and Smart (1974) did a factor analysis of the EPS and were able to expand on Houle's typology by identifying six factors as major reasons for participation: social relationships, external expectations, social welfare, professional advancement, escape/stimulation, and cognitive interest. Over the years, the EPS has been refined, with versions targeted to special populations (for example, older adults and adults with low literacy skills). Today it continues to be used widely.

Most of the research on participation to date has been most directly informed by psychology. Courtney (1991), however, has raised some concerns with this line of research. He suggests that sociology and, more specifically, social participation can be used to explain adult education participation by emphasizing a "reinterpretation of adult learning as an aspect of the person's totality of involvement with his or her community and society" (p. xv).

We believe that research on reasons for participation has made a valuable contribution to the field of adult education because it demonstrates the vast and varied reasons that adults choose to participate. This understanding is crucial to future efforts to develop adult education programs and activities that effectively respond to the motives of prospective learners.

What Are Some of the Barriers to Participation?

Just as research on why adults participate has been helpful in providing a more complete understanding of adult learning, so too is an understanding of those factors that deter adults from participation; this might be thought of as the flip side of research on participation. Two examples of this work are a distinction made by Cross and later expanded by Darkenwald and Merriam, and a series of research studies involving the Deterrents to Participation Scale.

Cross (1981) used data from a study by the Commission on Nontraditional Study (Carp, Peterson, and Roelfs, 1974) to identify three major categories of barriers to participation. *Situational barriers*, according to Cross, deal with factors in an individual's life circumstances at a given point in time. The most common of these are lack of time and money and home and job responsibilities. *Institutional barriers* are those practices, procedures, and policies that place limits on opportunities for potential adult learners to participate; these can include course scheduling, residence requirements, and bureaucracy. *Dispositional barriers* relate to "attitudes and self-perceptions about oneself as a learner" (Cross, 1981, p. 98). Examples include low confidence, negative past experiences, lack of energy, and fear of being "too old" to participate.

Darkenwald and Merriam (1982) have added a fourth category, *informational barriers*, to this typology. These barriers reflect a lack of information about available learning opportunities. To a large degree, this is a variation of Cross's institutional barriers, since it reflects problems that an institution may have in marketing its programs to a target audience of adult learners.

As a way of gathering survey data on what can limit adult education participation among allied health professionals, Scanlan and Darkenwald (1984) developed the Deterrents to Participation Scale (DPS). Darkenwald and Valentine (1985) developed a generic version of the instrument, called DPS-G, and Hayes (1988) created a version for low-literate adults, called DPS-LL. In a subsequent analysis of data from the DPS, Valentine and Darkenwald (1990) developed a typology of adult nonparticipants. They concluded that adults are deterred from taking part due to personal problems, lack of confidence, educational costs, lack of interest in organized education, or lack of interest in courses that are available.

In summary, we can conclude that research on participation in adult education has provided a rich source of information that contributes much to our understanding of the adult learner. While this line of inquiry is not without its limits, it does provide those who are new to the field with a thumbnail sketch of who participates, who doesn't, and why. Similarly, it offers a starting point for those currently practicing in the field who wish to more effectively target their efforts at serving the needs of adult learners.

Some Key Concepts in Adult Learning

The previous section provides a description of the adult learner. In this section, we shift our attention to five of the theories, models, and areas of knowledge that have helped educators work successfully with adult learners. Some of the concepts are the result of years of research and theory development, while others are drawn largely from the experiences of educators who have worked with adults in a wide range of settings. However, these areas share a common link in that each has helped educators gain knowledge, insight, and skill in working with the adult learner.

Andragogy

Andragogy is a term that "belongs" to adult education. Although its origins can be traced to Europe as early as 1833 (Nottingham Andragogy Group, 1983), and its earliest known use in the United States was in 1927 (M. L. Anderson and Lindeman, 1927), its current evolution grew out of writings of Malcolm Knowles in the late 1960s and early 1970s (Knowles, 1968, 1970). Essentially, andragogy is a way of thinking about working with adult learners. While it is sometimes described as a theory (see, for example, Knowles, 1986), it is most often thought of as "a set of assumptions and methods pertaining to the process of helping adults learn" (Darkenwald and Merriam, 1982, p. 14).

In his earlier writing, Knowles (1970) viewed andragogy as the polar opposite of pedagogy. He argued that pedagogy—which we use here to mean an approach to childhood learning—is inappropriate for adults and thus its use should be restricted to children. This view was based on four assumptions about self-concept, the role of experience, readiness to learn, and orientation of learning.

Andragogy was readily embraced by the adult education field, even to the point of being viewed by some as the theory of adult education. Yet during the 1970s, as andragogy came under closer scrutiny, several concerns were raised—one of which revolved around the distinctions between adults and children (Houle, 1972; London, 1973; Elias, 1979).

Are there not situations in which children can be self-directed or can draw from previous experience? Likewise, what happens when an adult entering an area of study (for example, a literacy student who found previous schooling painful) has low confidence or little or no experience in the area of study? Knowles responded by changing the subtitle of *The Modern Practice of Adult Education* from "Andragogy vs. Pedagogy" in the 1970 edition to "From Andragogy to Pedagogy" in the 1980 edition. Davenport and Davenport (1985) have also presented an informative summary of the "andragogy debate."

Over the years, Knowles has clarified, expanded, and modified his ideas about andragogy. Most recently, he has described six assumptions underlying the concept:

1. "Adults need to know why they need to learn something before undertaking to learn it."

2. "Adults have a self-concept of being responsible for their own lives . . . they develop a deep psychological need to be seen and treated by others as being capable of self-direction."

3. "Adults come into an educational activity with both a greater volume and a different quality of experience from youths."

4. "Adults become ready to learn those things they need to know or . . . to cope effectively with their real-life situations."

5. "In contrast to children's and youth's subject-centered orientation to learning (at least in school), adults are life centered (or task centered or problem centered) in their orientation to learning."

6. "While adults are responsive to some extrinsic motivators (better jobs, promotions, salary increases, and the like), the more potent motivators are intrinsic motivators (the desire for increased self-esteem, quality of life, responsibility, job satisfaction, and the like" (Knowles, 1989, pp. 83–84).

In assessing andragogy after twenty-five years, Pratt (1993) observes that andragogy has made a major contribution to adult education by serving as a "recognizable" concept that provides familiar ground for adult education. At the same time, Pratt acknowledges the limits of andragogy by concluding that

> its contribution to our understanding of adult learning is not as grand in substance as it is in scale. The widespread and uncritical adoption of a particular view of adults as learners should not be the only measure by which we assess andragogy's contribution. Further, while andragogy may have contributed to our understanding of adults as learners, it has done little to expand or clarify our understanding of the process of learning. We cannot say, with any confidence, that andragogy has been tested and found to be, as so many have hoped, either the basis for a theory of adult learning or a unifying concept for adult education [p. 21].

In summary, there can be little doubt of the impact that the development of andragogy has had on how educators understand and work with adult learners. For some, andragogy has become almost a way of forging an identity in the field. Yet we also believe that the concern raised by Pratt is insightful and important: this criticism does not negate the value of andragogy's contribution to adult education but rather helps to sharpen the focus on what andragogy has and has not contributed to our understanding of adult learning.

Self-Directed Learning

Some of the most important developments in adult education over the past three decades have been in the area of self-directed learning. Although it emerged as a major topic during the 1970s and 1980s, the idea of self-directed learning—that is, adults assuming control of their learning—is as old as history. Kulich (1970), for instance, provides examples of self-directed learning in such historical figures as Socrates, Alexander the Great, Caesar, and Descartes; and a study by Gibbons and others (1980) describes the self-directed learning efforts of more contemporary figures, including Frank Lloyd Wright, Amelia Earhart, Harry Truman, and Malcolm X.

The current emphasis on self-directed learning can be traced largely to the work of Allen Tough on adults' learning projects. Influenced by the "learning-oriented" participants in Houle's *The Inquiring Mind* (1988; originally published in 1961), Tough, in his seminal work *The Adult's Learning Projects* (1979; originally published in 1971), looked at the frequency and nature of self-planned learning activities among a sample of sixty-six adults. The major finding of Tough's study was that over two-thirds (68 percent) of all learning activities were planned, implemented, and evaluated primarily by the learners themselves. Numerous replications with diverse samples of adult learners have largely supported Tough's conclusion (see, for example, Brockett and Hiemstra, 1991).

There has been much discussion about what constitutes self-directed learning. Writers such as Tough (1979) and Knowles have tended to stress self-directed learning in the context of the systematic process of designing such activities. For instance, Knowles (1975) suggests that the term refers to a process in which individuals take the lead "in diagnosing their learning needs, formulating learning goals, identifying human and material resources for learning, choosing and implementing appropriate learning strategies, and evaluating learning outcomes" (p. 18).

Subsequent writers began to suggest that self-directed learning is much more complex—primarily because these definitions fail to consider either the internal state of the individual learner (Kasworm, 1983) or the social context in which such learning takes place (Brookfield, 1985).

Two models attempt to further expand our understanding of self-directed learning. Brockett and Hiemstra (1991) have developed the Personal Responsibility Orientation (PRO) model. Using "self-direction in learning" as an umbrella concept, the PRO model holds that self-direction is made up of two related dimensions: *self-directed learning*, which emphasizes elements of the teaching-learning process much in the way suggested in the Knowles definition above, and *learner self-direction*, which focuses on characteristics internal to the individual that "predispose one toward taking primary responsibility" for learning (p. 29). The PRO model also recognizes the importance of the social context in which learning takes place.

Another model that has increased our understanding of self-direction can be found in the work of Candy (1991), who has approached the subject from a constructivist sociological viewpoint. Candy distinguishes between self-direction as "a process or method of education" and as "a goal or outcome" (p. 19). He further divides self-direction into two domains: *learner control*, in which even though the learner maintains primary ownership of the learning, "there is still a residue, albeit small, of teacher-control" (p. 18); and *autodidaxy*, in which no teacher is present and the learner may not even be conscious that he or she is learning. The strength of this model is that it emphasizes the social context in which learning takes place—something that is often downplayed in other views of self-directed learning.

Like participation, self-directed learning has clearly emerged as one of the few knowledge areas in adult education to undergo systematic development over the past two decades. The literature has been reviewed in several places (see, for example, Brockett and Hiemstra, 1991; Caffarella, 1993). Brockett and Hiemstra have divided this research into three categories defined by research methodology: (1) *learning projects research*, descriptive survey studies derived from the methodology developed by Tough; (2) *quantitative measures of self-direction*, focusing on instruments designed to measure levels of self-directedness—the most widely used to date of which is the Self-Directed Learning Readiness Scale (Guglielmino, 1978); and (3) *qualitative studies* involving observation and in-depth interviews to build theory and provide rich descriptions of the self-directed learning phenomenon. Caffarella (1993), on the other hand, has categorized the research according to the form and process of learning, learner characteristics and preferences, and fostering learner initiative and control in formal settings.

Regardless of how the research is categorized, it seems clear that several key trends can be gleaned from the body of knowledge. First, self-directed learning, however defined, is the most frequent way in which most adults choose to learn. Second, there is a strong connection between self-directed learning and self-concept. Third, several other personality and social characteristics seem to have some connection to self-directed learning. Finally, this research has made it possible to gain a more holistic view of the adult learner.

In terms of implication for practice, the literature abounds with strategies for working successfully with self-directed learners. These include discussions of specific aspects of self-directed learning, such as the use of learning contracts (Knowles, 1975, 1986) and strategies for overcoming resistance to self-direction (Hiemstra and Brockett, 1994), as well as models for designing self-directed learning experiences. Two such models are the Staged Self-Directed Learning Model (Grow, 1991) and the Individualizing Instruction process (Hiemstra and Sisco, 1990), each of which identifies major phases and components of the teaching-learning process and presents practical strategies for promoting self-direction at each phase.

As we look to the future, self-directed learning by one name or another will most certainly be central to successful adult education practice. While much has been done in this area to date, much more needs to be done. We believe that, given the momentum that has evolved in the growth of self-directed learning, it is in the best interests of the adult education field to move forward and create new perspectives on self-direction.

Transformation Theory

Experience is central to an understanding of the adult learner. However, it is not the mere accumulation of experience that matters; instead, the way in which individuals make meaning of their experience facilitates growth and learning. This idea forms the foundation of transformation theory.

In 1975, Jack Mezirow and a group of colleagues from Teachers College, Columbia University, conducted a national study of reentry college women (Mezirow, 1975). Using structured interviews, Mezirow and colleagues identified a process of change in these women beginning with a disorienting dilemma—one in which old ways of thinking and responding are no longer effective—through a process of challenging and revising assumptions that ultimately led to a new way of engaging in their roles and relationships. Mezirow used the term perspective transformation to describe this change process.

During the next several years, Mezirow (1978, 1981) began to clarify and modify his thinking about perspective transformation. He described some of the influences on his thinking, who ranged from the German critical theorist Jurgen Habermas to philosopher-educator Paulo Freire to psychiatrist Roger Gould (Mezirow, 1981). At the time, he described perspective transformation as "the structure of psycho-cultural assumptions within which new experience is assimilated and transformed by one's past experience" (p. 6). Here he argued that critically reflecting upon our lives, developing an awareness of "why we attach the meanings that we do to reality," may be a unique characteristic of adult learning (p. 11, emphasis in the original).

Subsequently, perspective transformation gained a foothold and has moved to center stage in our understanding of the adult learner. Mezirow edited a volume in which several writers discussed strategies that can foster critical reflection in adulthood (Mezirow and Associates, 1990). In a subsequent book, Mezirow offered a detailed examination of his approach, which he began to refer to as "transformation theory" (1991a); here he states that the purpose of transformation theory is to "explain the way adult learning is structured and to determine by what process the frames of reference through which we view and interpret our experience (meaning perspectives) are changed or transformed" (p. xiii).

This approach to learning has some important implications for working with adult learners. M. C. Clark (1993) observes that what makes transformational learning different from other approaches is that it "produces more far-reaching changes in the learners than does learning in general, and . . . these changes have a significant impact on the learner's subsequent experiences. In short, transformational learning *shapes* people; they are different afterward, in ways both they and others can recognize" (p. 47, emphasis in the original).

Cranton (1994) has used Mezirow's research as a framework for discussing how educators can help learners engage in the process of transformative learning. She argues that empowerment and autonomy are a desirable outcome for adult learning and that transformative learning can serve as a process for empowering learners. Finally, an examination of how to develop critical thinkers (Brookfield, 1986) and a discussion of effective teaching and mentoring (Daloz, 1986) both draw extensively from the ideas of perspective transformation and transformation theory.

Transformation theory has provoked some insightful dialogue and debate within the field. For example, Collard and Law (1989) challenge the way in which Mezirow has linked his ideas to critical theory, because they believe that perspective transformation is "largely devoid of the socio-political critique that lies at the heart of that tradition" (p. 105). Another criticism argues that Mezirow's view of autonomy is limited because it reflects the middle-class, white-male-dominated culture in our society (Clark and Wilson, 1991).

Mezirow has contributed to the dialogue by responding to critiques such as these. In answer to Collard and Law's claim that the theory tends to ignore social change and social context, Mezirow responded that while social action may indeed develop out of the transformation process, the impetus for such action must come from the learner; for the educator to initiate a specific political agenda would constitute indoctrination (Mezirow, 1989). Similarly, he responded to the criticism of Clark and Wilson (1991) by clarifying his views on the relationship between social theory and learning theory and suggesting that the cultural context in which learning takes place is, in fact, a crucial element of his thinking about transformation.

We believe that transformation theory has been a major milestone in advancing understanding of adult learning. While specific elements of the approach will continue to evolve, the theory has refocused the interest of adult education on an aspect that may be truly unique among adult learners: the way in which experience can lead to fundamental changes in the learner's perspective.

Adult Development

From the discussion above on transformation theory, the connection between adult education and adult development is readily apparent. However, this link goes well beyond a single theoretical perspective. In an often-cited national survey of adult learning participation, Aslanian and Brickell (1980) conclude that life changes serve as a major trigger to adult learning and that, subsequently, most adult learning efforts are undertaken in response to a life transition. It makes sense, then, to look a bit further at this connection.

There is no shortage of theories intended to address development in the adult years, and it is not possible for us to provide detailed examinations of specific theories in this book. Bee (1995) and Kimmel (1990) offer detailed treatments of adult development theories, while Merriam and Caffarella (1991) and Tennant and Pogson (1995) explore the relevance of these theories to adult learning and education.

However, it might be useful here to make distinctions between the different *types* of adult development theories. Cross (1981), for example, has differentiated between theories that emphasize *phases* of the life cycle and those that focus on developmental *stages*. Phase theories often use the metaphor of seasons to describe the life cycle and emphasize "the responses people make to age and changing social expectations as they move through the phases of adulthood" (Cross, 1981, p. 168). Examples include the work of Daniel Levinson in

The Seasons of a Man's Life (Levinson and others, 1974); Marjorie Fiske and her colleagues (Lowenthal, Thurnher, Chiriboga, and Associates, 1975; Fiske and Chiriboga, 1990); and the best-sellers *Passages* (1976) and *New Passages* (1995) by journalist Gail Sheehy.

Those who emphasize stage theories have tended "to speak of continuous growth from simple to higher or more complex forms of life and from immaturity to maturity" (Cross, 1981, p. 168). This is a developmental approach in which subsequent stages build upon earlier ones. One of the earliest stage theories was proposed by Erik Erikson (1963), who divided the life span into eight stages, each of which centers on the resolution of a developmental crisis. The importance of his work for adult development is that by including three distinct stages representing the adult years, Erikson made a major departure from most of his contemporaries, who believed that the majority of significant developmental changes took place in the early years and that adult personality was merely an extension of earlier development.

In addition to Erikson, other stage theories have included Jane Loevinger's work on ego development (1976), William Perry's research on the stages of intellectual and ethical development (1970), Lawrence Kohlberg's work on moral development (1969), James Fowler's perspectives on faith development (1981), and George Vaillant's hierarchy of adaptive mechanisms (1977).

Other perspectives on development can be identified by distinguishing among three key concepts from the literature on adult development: sequential patterns of change, life events, and transitions (Merriam, 1984). The first of these notions, sequential patterns of change, views adult development as a series of stages or phases that adults go through (Merriam and Caffarella, 1991); most of the phase and stage theories we identified above fall within this category. Life events, the second concept, emphasizes adult development within the framework of individual and cultural events that occur throughout a person's lifetime—for example, marriage, childbirth, death of a spouse or companion, and social and historical events that occur throughout a lifetime. The third notion, transitions, involves "the natural process of disorientation and reorientation that marks the turning points of the path of growth" (Bridges, 1980, p. 5); the work of Mezirow and others, discussed in the previous section of this chapter, illustrate this concept.

A criticism of most theories of adult development is that they describe white, middle-class, and usually male perspectives of development. In response, there have been some recent efforts to look at the psychosocial development of women (Caffarella and Olson, 1993). Among the most influential of these is the work of Gilligan (1982), who argued that important sex differences exist in personality and moral development. A second example is found in the work of Belenky, Clinchy, Goldberger, and Tarule (1986) on women's "ways of knowing." From interviews with 135 women, Belenky and her colleagues found that their perspectives on knowing could be placed in one of five categories—ranging from "silence," which encompasses the feeling of being "mindless and voiceless and subject to the whims of external authority" (Merriam and Caffarella, 1991, p. 192) to "constructed knowledge," in which women view themselves as creators of knowledge and they value both objective and subjective learning strategies. While the authors stress that these categories are not developmental, this theory nonetheless contributes to our understanding of adult development because it helps us recognize differences in how women construct knowledge. Some of the most exciting developments taking place in adult education today center on understanding women as learners (Tisdell, 1995).

How can an understanding of adult development be helpful to those who work with adult learners? Perhaps most obviously, understanding the developmental stages, phases, tasks, and transitions can help educators better understand the life circumstances that trigger the need for learning. Recognizing that participation in adult education is often a response to a developmental change or crisis, educators are in a position to understand the learner from a holistic perspective.

Tennant and Pogson (1995) provide a detailed discussion of how such adult education practices as self-direction and autonomy, incorporating experience into the learning process, and the teaching role can be better understood through a developmental perspective. Similarly, Merriam and Caffarella (1991) suggest that "the more we know about adult learners, the changes they go through, and how these changes motivate and interact with learning, the better we can structure learning experiences that both respond to and stimulate development" (p. 119).

However, Courtenay (1994) raises an important challenge to those in the field who use adult development theories in their practice. He argues that assumptions about the importance of growth in developmental models, emphasis on the belief that "higher levels of development" are "better" (p. 151), and questions about the data on which most developmental models are built can limit the usefulness of such theories in the context of adult education practice. While we agree with Courtenay that these models must not be accepted uncritically, they are pieces of a puzzle in advancing our understanding of how adults learn and change.

Intelligence and Memory

How do the processes that influence adult learning ability change over the course of a life span? Because this question has been of interest to psychologists, gerontologists, and educators for many years, there is an extensive body of research on intelligence, memory, cognition, problem-solving ability, creativity, and so on. Readers who seek more detailed information on this research can refer to such sources as Birren and Schaie (1990), Schaie and Willis (1986), and Kimmel (1990), or periodicals such as the *Journal of Gerontology* and the *International Journal of Aging and Human Development*.

For purposes of this discussion, we will briefly highlight two areas that have particular relevance to working with adult learners: intelligence and memory.

Intelligence

At the beginning of the twentieth century, intelligence was generally believed to peak during the late teens and begin a downslide at about age twenty. Thorndike (1928), in the first major study of adult intelligence, concluded that intelligence remained stable between the ages of twenty and forty-five, after which a decline could be noted. During the ensuing years, researchers continued to push back a decline in functioning to the sixth or even seventh decade of the life span (Merriam and Caffarella, 1991). Yet there appears to be much controversy among those who conclude that intelligence either (1) declines in the adult years, (2) generally remains stable, or (3) declines in some areas while remaining stable or even increasing in others.

To a large extent, this controversy reflects how intelligence has been defined. Historically, it was viewed as a single "general" factor that explained performance on a wide range of tasks. An alternative explanation is that intelligence consists of multiple factors. Cattell's distinction (1963) between fluid (biologically based) intelligence and crystallized intelligence (based on education and experience) is an example. Researchers generally seem to agree among themselves that fluid intelligence peaks in early adolescence, while crystallized intelligence either remains stable or increases throughout the adult years (Hayslip and Panek, 1989).

Some of the most exciting recent developments in intelligence are linked to the idea that intelligence consists of multiple factors and that these factors are more closely related to everyday problem solving than to performance in artificial testing situations. Gardner (1983) has proposed a "theory of multiple intelligences," which holds that there are seven forms of intelligence: linguistic, musical, logical-mathematical, spatial, bodily-kinesthetic, and internal and external personal intelligences. The importance of Gardner's theory is that it argues against generalizing that an individual is bright, average, or dull; instead, a person may be highly intelligent in one or two areas while simultaneously much less so in other areas.

Another perspective on multiple intelligences has been offered by Sternberg (1985, 1988) in his "triarchic theory" of intelligence. This view suggests that there are three subtheories of intelligence: the componential subtheory, which emphasizes internal mechanisms of intelligence similar to more traditional theories; the experiential subtheory, in which experience with particular tasks may affect how an individual responds to similar situations; and the contextual sub-theory, in which intelligent behavior in a given situation is deter-mined by how well a person can "read" the external environment. The importance of Sternberg's theory is that it argues for a practical intelligence that is tied to real-life situations, where "street smarts" (contextual intelligence) is at least as important as "book smarts" and test-taking ability (componential intelligence).

As theories such as those proposed by Gardner and Sternberg help to redefine how researchers look at intelligence, it is likely that adult educators will be able to find new and creative ways to draw on the intelligence of adult learners in a way that was not previ-ously believed possible or worthwhile. Simply stated, the landscape of adult intelligence is being reshaped at this very moment; old ways of thinking are giving way to new approaches that will redefine how we think about intelligence in the coming years. And ulti-mately, these redefinitions should have clear and practical implica-tions for developing new ways to work effectively with adult learners.

Memory

Memory is generally thought of as having three different phases: the acquisition, the storage or retention, and the retrieval or recall of knowledge (Schaie and Willis, 1986). Considerable research has been conducted on changes in memory throughout adulthood, and it seems clear that a decline in certain functions of memory is a part of the normal aging process. In general, there appears to be little diminution in sensory or short-term memory, while long-term mem-ory is more susceptible to decline (Merriam and Caffarella, 1991). In the case of long-term memory, most changes are found in the acquisition and retrieval of knowledge; little evidence exists of changes in storage or retention of knowledge.

When examining the literature on memory, it is important to remember that most of this research has been conducted in a laboratory setting. Thus, as with earlier work on intelligence, the findings have been derived from an artificial setting. This leads to questions about memory in everyday situations, or in situations in which a person has acquired expertise (Kimmel, 1990); in such cases, the evidence points to less memory decline with age. Finally, as with intelligence, changing views of memory have the potential to add greatly to the knowledge of how acquiring, storing, and retrieving information is influenced by such factors as the context in which learning takes place and a person's motivation in a particular situation to engage in the processes of memory.

Emerging Concepts in Adult Learning

The themes that have been discussed so far in this chapter center on some of the main concepts that have contributed to current understanding of adult learning and the adult learner. In this section, we present five ideas that appear to be currently taking hold and that we believe will continue to emerge, in one form or another, as adult education moves into the next millennium: the learning environment, training and development, experiential learning, situated cognition, and critical and feminist pedagogy.

The Learning Environment

It should come as scant surprise that the environment in which learning takes place plays an important role in successful learning. Perhaps more surprising is that relatively little has been written regarding the physical, psychological, and social dimensions of the learning environment.

Physical environment refers to the actual space in which learning takes place. It is concerned with factors such as room size, temperature, lighting, acoustics, seating type and arrangements, and how technology is arranged and used in the learning space. It also refers to "proxemics"—how learners relate to one another in terms of body language and personal space (Vosko, 1984; Fulton, 1991). Not surprisingly, a learning space that is physically uncomfortable and with a layout that does not afford a comfortable degree of personal space will detract from the learning process.

Psychological environment centers on creating a climate in which both learners and teachers are able to engage in genuine exchange. For teachers, this typically means helping learners feel welcome and at ease in the opening minutes of the activity. It also involves attending to the fears and doubts that adults may be experiencing. And it recognizes that learners do not come to the learning situation with a "blank slate;" rather, they come with a range of life experiences—some of which can serve as possible learning resources and others (such as time pressures, difficult work situations, and domestic concerns) that can detract from learning.

Finally, *social environment* centers on the culture of the teaching-learning setting. This is where it becomes important to recognize the importance of factors such as race and sex in relation to how adult educators work with learners (Colin and Preciphs, 1991; Collard and Stalker, 1991; Fellenz and Conti, 1990). The social environment is central to discussions of critical approaches to adult education (such as critical and feminist pedagogies) because it emphasizes the place of social context in the adult learning environment, rather than an individual's response to the environment.

Taken together, the physical, psychological, and social elements of the learning environment are an important arena for improving adult education practice. In terms of how to engage in new practices relative to improving the learning environment, Hiemstra (1991) has offered several recommendations: Find ways to help learners control the learning environment, engage in practices that make it possible to evaluate and control physical spaces, incorporate computers into the learning environment, get to know the needs of learners in a way that can promote more effective practice, help learners feel at ease, take a proactive approach to bringing about change (particularly in issues of racism and sexism), and make "a personal commitment to change" (p. 96). The key point here is that the learning environment is an area ripe for research and innovative practice.

Training and Development

Rachal (1989) has stated that the workplace is a major force in the changing nature of adult education. Interest in adult learning in the workplace is certainly not a new idea. Yet its prominence within the sphere of adult education has never been stronger, and this direction is likely to continue.

We have addressed the relationship between adult education and training earlier in this book (see Chapters One and Two). For example, Malcolm Knowles (1986) and Leonard Nadler (Nadler and Nadler, 1989) have written for many years on behalf of building this link, which has sometimes been unclear and even strained: while some adult educators embrace the notion of training as a part of their identity, others have eschewed it. To be sure, adult educators may rightfully wish to question the motives of some training efforts. Is the purpose to serve the learner or the organization? Can both be served simultaneously? (Cunningham, 1993). At the same time, the training field has been a forerunner in the use of technology.

Two concepts from training that may also serve adult educators are performance-based learning and the learning organization. Within training and development, the *performance-based* (or competency-based) model of learning has been predominant because it stresses the attainment of measurable outcomes tied to established objectives. This is very consistent with the behaviorist philosophy we discussed in Chapter Two. In other words, with performance-based learning it is possible to observe directly the extent to which learning objectives are met. The strength of this approach is that it promotes accountability by emphasizing results that can be "seen."

On the other hand, critics argue that performance- or competency-based approaches can be overly prescriptive, can promote mediocrity, and can encourage conformity and control (see, for example, Knox, 1979; Collins, 1983; Newman, 1994). It is possible to deduce that this approach is not an effective way to address learning related to values and critical-thinking skills. This debate is not likely to dissipate in the coming years; however, adult educators who want to build on the strength of developments in this area must be willing to critically juxtapose the approach's potential benefits with its possible limitations.

A second area within training and development that has potential connections to adult education practice is the "learning organization" (Senge, 1990; Watkins and Marsick, 1993). According to Senge, the learning organization is a place "where people continually expand their capacity to create the results they truly desire, where new and expansive patterns of thinking are nurtured, where new and collective aspiration is set free, and where people are continually learning how to learn together" (p. 3). Senge identifies five technologies of the learning organization: systems thinking, personal mastery, mental models (assumptions or images that influence how we understand and act), building shared vision, and team learning. Watkins and Marsick build on Senge's approach by discussing principles and practices that can make it possible to "sculpt" the learning organization.

Experiential Learning

It is actually a bit inaccurate to include the topic of experiential learning in a discussion of "emerging concepts" in adult learning. The key role of experience in the process of learning has its roots in the progressive philosophy of John Dewey (see, for example, Dewey, 1938); it was also central to Lindeman's view of adult education's meaning ([1926] 1989) and is reflected in major contemporary approaches to adult learning (see, for example, Boud, Cohen, and Walker, 1993; Kolb, 1984). Here the idea is not merely that the accumulation of experience makes a difference; it is how learners attach meanings to or make sense of their experience that matters.

The idea of experience as a core aspect of adult learning is so pervasive in the theory and practice of adult education that it would be difficult to find examples that do not address the role of experience. Indeed, experience is central to *each* of the concepts we present in this chapter. Empirical research on experiential learning, however, is much less prevalent. Studies have been conducted on experiential learning in the workplace (Boud and Walker, 1991), the relationship between life experiences and developmental outcomes (Merriam and Yang, 1996), and learning that comes from the negative interpretation of life experiences (Merriam, Mott, and Lee, 1996).

Important theoretical contributions to our understanding of experiential learning have been made by Boud (1994) and Kolb (1984). Boud's three-part model is based on the assumption that "adult educators are working with many different learners and attempting to help them learn from their experience" (p. 49). The model, which consists of experiences prior to the learning event, during the event, and following the event, documents the process of learning from experience and also suggests how this kind of learning can be facilitated.

Kolb's model is presented as a four-stage cycle consisting of (1) gaining new kinds of *concrete experience*; (2) engaging in *reflective observation* that allows one to interpret experiences from different viewpoints; (3) forming an *abstract conceptualization* that leads to the development of theories about the experience and reflection; and (4) *active experimentation* with these theories in order to solve practical problems. Each of these four capabilities are reflected in different kinds of learning environments, and as such they reflect differences in the kinds of strengths that learners demonstrate in various learning styles. For example, an environment for effective learning is consistent with a concrete-experience style; reflective observation emphasizes a perceptual approach in which learners search for meaning; abstract conceptualization involves a logical systems view; and active experimentation is based on setting goals and taking risks to achieve them.

An important application of experiential learning can be found in some innovative efforts to work with adults who return to higher education. In this setting, "experiential learning generally refers to learning that takes place outside the classroom" (Rose, 1989b, p. 212) and includes arranging for learning activities outside the classroom (for example, internships), as well as awarding credit for prior learning, regardless of whether this learning was gained through "in-service training courses [or] voluntary activities or hobbies or the work experience itself" (p. 213).

While some critics have argued that experiential learning can diminish the value of a college education and can reinforce society's overemphasis on credentialing, supporters believe that the approach can open the doors of higher education to adults who otherwise would be unable to pursue such opportunities. Lewis and Williams (1994) suggest that three of the most important applications of experiential learning in the context of higher education include (1) field-based academic programs comprising internship and practicum experiences as well as cooperative education and community service; (2) granting credit for prior learning; and (3) classroom-based experiential learning, such as case studies, critical incidents, simulations, and games. At present, experiential learning opportunities are available for adults in many colleges and universities across the United States and Canada—including several well-established institutions whose primary mission is to serve nontraditional adult learners. Among these are Empire State College in New York, Thomas Edison State College in New Jersey, and Athabasca University in Alberta.

Today, in addition to its contribution to concepts such as andragogy and transformation theory, the importance of the learner's experience has helped shape techniques of *collaborative inquiry* (also called collaborative learning)—"a sharing of information in relationships of equality that promotes new growth in each participant" (Jackson and MacIsaac, 1994, p. 24). Under the rubric of "action inquiry technologies," Brooks and Watkins (1994a) have brought together a number of these concepts, including action research, action science, action learning, and participatory research; according to Brooks and Watkins, action technologies bring together theory and practice in a way that places greater emphasis on taking action and working with informal theories and people's experiences, rather than formal theorizing and reporting on research results. Thus, in an approach such as participatory research, those being studied are co-researchers who share in making decisions about why a study is being undertaken, who will be studied, how the study will be conducted, and how the results will be used. In general, action technologies play down the role of experts and emphasize the input of those whose lives and work are most directly affected by the problem under study.

A final illustration of how experiential learning continues to be an emerging concept can be found in the work of a faculty group at the University of Northern Colorado (Jackson and Caffarella, 1994). This group has proposed a process model that makes it possible to apply experiential learning in the teaching and assessment processes in a variety of settings. The model begins with an understanding of adult learners and experiential learning and includes both in-class and field-based experiential techniques; it incorporates an assessment process that concludes with the construction of a portfolio. Bassett and Jackson (1994) illustrate how this model can be applied to such settings as higher education (teacher education and educational technology) and the workplace (adventure programs, adult literacy classes, and diversity training).

Situated Cognition

The adult learner's real-life experiences play an important role in *situated cognition*, one of the most promising approaches to understanding adult learning. The key idea behind situated cognition is that context is central to how adult cognition is understood (Cervero, 1988; Wilson, 1993b). This approach "recognizes the inextricability of thinking and the contexts in which it occurs, and exploits the inherent significance of real-life contexts in learning" (Choi and Hannafin, 1995, p. 53). In other words, cognition (or knowing) is not merely something that goes on inside of the individual, but rather is tied to the surroundings and life experiences of the person. Wilson argues that in order "to understand the central place of context in thinking and learning, we have to recognize that cognition is a social activity that incorporates the mind, the body, the activity, and the ingredients of the setting in a complex interactive and recursive manner" (1993b, p. 72).

Situated cognition is based on the idea that what we know and the meanings we attach to what we know are socially constructed. Thus, learning and knowing are intimately linked to real-life situations. According to Wilson, situated cognition is based on three key ideas: (1) Learning and thinking are generally social activities; (2) thinking and learning abilities "are profoundly structured by the availability of situationally provided 'tools'"; and (3) thinking is influenced by interaction with the setting in which learning takes place (1993b, p. 72).

Current work in situated cognition focuses not only on the learning process itself, but also on how educators can effect a more authentic, real-life context for learning (through apprenticeships, for example) and can support the transfer of learning from one context to another (Choi and Hannafin, 1995; Resnick, 1987; Wilson, 1993b). While the premise behind this idea is not new, what appears to be of more recent vintage is the commitment of adult educators to expand their understanding of and interest in the adult learner beyond the limits of individual psychology taken out of the context of life experience.

Critical and Feminist Pedagogy

As we have stressed throughout this book, some of the most important recent developments in contemporary adult education can be linked to the introduction of the "critical" perspective into the theory, research, and practice of adult education. For purposes of this discussion, critical and feminist pedagogy are discussed together; however, it is important to recognize that there are some differences between the approaches.

The central theme of critical pedagogy is that for true learning to take place, it is necessary to ensure that the voices of those people who have traditionally been marginalized due to race, sex, or lifestyle factors are fully engaged in the learning process (see, for example, Hayes and Colin, 1994; R. J. Hill, 1995).

In Chapter Two on the philosophy and Chapter Three on the history of adult education, we addressed the contributions of such educators as Paulo Freire and Myles Horton. Both Freire and Horton exemplify the spirit of critical pedagogy, in that their work emphasizes giving voice to learners who have been marginalized or silenced by society.

A recent example of critical pedagogy can be found in the writing of bell hooks (1994). In her book *Teaching to Transgress*, hooks argues that education is "the practice of freedom" (p. 13). She emphasizes the notion of "engaged pedagogy," which is "more demanding" than critical or feminist pedagogies because it places emphasis on well-being: "teachers must be actively committed to their own well-being if they are to teach in a manner that empowers students" (p. 15). Similarly, a recent book by Vella (1994) argues that the most effective adult learning is achieved through dialogue.

Feminist pedagogy is both similar to and different from critical pedagogy. It shares with the critical approach a commitment to giving voice to those who have been silenced and to the intersection between reflection and action; yet it differs in that there is no single model of feminist pedagogy. Tisdell (1993a, 1995) distinguishes between liberatory and gender models of feminist pedagogy: here the liberatory model "deals with the nature of structured power relations and interlocking systems of oppression based on gender, race, class, age, and so on" (p. 94), while the gender model deals with socialization of women as nurturers and with emancipation "in the personal psychological sense," but not in terms of dealing with power relations (p. 97).

Critical and feminist pedagogy will likely play an important role in the future of adult education. Some educators may disagree with the radical action that these approaches often advocate, and there is the possibility that as traditionally silenced groups find their voice, other voices could in turn be silenced. If we are to learn from these approaches, we need to stress the ideas developed by Vella and hooks: that freedom is the goal of education, and dialogue is the means of ensuring freedom.

Summary

Educators who wish to work successfully with adult learners need to understand who adult learners are and how they learn. In this chapter, we have identified several questions, concepts, theories, and models that can offer a broad, general understanding of the adult learner. To begin, it is important to have some sense of who adult learners are, why they choose to participate, and what factors can limit their participation.

From this general overview of participation, we presented several of the major concepts that have informed our understanding of the adult learner. Andragogy, self-directed learning, transformation theory, adult development, and intellectual functioning are some of the ideas that have been most influential in recent years. For the most part, these concepts emphasize the individual learner, often from a psychological perspective.

At the same time, some new concepts have begun to take hold, including situated cognition and feminist pedagogy—as have some new perspectives on older ideas such as training and development and experiential learning. In these areas, the focus on the individual is complemented by greater emphasis on the social context in which learning takes place.

In this chapter, we have introduced brief discussions of the learning environment, training and development, experiential learning, situated cognition, and critical and feminist pedagogy so that we could project what we believe will likely be some of the most important directions to emerge in this realm over the next several years. An understanding of adult learners and the learning process is central to successful work in adult education—regardless of whether practitioners work directly with learners in an instructional setting or indirectly through program-development or administrative roles.

7

The Global Context
of Adult Education

We in the field tend to think of adult education in terms of our own particular role, whether it be health educator, college administrator, extension agent, or trainer. We may also regard adult education only in terms of the clientele we serve, the community in which we live, or the organization for which we work. Rarely does our vision of adult education extend beyond our immediate environment, yet the world is fast becoming a global community with shared concerns and interests. International trade agreements and tariffs, cable-television access in remote Third World villages, the Internet and the World Wide Web, terrorism, disasters and diseases such as earthquakes, Ebola outbreaks, and the AIDS epidemic all draw our attention beyond our own borders. Ignoring the rest of the world does not prevent it from having a profound impact on our daily lives; attending to the world beyond our own—in even just one arena of interest such as adult education—allows us to expand our vision and be proactive in constructing the kind of life we value.

Interest in international adult education has been long-standing and can be traced back to a number of events, including a 1919 publication on adult education in Great Britain, known as *The 1919 Report* (1980), that became an "instant classic" in Europe and North America (Houle, 1992). Other influential events include the short-lived World Association for Adult Education, which published an international handbook in 1929; and the worldwide literacy campaigns of Frank Laubach (1970) that spanned forty years from 1929 on and continue today in the work of Laubach Literacy International.

More recently, writers from several nations have called for the adoption of a worldwide vision of adult education (Cassara, 1995; Cookson, 1994; Cunningham, 1991; Draper, 1992; Duke, 1994b; Gelpi, 1985). Draper, for example, argues that such a worldview would emphasize "the commonalities between all aspects of adult learning, regardless of where it takes place or what is being learned"; that, in turn, "maximizes the potential sharing and transferability of experiences" (1992, p. 78). A worldview would also allow us to accommodate the many forms and diversity of adult education, help us focus on both the study and practice of adult education and generate more knowledge about it, and lead to a better definition of employment opportunities for those trained in the field.

Cassara (1994) suggests yet another reason for becoming informed about adult education globally: "the adult educator will serve clientele from many countries, even within his/her own country, and for this an international understanding is imperative."

A worldview would also allow us to see the contradictions both in our own society and in others. As Gelpi (1985) states: "The emergence of previously repressed civilizations and cultures along with the continued overt suppression of minority groups, the hidden manipulation through the mass media of local and national cultures, all assume new significance and meaning in our planetary and often consumer societies. Explosive contradictions exist; people are frequently both the subject and the object of cultural repression. Industrialised countries compete with developing countries, one age-group with another, local workers with migrants, urban workers with semi-urban and rural workers" (p. 17). Gelpi further argues that "teaching people how to live with these contradictions is perhaps the principal task of education today" (p. 15).

There would seem to be numerous reasons for acquainting ourselves with adult education worldwide; indeed, one would be hard pressed to argue against such a perspective. To become conversant, we would have to focus some effort in this area and, ideally, participate in some internationally based activity. Within the limited space of this chapter, our goal is to introduce readers to this aspect of adult education. First, we will describe what adult education is like in other parts of the world. Second, we will discuss how international adult education can be conceptualized as a forum for exchanging ideas and experiences. The third section of this chapter will look at international adult education through the lens of the academic discipline known as comparative studies of adult education.

Adult Education in Other Countries

What does adult education look like worldwide? What commonalities and differences are there in the provision of adult education in other countries or regions of the world? To what extent do nations with different political and economic systems and different cultures grapple with similar issues? In this section of the chapter, we are able to offer only a glimpse of worldwide adult education. Of necessity, our discussion will be in terms of general factors—how adult education develops, what its purposes or goals are, how it is structured, and what some of the relevant issues are worldwide.

At times, we will illustrate points related to these topics with examples from specific countries, but just as often our discussions will be in terms of industrialized countries versus Third World nations. Of course, a number of problems are inherent in dividing up the world in this manner, not the least of which is semantics. There is something of a common understanding that industrialized—or what Titmus (1989b) calls "developed"—countries are "significantly more advanced economically" (p. 389). Titmus includes among these countries Japan and those nations that can trace their roots to the European cultural tradition. However, such countries as Taiwan, South Korea, South

Africa, China, and perhaps Malaysia and Thailand are positioned to become—if they are not already—highly industrialized nations.

Naisbitt (1996), in fact, identifies a shift from West to East in the global center of economic, political, and cultural gravity as one of the megatrends of the 1990s. The term *Third World* is even more problematic, but in the literature it seems preferable to LDCs (less developed countries), *underdeveloped nation*, or *developing nation*, because in reality all countries are changing and "developing." When compared with industrialized countries, Third World nations are characterized by low per capita income, a low gross domestic product, poor health and nutrition, a high birthrate, and a primarily agricultural economy. About 70 percent of the world's people live in Third World countries.

The Development of Adult Education Worldwide

Planned and systematic instruction of adults has taken place since the formation of early societies. Titmus (1989b) provides an overview of these efforts. He notes, for example, that there were well-organized systems of education for adults in ancient Egypt, China, and India, and that in the Islamic world "a combination of Mosque universities, Koranic schools, organized study circles, book publishers, and book shops served as cultural centres and all fostered the culture of the time and created a condition and environment that can properly be assigned the title of 'a learning society'" (p. xxiv). From the eighteenth century on, adult education programs increased dramatically, although it was not until the late 1900s and early twentieth century that nations consciously identified their efforts as "adult education."

The development of adult education over time and across national boundaries has been shaped by similar forces. Titmus (1989b) explains:

> Some of the compelling pressures of change which evoked a response were religion; social or political revolution; new economic needs arising from changes in

technology, both in agriculture and in industry; the need
for training and education associated with changing military technologies and strategies; pressures and opportunities arising from transformations in class, occupation,
and place of residence; as well as the vast numbers of
migrant peoples beginning to move to cities or to countries far from their birthplaces. The organization of adult
education has been fuelled by faiths, by revolutions, by
migration, by inventions and renaissances, by national-
ist ardour, by internationalist organizations, and now by
the demands of high technology [pp. xxiv–xxv].

A quick look at our own country's history of adult education reveals
how accurate Titmus's analysis is. In Colonial America, adult education was driven by religion; the Revolutionary War shifted the
focus to civic education, and the Industrial Revolution—with its
attendant immigration and new technologies—led to adult vocational education as well as the formation of programs for immigrants. The global economy and advanced technologies are shaping
contemporary responses.

　While these influencing forces are universal, a particular country's response may be unique. History combined with culture can
often explain why certain forms of adult education appear at particular times in a nation's development. Puppet theaters in Africa,
a radio school for farmers in India, folk schools in Scandinavia, popular songs in South America, the Open University in Great Britain
are all examples of culturally specific delivery systems. Charters and
Hilton's (1989) comparative analysis of eight "landmark" programs
in eight Western countries underscores this point. While each program was "derived from the great events—economic, political and
social—of each society at a particular time in its history," each was
also "individually designed or adapted" for the particular society (pp.
176, 177). The Frontier College of Canada, to take one example,
was designed to meet the needs of workers in isolated parts of that

nation at the turn of the twentieth century. These workers lived in camps removed from both rural and urban life. The Frontier College provided literacy and social and cultural instruction by camp laborers who were trained as teachers. The college survives today, although its mission has expanded to include people who are isolated by factors other than geography, such as prisoners, native communities, and urban illiterate adults (J. Morrison, 1989).

History and culture shape adult education in particular settings. Cultural infusion can also create learning demands that can severely tax a nation's resources and ability to respond. This is particularly evident in today's world of instant communications, worldwide television, fast modes of travel, and the export or sharing of cultural forms. Duke (1994b) comments that "globalization itself will increase the necessity for more and more people to be lifelong learners, working in learning organizations in a learning society. The struggle will be over the direction and character of this learning, rather than about its existence and growth" (p. 315).

Globalization is affecting both the Third World and industrialized countries. Cultural influences "have engendered sharp divisions between the deep-rooted traditional culture that still dominates most rural areas [of developing countries] and the heavily westernized modern cultural beachhead in the capital city" (Coombs, 1985, p. 245). On the other hand, writes Coombs, industrialized nations "are caught in wrenching transitions" from modern to postmodern societies characterized by "far-reaching changes in the nature of work and lifestyles, by the rapid erosion of old values and social codes of behavior, and by the deterioration of long-established political, judicial, religious, and educational institutions, including the most basic of all educational institutions, the family" (p. 245).

The Goals of Adult Education

The stated goals of adult education in countries around the world are similar in the sense that each nation is concerned with improving the lives of its citizens. How this is to be achieved varies by social and political context. Some nations have a national agenda with priorities spelled out, while others implicitly endorse certain goals by the ways in which it allocates funding and other resources. According to Titmus (1989b), four major categories of purposes capture the goals of adult education worldwide:

(a) [S]econd-chance education, which offers adults who missed it the kind of education obtainable in the initial education system. This may range from basic literacy to mature entrance to university;

(b) role education, which is education for social function (outside employment) and includes social role education (e.g., as citizen, member of an association) and personal role education (e.g., as parent, spouse, retired person);

(c) vocational education, that is, education in the skills and knowledge required in employment;

(d) personal enrichment education, or education intended to develop the individual without regard to his or her social or economic function which includes, in effect, anything not covered by the other headings [p. 384].

These purposes are broad enough to encompass Third World and industrialized nations, democratic and totalitarian societies, ancient and emerging nations, and multiethnic and culturally unified societies. In the case of the third purpose—vocational education—for example, we could point to continuing professional education, on-the-job training, apprenticeships, and staff development programs, all of which are found in varying degrees in all countries.

While these purposes are common to all nations, Third World governments rarely support personal enrichment education, because "the over-riding purposes of adult education in these regions are to overcome illiteracy and help create a pool of skilled and aware labour for national development" (Titmus, 1989b, p. 423). It can be argued, however, that popular education—those forms of learning that originate with the people themselves—often address personal enrichment needs. We might also point out that even for many industrialized nations, this category of education enjoys little if any government support.

A number of writers have argued that government support for adult education nearly always promotes the national agenda and reinforces the status quo (Cunningham, 1995; Gelpi, 1985; Titmus, 1989b). Whether the education is for training a workforce to modernize to compete in world markets, for facilitating the upward mobility of those in the lower classes, or for inculcating the values and ideals of society, it is a very politicized activity. Minnis (1993) underscores this point in an article titled "Adult Education and the African State in the Post Cold War Era." For most African countries, adult education is highly centralized; "a 'social control' model has been the norm resulting in a state monopoly on adult education provision. The overriding objective of the state is to use adult education as a means to maintain and conserve the traditional ordering of society however unjust and inequitous [sic] these policies turn out to be" (p. 12). Education whose purpose is the transformation of the social structure is left to nonformal and informal forms of educational activity.

Adult Education Delivery Systems

Specific delivery systems—the ways in which adult education is structured—vary enormously from country to country. "The untidy structures which prevail in many countries are, in large part, a consequence of the diversity of initiatives and providers, mostly private until the second half of the twentieth century" (Titmus, 1989b, p. 381). Though not perfect, Coombs's categories (1985) of formal, nonformal, and informal adult education provide a template for organizing this diversity (see also Colletta, 1996).

Formal adult education is that which is institutionalized, usually as part of an existing system. Continuing higher education, vocational and technical schools, literacy programs attached to public schools, and government training programs are a few examples. Formal adult education is most often supported by public funds and thus contributes to carrying out the state's goals in the manner outlined above. The relationship between adult education and the state is not as simple as it has been presented, however. As Jarvis (1993) points out, depending on the political milieu at any point in time, "there have been occasions when the state has needed adult education, some when it has used it, others when it has supported it and still others when it has merely tolerated it" (p. 15).

Formal systems of adult education tend to be most visible in industrialized nations. External degree programs—some of which have been inspired by Britain's Open University, Scandinavian folk high schools, European workers' universities and education centers, Swedish study circles, and the U.S. Cooperative Extension Service— are types of formal adult education that are at least partially subsidized by government. They are also examples of delivery systems that have been adopted with modifications in other, usually industrialized countries (Charters and Hilton, 1989; Darkenwald and Merriam, 1982; Titmus, 1989b). Interestingly, however, even "the advanced countries, most of which have a long history of organized adult education, lack common structures, or even national structures directed to clear and coherent goals" (Titmus, 1989b, p. 423).

In all countries, but especially in the Third World, formal education is augmented with nonformal delivery systems. In the Pacific Islands, for example, most governments have diverted a large proportion of available resources to building Western-style formal education systems; nonformal education is provided by a variety of nongovernmental agencies and private voluntary organizations that are supported by external aid programs (Schoeffel, 1995).

As we defined it earlier (see Chapter One), *nonformal adult education* takes place outside the formal system; typically, it is less structured, more flexible, and more responsive to localized needs. It also is expressly concerned with social inequities and often seeks to raise the consciousness of participants toward social action. Community-based development projects and popular education characterize much nonformal adult education.

Coombs, who has promoted the distinction between formal, nonformal, and informal adult education, also recognizes that these forms are not always as discrete as the categories would suggest (1989). In fact, he gives several examples of "homegrown hybrids" of formal and nonformal education: "the second-chance program for out-of-school youth in Thailand; distance learning in Lesotho; MOBRAL in Brazil; community schools in Tanzania; the Centers of Integrated Popular Education in Guinea-Bissau; and versions of 'production schools' and community learning centers in a number of other countries" (p. 58).

Developing nations in particular have found formal education to be inadequate in raising the socioeconomic status of the under-class and in preparing people for work in a competitive world econ-omy. Nonformal education has been seen as a panacea for addressing many of the severe problems of developing nations, and while it has had an impact in specific areas, it "has been no more successful in achieving a more equal distribution of resources and power than has formal schooling" (Bock and Bock, 1989, p. 66). Some of the problems in attaining the goals of nonformal education include failure to reach the very poor and illiterate; uneven local leadership; resources that are spread too thinly, resulting in weak impacts; and a lack of follow-up in skills development and/or a lack of methods for implementing newly learned skills (Bock and Bock, 1989). Coombs (1985) adds that for many of these reasons, many nonformal programs "have limited survival power. They start with enthusiasm, run for a while, and then disappear" (p. 91).

Bock and Bock (1989) suggest that an assessment of the strengths and problems of nonformal education leads to several policy impli-cations. First, they argue, greater coordination and integration must be achieved with various other institutions, agencies, and programs, including the formal school system; they point out that nonformal education itself helps create the demand for more formal education. They also recommend greater national support, but without diluting grassroots participation, and they suggest that "this combination of top-down and bottom-up organization may be better able to accommodate unique geographical and cultural differences. It may also empower the poor clients of nonformal education to participate in those decisions which are critical to their well-being" (p. 68).

Though not technically a delivery system, *informal adult education*— "the spontaneous, unstructured learning that goes on daily in the home and neighborhood, behind the school and on the playing field, in the workplace, marketplace, library and museum, and through the various mass media"—is a major source of adult learning (Coombs, 1985, p. 92). It is learning that occurs naturally within the context of people's lives. Because it is such a source of learning—and perhaps the major source—Coombs makes the point that nations should attend to enriching their informal learning environments. This is happening in some areas of the world through the education of parents; through the increasing availability of books, magazines, and newspapers; and through radio, television, film, and computers.

Spaulding (1987) makes the case that for a country to address its learning needs in a comprehensive manner, even informal education must be included. He offers a model that nations can use for policymaking and planning in adult education, one that accounts for the great diversity of activities, including informal adult education. As Table 7.1 shows, the types of services and activities range from those that are tightly controlled by authorities to those "depending solely on the interest of participants" (p. 160).

Thus, at the bottom of the model are formal educational activities in which admission is carefully controlled and learning is certified by agencies that are external to the learner. As we move up Spaulding's model, the activities become less controlled and can be

Table 7.1. Model for Policy and Planning.

Range of adult education services and activities
Open, noncompetitive, nonselective (or self-selective) activities and services, depending solely on interest of participants for choice of what will be done, listened to, read, or studied; little formal structure in course format; little or no certification of achievement; immediate satisfaction from participation and/or immediate perception of usefulness of content.
Type VI Mass media and information services
Type V Clubs and participant-governed groups
Type IV Extension, community-development "Campaign"–type programs designed to attract and influence adults in a variety of more or less nonformal approaches.
Type III Short-course–oriented adult education and training programs.
Type II Second-chance, degree-oriented formal programs (open university, secondary, school equivalency, and the like) that have few age restrictions and minimal entry requirements.
Type I Formal education and training that limit participants to specific age ranges and carefully select those who can enter.
Closed, selective, competitive services, depending primarily on standards set by the authority as to who should (or should be allowed to) study what subjects at what ages; usually structured in the form of courses, with recognized certification of attainment; little immediately perceived usefulness of content; deferred satisfaction; acceptance of long-term goals.

Source: Spaulding, S. (1987). Policy and planning in adult education: The international dimension. In W. M. Rivera (Ed.), Planning adult learning: Issues, practices and directions (pp. 142–168). London: Croom Helm. Reprinted by permission.

characterized as nonformal—Type III, for example, includes short courses in adult education and training. At the top of the model are self-selected informal learning activities, such as what people might learn from the mass media (Type VI).

While it would be difficult to map the nonformal and informal educational activities of a particular country, Spaulding's model at least draws attention to the many possible ways in which the total learning environment can be harnessed to provide educational activities for adults.

Adult Education for Development

Pictures of adults in remote and sometimes exotic settings who are learning to read, practice better health habits, or farm more efficiently come to mind when we think about international development efforts. These endeavors typically flow from wealthier, more industrialized countries to less developed nations and reflect the social-movement philosophy underlying much of international adult education. As Duke (1994a) explains: "International adult education as a social movement strives to combine a concern for equity with efforts for economic development, particularly of the disadvantaged and marginalized groups" (p. 2947).

Duke goes on to point out, however, that "the majority of adult educators [work] on programs that lack any clear ideological purpose" (p. 2947). Furthermore, what is on the international agenda at any point in time reflects the larger global context. For example, following World War II the emphasis was on the tensions between East and West and on "North-South aid and development relations" (p. 2946). With the major political changes in the late 1980s, "the attention of Western industrialized nations has shifted . . . to investment in Eastern Europe," with North-South relations consequently threatened (p. 2946). In addition, the resurgence of nationalism (frequently based on ethnicity) and its attendant tensions and conflicts has altered international adult education's "agenda for discussion and action" (p. 2946).

That context plays a deciding role in the structuring of education is underscored by the recent changes in Europe. Oglesby and Bax (1993) list a number of challenges that "materially affect the adult education world," including "changing welfare policies in European countries and the implications for education in social and personal terms, . . . internationalism and competition throughout the whole of Europe," creating a "predominant emphasis on education for industrial and commercial ends, . . . changes in demographic patterns . . . industrial restructuring . . . new technology, [and] ecological awareness and its subsequent effects on social and industrial initiatives, especially in the energy field" (pp. 51–52).

Whether or not an individual educator, a program, or even a country has a strong social agenda or a "clear ideological purpose," this dimension of international adult education strives for economic, social, and cultural development. This goal has come to be interpreted as assisting countries not as developed as industrialized nations to change through the infusion of technical assistance and social and educational programs. More formal, top-down models of education with the aim of development have given way to nonformal education.

As defined earlier in the chapter, *nonformal education* consists of systematic and organized educational activities that occur outside the formal school system. It can deal with any area of life, including family, work, and health matters. Nonformal education also differs from *informal* education, which is learning acquired from daily living and "is limited to whatever [an individual's] personal environment happens to offer" (Coombs, 1985, p. 24).

Adult education for development is most often manifested as nonformal education. Ewert (1989) has identified four types of nonformal education common to development programs. The first is *critical consciousness*, which draws upon Freire's philosophy (see Chapter Two). This strategy engages people in critical reflection and discussion of their problems and the underlying sociostructural causes of those problems. This leads them to a greater awareness of their world and what might be done to change it for the better. According to Ewert, "Community educators influenced by the Freire paradigm facilitate learning by posing questions that stimulate reflection leading to action, rather than by sharing technical information that addresses local problems" (p. 90).

Comings (1995) describes a project in Ecuador designed to address the basic education needs of rural adults, which the formal school system was not addressing adequately. Twenty-six villages were involved, and each chose facilitators to manage the educational processes in their village. The facilitators were trained by project staff, but late in the process the more experienced facilitators became the trainers. They worked in their villages to identify needs and design educational programs around those needs using a Freirian problem-posing model.

A second form of nonformal international education that Ewert identifies is *education for mobilization*. This strategy seeks to mobilize an entire country around particular national goals. Some of these are development plans spanning several years and containing a number of projected goals; other are goal-specific—for example, Nicaragua's literacy crusade. All of the educational resources of the country, from cultural activities to the mass media to the formal educational system, are marshaled in support of the campaign.

Popular education, which can be part of a mobilization effort, is a third strategy used for development purposes (Ewert, 1989). Popular education rests on the assumption that knowledge resides with the people in their own community and "that using such unofficial knowledge is much more appropriate than consulting an outside expert for so-called official knowledge to solve community problems" (Hamilton and Cunningham, 1989, p. 445). Popular education values people's own culture and draws on the art forms of that culture—"theater, dance, storytelling, music, songs, poetry, and art—to stimulate reflection and analysis" (Ewert, 1989, p. 91). For example, role playing, collective drawing, cartoons, and storytelling have been used to identify experiences of women's oppression in South Africa (MacKenzie, 1993).

Popular education assumes not only that knowledge resides within the community but also that local people can create knowledge themselves. This process is known as *participatory research,* a process "by which the 'raw' and somewhat unformed—or at least, unexpressed—knowledge of ordinary people is brought into the open and incorporated into a connectable whole through discussion, analysis, and the 'reflected' knowledge gained with or without allied intellectuals and those who have both broader and deeper insights. . . . Participatory research can, through successive movements of popular analysis over time, move people from looking at more peripheral contradictions in the local reality to focusing more clearly on central contradictions that actually influence and control their lives" (Hall and Kassam, 1989, p. 538). The Netherlands' Center for the Study of Education in Developing Countries, for example, has linked with Latin American popular educators to document the pedagogical practices involved in popular education (Epskamp, 1995).

The fourth strategy for nonformal education is what Ewert calls *integrated community-based development,* and it views the community as a whole. Workers from this paradigm see development as more than learning to read or make drinking water safe; they attack the many aspects of improving the quality of life in an integrated fashion. "The process is an educational one with people learning how to prevent disease and to promote health through changed behavior [for example]. It becomes political when people attempt to change those structures that are ultimately responsible for the existence of these problems" (Ewert, 1989, p. 92).

As an example of integrated community-based development, residents of San Miguel Teotongo, a densely populated settlement in the eastern part of Mexico City, decided to organize a residents' union to remedy a lack of urban services, improve health conditions, and combat malnutrition. They began with the question

"What is the state of our environment?" and proceeded to examine specific conditions such as "garbage, lack of green areas, poverty, alcoholism, malnutrition, unemployment, and lack of community participation" (Soares de Moraes, 1995, p. 242). Through "years of continuous and systematic work," the residents have gained access to services, accomplished some of their goals regarding health conditions and malnutrition, and organized an infrastructure (p. 240).

There is much overlap, and there are many commonalities among these forms of nonformal adult education. Certainly, mobilization campaigns make use of popular culture, and community-based development can have a consciousness-raising agenda. Knox (1993) notes that these programs vary widely depending on the political context:

> In countries and subcultures that are democratic and egalitarian and that have a relatively equitable balance of power, societal equilibrium has been assumed, and organizational and community development activities have been focused on individual change to achieve agreed-upon goals of modernization and improvement of human capital with a minimum of structural change in the political and economic system. By contrast, in totalitarian and oppressive countries and subcultures in which people feel exploited, revolutionary structural change sometimes seems to be the only solution. . . . Under such circumstances, adult education is often employed to empower people with unredressed grievances through emphasis on ideological solidarity and training for guerrilla war [pp. 414–415].

What all of these programs have in common, however, is a trust in the people's own culture and knowledge as a source of problem solving. Participation and the empowerment that derives from it results in action that can change individuals as well as the nation itself.

Many challenges face adult education worldwide. Some are specific to a particular country or region, while others are implicit in the nature of adult education itself. If, for example, we include formal, nonformal, and informal education in our definition of the field, it becomes virtually impossible to chart with any specificity the provision of adult education in any country. This has implications for organizing and coordinating adult education programs. Most countries, whether industrialized or part of the Third World, lack a national policy for adult education or lifelong learning (which includes all levels of education). The result is a fragmented, usually short-term effort to address pressing needs.

As we might expect in an area as diverse as international adult education, a number of tensions and issues plague the field. Shifting alliances and power bases, including the breakup of the Soviet Union, the formation of the European Community, and the sea change in South African society, necessitate the rethinking of adult education priorities. Duke (1994a) notes the "concerns that the wealthy nations will ignore the needs of the South" due to a shift in support to Eastern Europe (p. 2950). Another problem is the distribution of development efforts among private, national, and international agencies. With no overall strategy for development even within some individual nations, the efforts can be fragmentary, redundant, or uneven at best.

A final source of tension is philosophical, but no less real: the differences between those who are dedicated to fundamental social change and those who emphasize technical aid. Adult education, Duke (1994a) explains, is "inherently political and ideological in orientation, and yet efforts to professionalize the adult education service customarily place emphasis upon the technical skills related to teaching and facilitating learning, and often tend to be quite apolitical" (p. 2951). While the "universal stress on economic survival and competition . . . could threaten those characteristics peculiar to the movement which have distinguished and energized international adult education," there are still needs that require a response. "These include the persistence of illiteracy, of social and economic deprivation, and of racism and ethnocentrism in old and new forms. To these may be added the problems of the environment" (p. 2951).

Finally, all countries are challenged by issues of access and participation. The rural poor, women, illiterate adults, ethnic minorities, immigrants, and people with disabilities are commonly underserved in both industrialized and Third World nations. Minnis (1993) explains how the disparity of resources between urban and rural areas in Africa disadvantages a large portion of the population:

> Urban areas tend to get the lion's share of resources. Capital cities are especially well placed and often account for 50 percent or more of the secondary school intake (World Bank, 1988). Universities are more often than not located in urban areas, often in capitals, close to the seat of governmental power, the headquarters of NGOs (nongovernmental organizations) and influential donor agencies. Paradoxically, farmers who make up 75 to 80 percent of the population of many African countries, and who are responsible for generating a significant portion of national income, are virtually excluded from the policy-making process. This group tends to have the highest literacy rate and their children constitute only 25 percent of the secondary school intake [pp. 14–15].

Issues of access and opportunity are complex as well as frustrating, and there are no easy solutions. The first step is, of course, to at least acknowledge the existence of this and other challenges to providing adult education. We discuss these issues in more depth in Chapter Eight.

An International Forum

Duke (1994a) has defined international adult education as "those aspects of the education of adults which include some dimension of international exchange or comparison" (p. 2946). This definition encompasses the notions of adult education both as an international forum for the exchange of ideas and as a field of comparative studies.

International adult education as a forum for exchange encompasses the literal exchange of ideas, personnel, and practices among and between countries. Most exchanges are between individuals sponsored by universities, private consulting firms, businesses, or government agencies. Also, a number of intergovernmental organizations and international nongovernmental organizations facilitate international adult education activity. While it would be impossible to cover all such agencies in this chapter, we will mention some of the most prominent.

The United Nations Educational, Scientific and Cultural Organization (UNESCO) is probably the most widely known intergovernmental organization dealing with education in general and adult education in particular. Some of its work has been cut back recently due to budget reductions, but it still publishes *Adult Education Notes and News* and promotes development worldwide. UNESCO has also supported four major international conferences on adult education, the latest in Paris in 1985. (In addition, UNESCO sponsored a world conference on literacy in Thailand in 1990.) Belanger (1995) writes that UNESCO in the 1990s has broadened its scope beyond literacy activities to include "nonformal education for international understanding, retraining, and continuing education, distance education for out-of-school learners, and adult participation in university-level education" (p. 18).

Other organizations of which adult education is a major but not sole component include the World Health Organization, the International Labor Organization, the Food and Agriculture Organization, the World Bank (see Holden and Dorland, 1995), and the

European-focused Organization for Economic Co-operation and Development (OECD). Duke (1994a) comments that "the reshaping of Europe after 1992 raises questions about the membership and role of both [the] OECD and the European Community, and consequently about the means whereby international adult education will be promoted among industrialized nations within and beyond Europe" (p. 2948).

By far the most prominent nongovernmental organization dealing with adult education is the International Council for Adult Education (ICAE), which was founded in 1973 by Roby Kidd, a Canadian. Its world headquarters are in Toronto, where the association's international journal, *Convergence*, is published.

The ICAE divides the world into seven regions, with representatives from each region on its Executive Committee. Approximately one hundred countries are ICAE members, as are nearly one hundred "cooperating nongovernmental and intergovernmental organizations," as well as numerous networks representing peace, criminal justice, adult education history, older adults, and research (Cassara, 1994, p. 115; see also Cassara, 1993, 1995). Individuals can become members through a group called International Associates (Boucouvalas, 1994). The ICAE has sponsored five international conferences, most recently in Egypt in 1994. Recent priority concerns established by the ICAE are the education of women, peace and human rights, environmental education, and literacy.

Duke (1994a) points out that intergovernmental organizations (IGOs) and international nongovernmental organizations (INGOs) have different but complementary strengths. IGOs, for example, "have the authority of government behind them and, directly or indirectly, can influence the flow of . . . funds" (p. 2949). By contrast, INGOs have the advantage of "flexibility and rapid responsiveness to new situations and new needs" (p. 2949). Both promote and participate in information exchange, research, lobbying, professional development, and aid.

Various writers have offered specific suggestions as to how individuals can get involved in international adult education (Boucouvalas, 1994; Cassara, 1993; Cookson, 1994); Cookson has even presented a three-stage model of the process. The first stage is exploration, in which initial contacts are made based on "recognition of mutual interests and concerns" (p. 106). The second stage is the expansion of interlocking spheres of interest. Here a sense of emerging interdependence develops, in which "cooperative activities are identified, planned, and carried out" (p. 106). The final stage, commitment, is the evolution of a "general expectation . . . that the relationship will continue. Earlier activities tend to be repeated and reinforce the perception of an equitable balance of mutual efforts" (p. 106).

For example, the University of Georgia has entered into a formal, cooperative agreement with a university in Malaysia. The idea emerged from conversations with a Malaysian doctoral student in the University of Georgia's department of adult education who held a faculty position in a similar department at the Malaysian university. Exchange visits between faculty from both institutions resulted in the signing of the agreement, as well as in identifying and planning for collaborative activities to be pursued by students and faculty at both universities in the coming years.

Comparative Studies

Comparative adult education can be seen as a subset of the field of comparative education—or, as we are presenting it here, as an aspect of the international dimension of adult education. Such studies are, of course, a form of exchange and international cooperation; they can also inform policy in particular countries or geographical regions. Charters and Associates (1981) argue that educators "can benefit in their planning and execution by some understanding of lifelong education in other countries. The benefits include a better understanding of oneself, of one's own culture, and of others whose ideas and experiences may prove useful. The goal of the emerging discipline of comparative international adult education is to help the educators of adults in all countries learn from each other" (p. xiii).

Comparative international adult education, Charters further explains, "is not the mere placing side by side of data concerning one or more aspects of adult education in two or more countries" (p. 3); it also involves identifying the extent to which these aspects are similar or different. Then "the real value of comparative study emerges": "the attempt to understand why the differences and similarities occur and what their significance is for . the countries under examination," as well as other relevant settings (p. 3). For example, one project has developed out of the cooperative agreement between the Malaysian and American universities mentioned above—a comparative study of distance education in Malaysia, Australia, and the United States. Of particular interest is how context and culture shapes the form that distance education takes in each country.

Comparative adult education often begins with factual descriptions of adult education in individual countries. Sometimes these reports take the form of impressionistic "travelers' tales," while others are more systematic explorations of a nation—for example, a study of China conducted by Wang, Lin, Sun, and Fang (1988), or a single institution or program (Cookson, 1989). Examples of a systematic study of a single institution or program are J. E. Thomas's study (1985) of social education in Japan, and V. Miller's study (1985) of the Nicaraguan literacy campaign.

Truly comparative work involves contrasting the provision of adult education in two or more countries or comparing an institution, program, or concept across several countries. Roberts (1982), for example, compared adult education programs in Alberta and Quebec, two very different provinces of Canada. Lowe's *The Education of Adults: A World Perspective* (1975) is a comprehensive analysis of international issues. Charters and Hilton's edited book (1989) is a comparative study of exemplary programs in eight countries; the landmark programs include folk high schools, Swedish study circles, workers' universities, and the Cooperative Extension Service. In a more recent comparative study, Knox (1993) draws from case studies from more than thirty countries to examine how leadership and strategic planning can strengthen programs worldwide.

A number of writers believe that the state of scholarship in comparative adult education has not yet advanced to the level of analysis needed to have a substantive impact on policy (Cookson, 1989; Kidd, 1981; Titmus, 1989a). One explanation for the lack of work in this area is the low level of common understanding about the phenomenon to be compared; that is, "the breadth and diversity of what is comprehended within the term 'adult education' . . . varies from country to country, if indeed a concept of it as a distinctive process or system exists at all" (Titmus, 1989a, p. 543).

Second, in contrast with preadult education, adult education is so embedded in a wide variety of activities and organizations, both formal and nonformal, that it is difficult to identify or study apart from the wider and vastly complicated context in which it exists. Furthermore, many countries do not keep accurate data (or any at all) on adult education; nor are data comparable from country to country. Finally, Cookson (1989) points out that most adult educators lack training in the social sciences. "Grounded" as they are "in the field of practice, such practitioners do not typically place a high priority on empirical research" (p. 80).

Summary

In a speech on international education, Groennings (1986) tells of a cartoon depicting two butterflies, one new to the winged status. The older one says to the younger, "But you still think like a caterpillar." With globalization and its inherent international concerns of peace, environmental protection, migration, disease, terrorism, and the like, we cannot afford to think like caterpillars. Adult education worldwide deals with common concerns and has experienced successes and failures—knowledge of which can inform our practice here in North America.

In the first half of this chapter, we explored the provision of adult education worldwide. This brief overview described how adult education evolves in particular countries, what its overall goals are worldwide, and how it is delivered through formal, nonformal, and informal means. We also discussed the concept of adult education for development—the infusion of personnel, programs, and other resources to aid in a nation's development. In the usual model for this type of adult education, industrialized countries assist less economically developed countries.

We discussed two other components of international adult education in this chapter. First, it can be seen as a forum for the exchange and sharing of information through collaboration, travel, conferences, and publications. The second component we addressed is the field of comparative adult education, which involves studies of particular countries or of practices across national boundaries. These two components are, of course, interrelated. Comparative studies, for example, can offer guidance into the most effective ways to aid in a nation's development. Likewise, the exchange component may involve conducting comparative studies.

8

Examining Access and Opportunity

In a poignant scene from Joseph Heller's *Something Happened* (1975), Bob Slocum, the successful, middle-aged businessman, can't decide whether "it's more boring to do something boring than to pass along everything boring that comes in to somebody else and then have nothing to do at all" (p. 28). He cannot find meaning in life, which, he says, is just like work—"one damned sterile office desk after another" (p. 337). In today's world, where the rapid rate of change soon renders our knowledge or skills obsolete, where "the mental demands of modern life" soon have us "in over our heads" (Kegan, 1994), Slocum's alienation is not uncommon. If he had so desired, he could have addressed his problem through continuing professional education activities; and as a white, educated, middle-class businessman, he would have had easy access to an abundance of learning opportunities.

Unfortunately, the millions of other adults who fail to fit the profile of the typical participant are not so lucky. The latest government figures of participation in the United States show that seventy-six million adults (40 percent) aged sixteen and over were engaged in part-time educational activities. However, there is a wide disparity between groups represented in this figure, with younger, middle-class, and better-educated adults overrepresented in proportion to older, nonwhite, and working-class adults (Kim, Collins, Stowe, and Chandler, 1995). These figures, of course, do not reflect the learning that goes on in nonformal settings or when people learn on their own. But as we shall see, even less-formal learning activities can exhibit and perpetuate some of the disparities found in organized learning.

The increasing need for learning, combined with the question of who has access to formal learning opportunities, has made the ongoing issues of access and opportunity more pressing than ever. Why more adults—particularly in underrepresented populations—don't take part, and how to increase participation, are questions that have beset the field of adult education since its inception, although it has only been since the mid-1960s that these questions have been approached systematically (Johnstone and Rivera, 1965).

Research and theory have underscored the complexity of the issue. Participation is not solely a matter of individual motivation, although that does play a role. Whether or not an adult has access to learning opportunities is also shaped by what Cropley (1989) calls "framework conditions," which "are largely a function of the circumstances in which people live, especially of factors such as the values, attitudes, habits, priorities and the like of the social groups to which they belong, the economic structure of their society, even features of the education system itself" (p. 146). As a result of these conditions, "some individuals are more equal than others in the choices available to them. . . . How to intervene effectively to counteract this divisive process is one of the major policy issues for the coming decade" (Gerver, 1992, p. 106).

The purpose of this chapter is to explore some of these framework conditions, or factors that limit adults' access and thus their participation in organized adult education. And because the issues of access and opportunity are international in scope, this chapter is framed from the global perspective of Chapter Seven. In the first half of the chapter, we will discuss four conditions: geographical, demographic, socioeconomic, and cultural. Each of these conditions manifests itself in terms of power and control. That is, the group that holds power by virtue of geography, socioeconomic status, and so on, controls others' access to education. The second half of the chapter analyzes three broad areas of response to these issues: political, educational, and technological.

Conditions That Limit Access

Research has demonstrated that removing perceived barriers to participation in adult education, such as making a program cost-free or offering an on-site class, has little overall effect on increasing participation. Deeper and more subtle conditions shape participation. Where one happens to live, what color or sex one happens to be, what one does for a living, and which ethnic group one is a member of—all contribute to explaining the skewed participation patterns in adult education worldwide. Although we discuss geographical, demographic, socioeconomic, and cultural factors separately to help unpack the complexity of the issue, keep in mind that in reality there is considerable overlap and interaction among these factors.

Geographic Conditions

Access to learning opportunities is partially determined by where people live. The "rhetoric" of geography has traditionally divided the world into North and South, with the North representing the more industrialized nations of North America, Western Europe, and Japan. With dramatic changes in Eastern Europe, more recent attention has framed the world in terms of an East-West split. Vio Grossi (1994) speaks to "the madness of geography" for defining policy. Most of us grew up in a world ordered by "a developed North and an impoverished South, a revolutionary and socialist East and a capitalist and liberal West" (p. 66). However, this order has changed: "The North and the South move, mix and intercourse. The South exists in the North, in the form of the growth of unemployment, poverty and the exclusion of immigrants. The South has its North, with its transnationalized oligarchies that manage the cheap labor. The East wants to begin a journey toward the North, but we all have a certain premonition that they will lose course and end up in the South; Africa appears to have disappeared and Latin America suddenly emerges as a continent in accelerated modernization" (p. 67).

A more viable means of assessing geography's role in issues of access and participation is in terms of the visible discrepancy between rural and urban. Within rural-urban, further distinctions can, of course, be made such as between prosperous and poor cities, between rural and isolated villages, between different constituencies within each setting, and so on. There are also migrant, transient, and homeless populations that are not in any location long enough to become aware of, let alone take advantage of available educational opportunities.

What constitutes *rural*, *urban*, and *suburban* is debated in the literature; however, most people hold an image of rural life as more agrarian than industrial, more sparsely populated, and more distant from services, including most levels of education (Van Tilburg and Moore, 1989). Although estimates vary, the majority of the world's population lives in rural areas. This is particularly true of less developed regions, where 65.7 percent of the people live in rural settings, in contrast to the developed countries such as the United States, where only 27.3 percent are classified as rural (United Nations, 1993). With few exceptions, formal adult education in rural areas of Third World countries is sporadic to nonexistent; efforts are concentrated at the primary school level. Even at the primary level, "schools in the hinterland generally have insufficient textbooks and other training materials and equipment and a disproportionate share of untrained and unqualified primary teachers" (Coombs, 1985, p. 223).

Coombs also points out that the discrepancies between rural and urban secondary and postsecondary schools is even greater than at the primary level. In the Third World, "the probability of a rural child of either sex getting an equivalent *quality* of education to that of an urban child is very low. The statistical probability of an urban boy climbing to the middle or top of the educational ladder is vastly greater than that of an equally bright and motivated rural boy. The prospects for a rural girl are even smaller in relation to an urban girl" (1985, p. 224, emphasis in the original).

In industrialized nations, the discrepancy is likely to be most acute in postsecondary and adult education settings. Contributing to the improved opportunities in rural areas of industrialized nations is a "shrinkage of rural populations, improved parental education, better transportation and communication, and strong public policies aimed at equalizing educational access" (Coombs, 1985, p. 218). Nevertheless, rural areas even in the most industrialized countries of North America, northern Europe, and Australasia rarely have the rich diversity of options for higher and adult education, the trained personnel, or the support services and resources found in more urbanized areas. Somewhat ironically, writes Coombs, in these most industrialized nations reside a segment of the urban population that fares less well than rural youth and adults—the disadvantaged people "trapped in the decaying inner core of major cities" (p. 218).

In addition to the rural-urban split, geography functions as a barrier to access and participation for migrant, transient, and homeless adults. Although major differences exist among these groups, what they have in common is a lack of geographical "place" that allows for access to social services and formal education. Velazquez (1994–1995), for example, writes: "Migrants are the most undereducated major subgroup in the United States. Mobility, language, and cultural differences experienced as they move from one community to another, combine with health and nutritional problems to have a negative effect on school achievement" (pp. 33–34).

Norris and Kennington (1992) address the challenges of providing literacy instruction to homeless adults when they have no consistent place to stay. Furthermore, the conditions of emergency shelters are hardly conducive to instruction: "Instructors may literally teach off an ironing board or a console television top. Instructors would likely be carrying all instructional materials in the trunk of a car, including audiovisual equipment. Cold weather or emergencies may result in a designated instructional space being used instead for extra beds" (p. 2).

Demographic Factors

Demographic variables have been associated with participation patterns in adult education. In particular, young people participate in greater percentages than older adults, and except in the most industrialized nations, men have a higher participation rate than women. We will discuss each of these variables in the following sections.

Age

U.S. government statistics on participation by age reveals that "rates gradually increased from 28 percent for adults age 17 to 19 to 48 percent for those age 40 to 44 and then decreased to 11 percent for those 65 and older" (Kopka and Peng, 1993, p. 2). It could be argued that older adults who have potentially less family and work responsibilities and more time and income should have higher rates of participation. There are, however, a number of other factors that mitigate against fuller participation. Older adults have less formal education on average than younger adults—and previous education level has shown to be highly correlated with continued participation. Also, the majority of adults report engaging in formal adult education for work-related reasons, which becomes less of an issue the closer a person gets to retirement. Studies have shown, in fact, that older adults favor liberal arts courses in higher education, and personal growth and leisure activity courses overall (Courtenay, 1989).

Several age-related concerns tend to limit access. Studies have found that several factors influence participation, including poor health, "fear of being out at night, lack of transportation, and being tired of school," as well as "the absence of a companion and lack of information about the activity," parking availability, and location of the program (Courtenay, 1989, p. 528). With regard to setting, geography as a barrier overlaps with age. According to Courtenay, older students prefer settings that are "accessible and familiar. Fisher (1986) discovered that awareness of sites where education is available is the best predictor of participation" (p. 529).

In other parts of the world, life expectancy is not as great as in industrialized nations. For example, the average life expectancy in the United States is 75.2 years, while in less developed countries it is 60.7 years (United Nations, 1993). Also, while the population in industrialized nations is aging (by the year 2000, people over the age of sixty-five will represent 13.5 percent of the population), it is still quite young in less developed countries, where by the year 2000 only 5.1 percent of the population will be over sixty-five; 21.9 percent will be under fourteen years of age (compared with 13.5 percent in more highly developed countries) (United Nations, 1993). This combination of factors renders the participation of older adults nearly invisible in nonindustrialized nations. The emphasis on preparing young adults to engage in the urgent task of national development takes precedence over attending to the learning needs of older adults (Knox, 1993).

Sex

In addition to age, a person's sex can preclude full participation in adult education. In most countries of the world, women's rates of participation at all levels of education are lower than men's, or the nature of women's participation is qualitatively different from—and usually inferior to—men's (Coombs, 1985; Oglesby, Krajnc, and Mbilinyi, 1989). The disparity in education reflects "the position of women globally. . . . Women make up over 30 percent of the 'official' labour force, perform 60–89 percent of all agricultural work, and produce at least 50 percent of all food, receive 10 percent of the world's income, and possess less than 1 percent of the world's wealth. Women and girls constitute 50 percent of the world's population and 75 percent of the world's undernourished" (Oglesby, Krajnc, and Mbilinyi, 1989, pp. 322–323).

Coombs (1985) has delineated five interrelated propositions that help account for the sex disparities in education in both industrialized and Third World countries. The first is that the lowest rates of participation are found in countries where participation overall is exceptionally low; higher overall rates mean higher rates for women. Thus, in countries such as the United States, where participation of both men and women is relatively higher than in developing countries, there is no difference in participation rates between men and women (Kopka and Peng, 1993).

Coombs's next three propositions refer to higher education. The second is where there are disparities, "they are always greatest in higher education," and disparities at this level reflect the "sorting out" by sex that takes place at secondary and primary levels (1985, p. 226). Coombs's third proposition is that even in Western nations, where parity in higher education appears to be the case, a closer look reveals "sizable sex disparities in enrollments between different types of postsecondary institutions and different fields of study" (p. 227). Fourth, sex biases in higher education are linked to employment practices. Women prepare for traditionally women's fields, which tend to pay less, thus perpetuating the cycle of women's oppression even in highly industrialized countries (Rice and Meyer, 1989).

Coombs's fifth and "most fundamental" proposition explaining sex disparities in education is that they "grow primarily out of the traditional culture, customs, and taboos of each particular society" (p. 228). Males hold the power and are the primary breadwinners in most societies, so not only are male children preferred—they are given preference when choices have to be made as to who can take advantage of educational opportunities.

While women's access to higher and adult educational programs has substantially improved in recent years, most writers in the field think that there is still much to be done, even in industrialized nations. "[A]lthough women share equally with the men the problems associated with modernization and technological change, and the dependency and exploitation resulting from poverty, in addition they are subjected to the cultural, social, and domestic pressures of being women" (Oglesby, Krajnc, and Mbilinyi, 1989, p. 331).

For example, managerial and professional workers and all nonmanual workers are much more likely to receive training than are manual workers. Since women are underrepresented in these higher-level positions, they receive less training than men. Furthermore, "women are less likely to receive formal, employer-sponsored training [of any kind] than men," placing them in a "disadvantaged position when seeking promotion" (Stacy and Duc-Le To, 1994, p. 107).

In summary, the demographic characteristics of age and sex constitute powerful barriers to participation in adult education. Even where some equality exists in participation, the nature of the experience may differ, revealing yet another layer of disparity between young and old, and male and female.

Socioeconomic Conditions and Education

In both industrialized and Third World countries, socioeconomic conditions in conjunction with geographical and demographic factors account for "the most widespread and intractable disparities in all education" (Coombs, 1985, p. 230). Hinzen (1994) points to the finding that "rich countries are becoming richer, and the rich people in the rich countries are becoming richer. The same could be said in reverse of the poor countries and poor people" (p. 45). The result, he argues, is "movement towards a two-thirds world. Two-thirds of humanity have to fight to survive. The remaining third lives in relative luxury. . . . And this two-thirds relationship is reflected within individual countries. In the rich countries, it will soon be a third of the population who fall through the widening holes in the social net; in the poor countries, the proportion is the reverse" (pp. 45–46).

This widening gap between rich and poor is reflected in studies of participation in adult education that consistently link participation with socioeconomic status and previous levels of education

(Kopka and Peng, 1993; Merriam and Caffarella, 1991). The pattern is particularly difficult to break because it is perpetuated by families through the generations, as well as by the institutions of society itself. Coombs (1985) explains that "in virtually all nations today children of parents high on the educational, occupational, and social scale have a far better statistical chance of getting into a good secondary school, and from there into the best colleges and universities, than equally bright children of ordinary workers or farmers. . . . The children of less-educated, lower income parents are heavily overrepresented in the vocational training schools and grossly underrepresented in [programs] for university entrance" (p. 230). Part of the problem is a long history of alienation and "deliberate noninvolvement" of low-income parents with the educational system (Nardine, 1990, p. 79). Noninvolvement not only perpetuates the socioeconomic discrepancy in participation from generation to generation, it also acts as a barrier preventing parents themselves from taking part in organized education.

A number of writers have addressed how education functions to preserve a society's economic and political systems. This interlocking of education and economics maintains the status quo—which, with regard to access and participation, means vast disparities. Beder (1992), for example, argues against allowing adult education in the United States to be market driven, because doing so perpetuates inequality. Because the more advantaged adults in society have "more resources to exchange for adult education offerings," they are more likely to participate, resulting in their becoming even further advantaged (p. 71). On the other hand, the disadvantaged "who might benefit the most from participation" have fewer resources and "prerequisite learning skills" to exchange (p. 71).

The educational system itself is a product of the dominant, middle-class culture. "People from other backgrounds tend to find the system difficult to understand, or frequently find that there is a conflict between its norms and those which prevail in the informal system" (Cropley, 1989, p. 146). By contrast, those born and socialized into the dominant society have the "cultural capital" to take advantage of the educational system (Jarvis, 1985, p. 138). Cropley explains how unequal access functions in adult education: "Participation in adult education is thus affected by the role [that] people play in the groups to which they belong, by the tactics they prefer for dealing with the external world, by their degree of willingness to accept certain kinds of external authority, [by] their preference for particular learning strategies, and so on. Furthermore, these characteristics are shared with other people, are acquired in group settings, and are reinforced by the groups to which people belong, social classes being among the most important groups" (1989, p. 146).

Formal schooling, as part of the system that perpetuates the status quo, acts in and of itself as a barrier to participation in adult education. According to Cropley, this is because "there is a strong tendency for formal, school-like learning to be regarded as the only really worthwhile form of learning" (1989, p. 146). This is a common perception worldwide. Even in the United States, formal educational institutions that dispense degrees and credentials are valued more than activities of a less formal nature. Rubenson (1989) points out how this tendency reinforces socioeconomic discrepancies: "[T]he better an education pays off in terms of income, status, occupation, political efficacy, cultural competence, and similar matters, the greater the differences in socioeconomic status between participants and nonparticipants" (p. 64).

Even adult education that purports to address inequities can be seen as supporting the status quo. For example, remedial education, which is meant to offer a second chance to those wishing to acquire basic skills, merely "produces an appearance of greater equality of opportunity and, hence, reinforces the existing social structures" (Jarvis, 1985, p. 143). Literacy education in the United States is a case in point: while it purports to provide an opportunity to redress deficiencies in this area, "the federal adult literacy program currently serves about 7 percent of those eligible per year" (Beder, 1992, p. 72). We need also to be wary of adult education that seeks to empower and liberate individuals, for such programs "may actually be designed to enable people to fit more easily into the existing social system" (Merriam and Caffarella, 1991, p. 275).

Cultural Determinants

Most societies are made up of various subgroups or subcultures. People in each subgroup have some factor in common, such as race, religion, language, or ethnicity, and members usually share certain values, beliefs, and practices. In every society, certain of these groups enjoy a higher status, have more power, and thus command more control over educational opportunities than other groups. The group in power may or may not represent the majority population. Historically, colonized countries of Africa, for example, have been controlled by a white minority; and the French in otherwise English-speaking Canada have maintained control over Québec.

In most contemporary societies, however, those with less power—those having *minority* status—are also less in number than the *majority* in power. In the United States, this factor plays out predominantly in terms of whites participating to a greater extent than black, Hispanic, Native American and other minority populations. In other countries, different dynamics are at work. For example, in Colombia the eighty or so indigenous groups have lower participation rates than either blacks or Spaniards (Tamayo R, 1994); in Hungary, the Gypsy ethnic group participates less than Hungarians (Bathory, 1994); and throughout the world, immigrant populations are much less represented in adult education than are native-born adults (Knox, 1993).

Being a member of a particular social group may affect a person's attitude or interest in education. For example, being a member of a social group that does not value education, inexperience with the educational system, or previous experiences that jeopardized self-esteem or self confidence may lead to a lack of confidence or interest. Ross-Gordon (1990) discusses these factors with regard to the minority adult, who when "considering participation in an educational activity begins with a self-evaluation. This self-evaluation is influenced by the individual's attitudes toward education, which arise both directly from the learner's own past experience and indirectly from attitudes and experiences of friends and 'significant others.' Negative attitudes due to previous educational failure or attitudes of the reference group may prevent further consideration of the learning opportunity. . . . If a minority adult doubts that participating in the educational experience will lead to any tangible changes in his or her life situation, motivation to participate may be reduced" (p. 10).

Of course, more is involved here than just being of minority status. Ross-Gordon observes that in the American workplace, for example, "the disappearance of the industrial economy and its replacement by a technology-based information economy may have a major impact on the economic status of minority workers . . . without a significant increase in their college participation rates or adult education experiences to provide further education, many from this growing minority segment of the work force will find themselves relegated to low-level service occupations" (1990, p. 8). And in turn, employers tend not to support training and continuing education for workers at this level.

Recent incidents of racial, religious, or ethnic violence throughout the world underscore the issue. In an article titled "Migrants and Ethnic Minorities: A European Challenge to Adult Education," Leumer (1994) points out that the "overall picture can easily be broken down by country, occupational structure and socio-political peculiarities. It is common to all cases that the reality of multiculturalism is insufficiently accepted by the mass of the population. . . . Racism does not trouble with statistics and fine differentiation: to a racist, every 'foreigner' is one too many" (p. 236).

Leumer goes on to note that cultural groups having little or no power in a society generally have a lower standard of living, higher unemployment, and a higher proportion of criminality and family breakdown; they are physically and socially separated from other segments of society and have experienced more acts of aggression toward them than the ruling cultural group. The majority society, according to Leumer, is uncomfortable with multiculturalism because of racism, stereotyping, fear of anything foreign, and "the phenomenon that the victims of aggression and violence are blamed for their own social situation" (p. 237). Leumer suggests three strategies for learning to live in a multicultural society: antidiscrimination training, improving access to education and employment for foreigners and ethnic minorities, and strengthening these groups' ability to organize themselves.

To summarize this section, which has focused on conditions affecting access and participation in organized adult learning, a number of social-structural factors combine to help explain the fact that worldwide, better-educated adults of higher social status disproportionately participate in adult education. Cropley (1989) raises an interesting question regarding the discrepancies in participation. He asks whether we should assume that higher rates of participation are desirable when most countries could not accommodate such an increase. He suggests that "convincing arguments need to be found which indicate that rates should be raised (i.e., there should be a quantitative change in participation) or else that the 'right' people need to be encouraged to make use of available resources (i.e., a qualitative change). Such arguments would be most convincing if they were based on a clear statement of the role of adult education in the modern world" (p. 147).

Responses to the Dilemmas of Access and Participation

Worldwide, there have been a number of efforts to address the imbalance of participation in adult education. Some of these efforts have originated at the national level with legislation and policy; others started at the local level with adult educators themselves. To organize these responses for discussion, we have divided this section of the chapter into three parts: the political response, the educational response, and the technological response. As with the conditions and factors contributing to the problem, these three responses are in reality quite interrelated to one another. Furthermore, none of them provides a panacea to the problem, and each has some controversy associated with it.

The Political Response

For lack of a better term, the *political response* is meant to encompass "official," usually governmental-sponsored, legislation and policies to combat the inequities in participation. Some countries—especially but not limited to those in the Third World—have had nationally mandated literacy campaigns sponsored by the government; others have instituted national programs for minority and native groups; and still others have put efforts into large-scale community development projects with the aim of improving the quality of life for everyone. These responses are easier to effect in smaller, more homogeneous nations (such as Scandinavian countries) and in more socialist or totalitarian nations (such as China).

In multiculturally diverse and social-democratic countries, the number of competing interests and levels of government results in a complex political response. A recurring debate in the United States, for example, is the extent to which a national system—or at least national-level coordination—of adult education should be implemented. One assumption underlying the debate is that either strategy both promotes and impedes access. More than twenty years ago, Knowles (1977) laid out the pros and cons of greater national coordination, which was meant to address the overlapping of service, duplication of programs, and competition for participants. Furthermore, "the marginality of the adult educational role in most institutional settings induces adult educators to seek mutual support, status, and problem-solving help across institutional lines" (p. 265). In addition, there is a commonality of interests among different segments of adult education, and linking together would promote professionalism as well as gain recognition and status for the field as a whole.

Arguments against coordination center on the diversity of the adult education field in terms of goals, differences in the training and experience of personnel working in the field, and perceptions of differences in status of various groups (Knowles, 1977). Also, "without a clear and comprehensive map of the field to be coordinated, it is difficult to construct a coordinated organizational structure in which the component parts of the field feel represented and in which a functional division of labor is possible" (p. 268).

McCarten (1987) also notes that in the United States, responsibility for education falls to the states. In fact, some states have addressed barriers to participation by targeting subpopulations and increasing delivery to isolated or underserved areas.

While the argument for more or less control and coordination at the national level has waxed and waned over the years, in practice the provision of adult education in the United States continues to be fragmented and diverse. McCullough (1980) points out that adult education is in a state of "creative anarchy" in which adult educators have "gone about their business within their individual organizations or associations, either unwilling to grapple with such a task [of centralizing] or unaware that it even exists" (p. 162).

However, even with such a decentralized system as that in the United States, there are ways in which control exists at the national level. "Adult education is given public support when the public can see the connection between education and the solution to a threatening situation" (Griffith with Fujita-Starck, 1989, p. 172). The present emphasis on job training and basic skills reflects the country's concern with staying competitive in a global economy.

How job training and vocational and adult education will be structured in the future remains unclear. Collins and Long (1989) believe that for both the United States and Canada the "trend [is] toward greater rather than less involvement by federal agencies in the education of adults" (p. 385); however, current discussions in the U.S. Congress on the federal government's role center on the feasibility of turning educational functions over to individual states through block grants.

Interestingly, the radical changes taking place in central Europe and the Baltic states signal movement in the opposite direction, from centralization to decentralization:

> Systems and structures are moving away from central direction by the State to provision for target groups and basic education by state, private and non-profit making sponsoring bodies at the price of restricting access so that not everyone can still take advantage of a complete and thorough education and training. In this process of transforming adult education structures, there is still great uncertainty over the range and nature of varying forms of organization and what they provide. The role of the State and of sponsoring bodies, and the importance of individual initiative, have to be recognised and redefined [Strewe, 1994, p. 295].

Coombs (1985) also argues for the "decentralization of planning, curriculum development, teacher training, and financial discretion" to deal with disparities based on geography in particular (p. 233).

Correcting disparities based on sex, minority status, and socioeconomic conditions would seem to warrant more systemic changes that require societywide policies and programs best implemented at the national level. This is, in fact, what Oglesby, Krajnc, and Mbilinyi (1989) recommend to improve women's access to adult education: "[M]en must be partners in the women's development process, as men's image of women and women's image of themselves can prove a major barrier to equality of access to educational opportunity. Greater continuity and coordination of education and training programmes and research projects is necessary, between the providing agencies, to avoid duplication of effort and to provide an integrated provision which women can use to aid their educational progress" (p. 332).

Education that is mandated by government at whatever level or by a nongovernmental regulatory body would seem to be another way of addressing the inequities in educational access and participation. Some countries have mandated that all citizens learn to read and write, others that all must participate in political activity. In the United States, mandatory education has taken a slightly different route. Most professions require updates and recertification, making continuing education mandatory. In addition, education is sometimes mandated for welfare recipients, traffic violators, prisoners, and others. The issue of whether any continuing education should be mandatory is a topic of debate in the field (Brockett, 1992; LeGrand, 1992).

In summary, government involvement in adult education has been one response to the inequities of access and opportunity. The picture is not simple, however, as economic, cultural, and political antecedents drive such efforts.

The Educational Response

The *educational response* to disparities in participation has come primarily from community-based, nonformal alternatives to the formal educational system. However, some developments occurring in the formal system also seek to address these disparities. Formal responses have come in the form of specific policies and programs targeting the conditions and factors we discussed earlier in this chapter. For example, Australia, Canada, and Great Britain have established national policies on multiculturalism. Women's studies, reentry, and displaced-homemaker programs in postsecondary and higher education target women in industrialized nations. Retirement-age adults can participate in the University of the Third Age, Elderhostels, and other institutions—again primarily in developed countries. And the community college system serves women, rural adults, and minorities in the United States.

While it cannot be denied that these formal modes have opened up access to education for many adults, these opportunities exist primarily in highly industrialized nations, and they still tend to attract the more educated and socioeconomically well-off adults. Older adult special programs that are designed to attract women to higher education are an unaffordable luxury for women at or below the poverty level. Such programs have been criticized for drawing mainly well-educated, white retirees (Courtenay, 1989; Withnall and Kabwasa, 1989).

The community college is perhaps one example of an organized educational system that does serve to broaden participation. However, it is still a postsecondary institution, and even in the United States, some 11 percent of white, 17 percent of African American, and 36 percent of Hispanic youth fail to complete high school, thus limiting their access to community colleges (U.S. Department of Education, 1994).

In underdeveloped countries, formal educational responses are often viewed as tools of the educated elite to transmit their culture and ideology; what goes on in "school" may be seen as irrelevant and unnecessary to a particular community's vision of the world. Tamayo R (1994) notes, for example, that for indigenous peoples of Colombia the very concept of "school" as a place for learning is somewhat foreign:

> [School] is a space that can exist anywhere—in the jungle, the mountains, or at home. And it is not just for children, but for everyone. This is illustrated, for example, in the area of traditional medicine. In the Embera culture, the traditional medicine man, or "Jaibana," learns the area of medicine through other more experienced Jaibanas. The period of time it takes him to learn is determined by his individual ability. Learning takes place in the jungle, on the river, at home, and even in dreams. When the idea of school is

introduced, it presents a problem for indigenous people [p. 197].

One alternative to formal programs that has achieved some success in increasing access and participation goes by a variety of names, including *nonformal education, popular education, community-based education,* and *community development education* (Galbraith, 1990; Hamilton, 1992; Hamilton and Cunningham, 1989). Briscoe (1990) lists several characteristics of community education that also apply to the other forms. This type of education welcomes participants in the planning and decision-making processes, promotes the notion of learning as a lifelong pursuit, promotes ease of access to activities by locating them in the community, and fosters collaboration and cooperation "with agencies that have similar goals and that share similar clientele [to] ensure an integrated delivery system" (p. 85).

Nonformal, community-based programs that deal with issues of vital concern to residents of the community, for example, can bring about what Brookfield (1992) calls "political" learning. Responding to "initiatives to establish hazardous nuclear and toxic waste disposal sites; proposals to build highways, nuclear power plants and high voltage power lines; efforts to convert recreational land to commercial use; foreclosures on family owned farms; and plans to close down factories in single-industry communities" can be the forum for adults to "acquire their political knowledge and skills" (p. 146). Community action groups also "cut across class, ethnic, and regional lines" (p. 147).

Nonformal, community-based programs constitute a major response to reaching underserved populations of adults. Regarding just one of these populations—out-of-school youths—Coombs (1985) notes that "flexible and responsive nonformal education programs can provide important opportunities, both by making up for formal educational deficiencies and by providing usable occupational and other practical skills for these young people whose needs in most countries lie beyond the sphere of responsibility of any particular ministry" (pp. 238–239).

They are many "model" programs, some of which have been mentioned in previous chapters, that exemplify the characteristics of the nonformal, community-based response to access and participation in both Third World and industrialized nations. The Kettering Foundation's National Issues Forum, study circles (Oliver, 1987), self-help groups, and community literacy programs are a few American examples. In assessing what makes these kinds of programs successful in reaching minorities in the United States, Ross-Gordon, Martin, and Briscoe (1990b) cite several elements:

1. Preserving cultural distinctness of groups in programming
2. Accommodating preferred learning strategies or learning environments
3. Utilizing existing social networks
4. Empowering learners to change their lives and communities
5. Preparing learners for life and career development beyond short-term occupational goals
6. Supporting minority families in their pursuit of learning goals
7. Reaching out to the most disenfranchised
8. Utilizing creative financing of adult learning opportunities
9. Sponsoring activities that increase the level of intercultural sensitivity of staff [pp. 102–104]

As with the political response, nonformal education is not without its problems. Sustaining a program built with minimal financial investment and training of staff, and tailored to meet highly specific and perhaps totally unique situations is a challenge not easily met. Furthermore, as we mentioned earlier in this chapter, many nonformal efforts are seen as marginal to "real" education; that is, they do not provide the certificate, degree, or credential needed to improve an individual's socioeconomic situation.

Coombs (1985) perhaps sums it up best when he acknowledges that nonformal education is not a "miracle drug. . . . [It] will not produce sweeping changes overnight. Even with a concerted effort and accelerated time schedule, and with all the best will in the world, the reduction of deep-seated educational inequalities is at best a gradual process. This is why we have repeatedly spoken in terms of the reduction, rather than the eradication of such disparities" (p. 239).

The Technological Response

Educational technologies hold great potential for addressing inequities in participation worldwide. There is also concern, backed by some empirical research, that these same technologies may actually intensify the gap between the haves and the have-nots, between the sexes, between young and old, between majority and minority populations, and between rich and poor nations.

The use of technology to address educational issues is commonly linked with forms of distance education that "at its simplest . . . connotes a separation between the learner and the instructor within a formal educational structure" (Rose, 1995, p. 5). In fact, educational technologies in the form of computers, audio-video, and telecommunications are central to modern distance education systems. Bates (1995) has identified three stages, or "generations," of development in the relationship between technology and distance education. The first is characterized by the predominant use of a single technology (initially correspondence by mail, subsequently radio, then television), and lack of direct student interaction with the teacher originating the instruction" (p. 1574). In second-generation distance education, learning materials are more multimedia in nature. For example, Britain's Open University uses print, television, audiocassettes, and face-to-face tutorials—as do such universities "without walls" as Empire State College and Thomas Edison College in the

United States. Third-generation formats are "based on two-way communications media which allow for direct interaction between the teacher who originates the instruction and the remote student" (p. 1574). Typical technologies of third-generation distance education include computer conferencing and networking, audio and video conferencing, and interactive two-way television.

Throughout the world, technology is opening up access to learning opportunities. In developing countries, primarily first-generation technology is being used to provide basic skills training, curriculum at the primary and secondary school levels, and teacher training. For example, the National Open School in India provides secondary school instruction to people over fourteen years old; at least fifty-three developing countries use distance education for teacher training; countries in Latin America and Africa use radio for literacy instruction and for government-sponsored mass campaigns in health, family planning, and agriculture; and China uses a nationwide satellite TV network for secondary education, vocational education, and teacher training (Moore, 1994). Clearly, millions of people who for various reasons would not participate in the formal educational system are being reached through this medium.

Besides increasing access, other benefits accrue from the integration of technology and distance education. Thach and Murphy (1994) point out that this medium "is pulling people around the globe into new and unexpected forms of collaboration," in that it often requires group effort: "Suddenly, separate cultures, laws, regulations, and customs have been brought together in a kaleidoscope of learning. The result is chaotic, fun, challenging, and anxiety producing; it challenges all those who work in the field of distance education to broaden their perspectives; to strive for the implementation of best practices; and to encourage collaboration while respecting individual, group, and institutional integrity" (p. 17).

In addition to collaboration and exposure to other cultures, educational technologies can also be used to serve empowerment, critical thinking, and social change. Brookfield (1994) reports on one study of how learning journals were used to encourage critical reflection in an Australian distance education course, and on another proposal for using experiential learning technology to empower "'the scattered, oppressed adult population of South Africa'" (p. 167).

In terms of politics, Frederick (1994) reviews how technologies played a major role in informing the world about the Tiananmen Square uprising, the attempted coup in the Soviet Union in 1990, and the 1991 Gulf War. In addition, the Association for Progressive Communications, a global computer network dedicated to peace, social justice, and environmental protection, oversees approximately "nine hundred electronic conferences . . . on subjects from AIDS to Zimbabwe" (p. 292).

Not everyone believes that technology will create growing schisms between the haves and the have-nots. For example, de Sola Pool (1990) makes the point that poorer nations can accelerate their development "because of the advantage of coming second and being able to borrow rather than invent advanced technology" (p. 170). Peter Drucker, one of the architects of the discipline of management and an observer of changes in American society, "believes that access to information will help dispel inequities between the rich and the poor" (M. Johnson, 1995, p. 12). Fear that the poor cannot afford computers and so will be left behind, Drucker points out, is reminiscent of the debate in the 1940s and 1950s about television—and fifty years earlier about the telephone.

Despite the indisputably positive impact that technology is having on access and participation, concerns remain at two levels: one with access *between* nations and the other with access of different groups *within* a country. Many people feel that technology is widening the gap between rich and poor nations. Frederick (1994) dramatizes this disparity:

- An estimated 95 percent of all computers are in the developed countries.

- While developing countries have three-quarters of the world's population, they can manage only 30 percent of the world's newspaper output.

- About 65 percent of the world's population experiences an acute book shortage.

- Readers of the New York Times consume more newsprint each Sunday than the average African does in one year.

- The only third world country to meet UNESCO's basic media standards for per capita numbers of newspapers, radio, and cinema is Cuba.

- Only seventeen countries in the world had a gross national product larger than total U.S. advertising expenditures.

- The United States and the Commonwealth of Independent States, with only 15 percent of the world's population, use more than 50 percent of the geostationary orbit. The third world uses less than 10 percent.

- Ten developed countries, with 20 percent of the world's population, accounted for almost three-quarters of all telephone lines. The United States had as many telephone lines as all of Asia; the Netherlands, as many as all of Africa; Italy, as many as all of Latin America; Tokyo, as many as all of Africa [Frederick, 1993; cited in Frederick, 1994, pp. 287–288].

With respect to computers alone, studies have demonstrated that availability of computers is correlated with a country's per capita income—a fact that jeopardizes Third World countries and suggests "how difficult it will be to achieve global computer equity" (Anderson, Lundmark, Harris, and Magnan, 1994, p. 374).

Even in the most technologically advanced countries like the United States, there are demonstrated inequities in access and usage. Those who have gained computer skills have a distinct advantage in the workplace, thus creating a growing economic schism between skilled and unskilled workers. The roots of this disparity lie in the very same access-limited factors we explored in the first part of this chapter. Typically, technological learning—and in particular computer learning—favors males over females, the young over the old, and the white middle-class over minorities and the working class. In a review of the research on variables affecting equitable access to computing, Anderson, Lundmark, Harris, and Magnan (1994) summarize as follows: "Our systematic review of the data from large, representative studies has found strong evidence of persistent patterns of computer inequity among gender, income, and racial groups. . . . While the quantitative evidence for widespread computer inequity is substantial, the qualitative studies reveal that the actual inequities probably are vastly greater than the statistics indicate" (p. 381).

Furthermore, technology in industrialized nations is widening the social class gap. The technologically skilled can "secede, at least mentally, from institutions they do not like" (Tenner, cited in Levison, 1995, p. B5) and can insulate themselves "from disturbing news and contrary opinions [and] the concerns and problems of the nation's have-nots" (Levison, 1995, p. B5). Finally, technology may be creating "a new kind of social snobbery" in which "a young American without computer literacy, an e-mail address and log-on privileges to several networks may risk . . . social ostracism" (p. B5).

Thus, while technology appears to be addressing the issues of access and participation on the one hand, it also is contributing to these very same inequities.

Each of the three responses we have discussed in this chapter—political, educational, and technological—has its problems and limitations as a solution to access and opportunity issues. However, this should not obscure the fact that each has also opened up learning opportunities to adults who do not fit the profile of the "typical" learner. Millions have been taught to read through national literacy campaigns; women have improved their status through a wide variety of nonformal, community-based initiatives; ethnic minorities and adults from lower socioeconomic classes have taken advantage of job training and other opportunities; and learners in remote areas have linked together with resources through technology.

What we have tried to do in this chapter is first have you consider what structural barriers may be contributing to the problem. Where one lives, what one's sex and ethnicity are, and so on are factors that individuals have little if any control over. In North America, at least, we tend to frame issues such as participation from an individual, psychological perspective. Unfortunately, that approach can lead to seeing individuals as somehow deficient and personally at fault for not taking advantage of learning opportunities. The problem of access thus becomes "their" problem, not ours as responsible educators.

However, looking at the issue from a structural perspective, as we have done, raises different possibilities with respect to our own practice. How can we reduce the power of these barriers such that potential participants first become aware of opportunities and then are comfortable responding to them? Some political, educational, and technological responses and some model programs combining these responses have been successful (technology, for example, cuts across the political and educational). We can learn from them while we search for creative ways to adapt our own practice to address the inequities.

Summary

Despite a growing awareness of the problem, as well as interventions to counter inequities, the issues of access and participation continue to plague the field of adult education throughout the world. The substantial disparities between who has access and who does not—and who participates and who does not—are the result of a complex set of conditions and circumstances. In this chapter, we reviewed a few of those conditions and discussed macro-level responses.

We outlined four conditions that help explain some groups' limited access to adult education. Geographical conditions—usually construed in terms of rural versus urban but also including migrant, transient, and homeless people—was the first factor we presented. The second factor, demographic characteristics, included a discussion of age and sex as determinants of access and participation. The third factor was socioeconomic status; we included education in this category because it is so tightly embedded in social and economic class. The fourth factor, cultural background, also determines who has power and who controls access to education. Although they were each presented separately, we acknowledged the interrelatedness of these four factors.

The last part of the chapter was organized around three global responses and the issues surrounding each. First, we reviewed political responses—usually in the form of mandates by various levels of government—policies, and laws, along with the concomitant issue of centralization versus decentralization of policies and delivery systems. Education was the second response we presented, with both formal and nonformal, community-based options reviewed. The final response was labeled "technological" and included the integration of technology with distance education. While this response has made great strides in opening access to millions of people, it also by its very nature is contributing to the problem.

Part III

Developing a Professional
Field of Practice

In Parts One and Two, we outlined the role and scope of adult education in contemporary society and explored some key concerns related to practice. In Part Three, we shift our attention to an examination of adult education's status as a professional field. We believe that an understanding of the profession is essential to those who seek to identify with and make a commitment to adult education.

In Chapter Nine, we explore the current status of adult education as a profession. We take a brief look at the meaning of professionalization and the debate over it within the adult education field, and consider some central aspects of the profession—including the role of professional associations in adult education, the professional literature of the field, and graduate study in adult education. The emphasis of this chapter is on what is sometimes described as "mainstream" adult education.

As should be clear from the previous chapters, the adult education field is characterized by a multitude of perspectives. Some of the most innovative approaches to serving adult learners are undertaken by practitioners who work outside the mainstream. In Chapter Ten, we examine the practice of those who typically do not identify themselves with the professional movement of adult education. We discuss practitioners who have been marginalized; whose voices are rarely heard due to ethnicity, race, sexual orientation, or disability; and whose practice is largely invisible to mainstream adult education.

Finally, we bring the book to closure in Chapter Eleven by reframing the discussion of professionalization in a way that recognizes and highlights contributions of both the mainstream and "invisible" sides of the field. We revisit the three components addressed in Chapter Nine, but do so vis-à-vis the perspectives we present in Chapter Ten. In addition, we consider two more issues that have received increasing attention in recent years and that will likely play a role in future directions of the field: certification and ethics. This discussion of reframing professionalization comes full circle with a brief description of how the notion of reflective practice can help us rethink professionalization in the future. Finally, the chapter concludes with a reflection on what is possible for the future of the field.

9

Adult Education
as a Developing Profession

In the previous chapters, we attempted to sketch the landscape of adult education in broad brush strokes. As we have seen, adult education permeates the entire fabric of contemporary society. Yet these developments do not simply take place in a vacuum. Often, they are the result of deliberate actions on the part of individuals and institutions that see value in the education of adults and that are committed to actively supporting it. Such efforts most commonly find expression in how a given field professionalizes. The specific purpose of this chapter, then, is to explore the professionalization of adult education.

This discussion will be framed around three key questions. First, what does it mean to professionalize? In the first part of the chapter, we will briefly describe the concept of professionalization and will highlight how this issue has been a source of much debate and disagreement in the adult education field. Second, how has the adult education field professionalized so far? Three important elements of professionalization in the field have been professional associations, professional literature and information resources, and graduate study. Third, does professionalization make a difference? A brief discussion of this question will serve as a transition to the final two chapters, where we look at adult education from a different perspective and attempt to assess the "state of the field." As you read these last three chapters, we invite you to reflect on the questions we've asked and on where you see yourself relative to the professionalization of adult education.

The Nature of Professionalization in Adult Education

Professions have become a central force in contemporary society. Today, professionals "represent over a quarter of the work force and are the primary decision makers for society's major institutions" (Cervero, 1988, p. 1). As such, professionals wield great power in determining what goes on in our society. In this section of the chapter, we will first define and describe general characteristics of professions; then we will turn to the current debate surrounding professionalization of adult education.

What Is a Profession?

In attempting to define what a profession is, Cervero (1988) has distinguished among three kinds of definitions. Each offers a response to the question of what it means to professionalize.

The earliest approach to defining professions is what Cervero calls the *static* approach. In this view, professions are defined according to specific objective standards. Flexner (1915), a pioneer in this approach, argued that to be separated from occupations, professions must "(1) involve intellectual operations, (2) derive their material from science, (3) involve definite and practical ends, (4) possess an educationally communicable technique, (5) tend to self-organization, and (6) be altruistic" (Cervero, 1988, p. 6).

A second way to define professions is through the process approach, in which emphasis is placed on the circumstances by which an occupation professionalizes. Houle (1980) has identified fourteen characteristics of the professionalization process: concern among members for clarifying the mission and function(s) of a profession, mastery of theoretical knowledge, capacity to solve problems, use of practical knowledge, self-enhancement, formal training, credentialing, creation of a subculture, legal reinforcement, public acceptance, ethical practice, penalties, relations to other vocations, and relations to users of the service. This perspective differs from the static approach in that it defines a profession by *the extent to which* the criteria are met. Thus, while in the static approach a field is categorized as either a profession or an occupation, the process model establishes no clear-cut boundaries between professions and occupations.

The *socioeconomic approach* is a third way of defining professions. In this model, the idea of *profession* is viewed as a "folk" concept, in that an occupation is a profession only to the degree to which it is regarded so by the general public. Paraphrasing Larson (1977), Cervero describes the socioeconomic view of professionalization as "the process by which producers of special services constitute and control the market for their services" (1988, p. 9). He then goes on to note that "an occupation's level of professionalization can be assessed by the extent to which public and political authorities accept its credentials as necessary to provide a specific type of service" (p. 10).

Today, while professions permeate and define many aspects of contemporary society, Schön (1987) argues that there is a "crisis of confidence" about the public perception of professions (p. 3). According to Schön, this crisis centers on the nature of professional knowledge and how that knowledge is disseminated. For instance, some professions have been challenged on whether they actually possess a rigorous base of knowledge. In a similar vein, Schön notes that professional education has sometimes been challenged on the grounds that it stresses the mastery of rigorously developed technical skills over "the rudiments of effective and ethical practice" (p. 8).

There are many ways to examine the relationship between the professions and society. Cervero (1988) presents three such perspectives: functionalist, conflict, and critical. The *functionalist* view holds that professions "are service- or community-oriented occupations" that apply a systematic body of knowledge to practical problems of relevance to society (p. 21). The functionalist view holds that professions are a generally positive force in society. The *conflict* viewpoint sees professions as a vehicle for controlling knowledge and services. This perspective is based on the idea that issues of conflict and power exist across various groups in society, and that professions serve to maintain social inequality. Finally, the *critical* perspective "shares with the conflict viewpoint a recognition of problems inherent in professional practice." But rather than seek to eliminate professions, the critical perspective stresses finding ways to minimize these problems.

Taken together, an awareness of how professions are defined and how society views them can give us an understanding of what it means to professionalize. As we will see in the next section, this discussion has clear implications for the adult education field.

Debating the Professionalization of Adult Education

Professionalization has been one of the most perplexing concerns facing those who engage in the education of adults. Indeed, since the 1920s few issues have provoked more debate and controversy in adult education than whether or not professionalization is good for the field.

Today, the debate largely centers on the extent to which professionalization really contributes to improved practice or whether instead it sets narrow parameters as to who can practice and what is considered "good" practice (see, for example, Carlson, 1977; Collins, 1991, 1992; Cervero, 1988, 1992). In essence, the case against professionalization runs parallel to the conflict view of professions discussed by Cervero because it is grounded in the belief that such a direction will create an elite that perpetuates itself through a limited definition of who is a "real" adult educator and what constitutes legitimate practice. Some in the field fear that we may even create a situation in which learners become disempowered and, as a consequence, dependent on professionals.

On the other hand, some people believe that professionalization is essential to helping adult education play a more central role by increasing the visibility of the field and its influence throughout society. This belief holds that until adult education is more integrated into the fabric of society, it will continue to be seen by many as a marginal activity. This split between visibility and perceived concerns over elitism has clearly influenced both the image portrayed of the field and the impact of adult education in society.

While the debate continues, there have been some efforts to move the discussion in a different direction. Cervero (1992), for example, suggests that the debate over whether adult education should professionalize is basically a moot issue, because the field has already done so. Instead, Cervero believes that adult education must turn its efforts toward finding a model of professionalization that best reflects the values and philosophies of our practice. He argues that it is possible for adult education to avoid a more traditional model of professionalization and instead move toward a view that questions authoritative assumptions about the field and reduces overdependence on professionals.

Each of us who is involved in the education of adults has a stake in the debate over professionalization. While a simple solution to this issue will not likely be on the horizon soon, we must each be willing to examine the question of what it means to professionalize and, more specifically, what it means for *adult education* to professionalize.

Some Elements of Professional Adult Education

Turning now to the question of how adult education has professionalized to date, the *process* definition of profession that we presented earlier is particularly helpful because it emphasizes the *degree* to which adult education has professionalized. In this part of the chapter, we will turn our attention to a description of three areas that demonstrate clear evidence of movement toward professionalization: professional associations, professional literature and information resources, and graduate study.

Professional Associations in Adult Education

While the idea and spirit of adult education have existed for centuries, the roots of the profession in North America can be traced to the early 1900s. Professional associations, which are one central component of the professionalizing process, have played an active role in the development of the U.S. adult education movement for most of the twentieth century. For example, the National University Continuing Education Association (NUCEA), which today is one of the major associations for professionals in the area of continuing higher education, was founded in 1915 as the National University Extension Association (Rohfeld, 1990a).

For several decades the field has struggled to develop and support an umbrella association at the national level. (By *umbrella* we mean encompassing the many different segments of adult education—rather than, say, the NUCEA, which serves a specific segment of the field.) Knowles (1977) has provided an extensive discussion of the early development of this effort; however, we will highlight this history here.

Toward a Comprehensive Professional Association

The National Education Association (NEA) first became interested in adult education through the development of literacy programs, primarily among immigrants. In 1921, the NEA established a Department of Immigrant Education, which in 1924 was renamed the Department of Adult Education (Luke, 1992). At about the same time, the Carnegie Corporation began to see adult education as a way of fulfilling its role in "the advancement and diffusion of knowledge" (Stubblefield, 1988, p. 22).

In 1924, Carnegie President Frederick P. Keppel convened a group of experts to help explore what role the corporation might play in adult education. Two years later, financial support from Carnegie led to the founding of the American Association for Adult Education (AAAE). Unlike the NEA, whose main focus was on literacy, the AAAE was more involved in "supporting the continuing liberal and general education of individuals with an established educational background" (Luke, 1992, p. 19), and it implemented its program "through studies, research, demonstrations, and experiments" (Stubblefield, 1988, p. 25).

Over the next two decades, the AAAE and the NEA Department of Adult Education continued to operate as essentially separate associations. While some overlap existed in membership and programming, there appear to have been elements of conflict between the two groups during much of this time (Luke, 1992; Knowles, 1977). However, major events of the 1930s and 1940s—namely the Great Depression and World War II—influenced the funding of both associations considerably. Thus, during the late 1940s the two groups engaged in a series of discussions that led to the founding of the Adult Education Association of the U.S.A. (AEA/USA) in 1951.

According to Knowles (1977), the AEA/USA departed from its predecessor associations in several ways. Perhaps most notably, it tried to promote a democratic approach to leadership, with all delegates elected rather than "hand-picked" (p. 218). The association was clearly committed to collective decision making and experimentation. Howard McClusky, who served as the first president of the AEA/USA, offered the following reflection more than three decades after its founding: "One could not have participated in the years of negotiation which led to the merger of the AAAE and the National Education Association Department of Adult Education without [being] impressed with the emphasis on the 'democratization' of participation in the life of the organization—a concept to which the AEA was 'fiercely' committed" (1982, p. 9).

Still, the tensions that had prevented an earlier merger between the two associations remained. Knowles (1977) observes that although "the general spirit [at the AEA/USA founding assembly] was one of good will and optimism, an underlying resentment against absent ghosts of the past strongly influenced the deliberations" (p. 218). Indeed, in 1952 the National Association for Public School

Adult Education (NAPSAE) was approved by the AEA/USA delegate assembly to focus on the needs of those educators of adults working in public school settings (essentially the same group that had previously been served by the NEA Department of Adult Education).

During the ensuing three decades, NAPSAE evolved into a separate entity and subsequently changed its name to the National Association for Continuing and Adult Education (NAPCAE). Over the years, however, the AEA/USA and NAPCAE worked on various joint projects and eventually began to hold joint national conferences. In the late 1970s, recognizing that both groups shared many members and goals but only limited resources, they again considered a possible merger. In 1982 the AEA/USA and NAPCAE were dissolved to form the American Association for Adult and Continuing Education (AAACE), which today continues to serve as the primary umbrella association for adult education. Although its membership has remained consistent at about only three thousand members, the AAACE's goals and structure provide a place to serve a wide range of interests and audiences in adult education.

The Role and Scope of Professional Associations

Professional associations play a variety of roles, including addressing "a need for status, a sense of commitment or calling, a desire to share in policy formation and implementation . . . a feeling of duty, a wish for fellowship and community, and a zest for education" (Houle, 1980, p. 171). Adult education professional associations have tended to play a role in informal leadership for the field, while not engaging in the regulatory functions found in professions such as medicine and social work.

Many different types of professional associations serve the adult education field today. Some of these, such as the AAACE and the American Society for Training and Development, aim to serve the needs of individual adult educators. Others direct their services toward either institutions that provide services for adult learners or,

like the Coalition of Adult Education Organizations, toward linking several adult education professional associations (Smith, Eyre,
and Miller, 1982).

Not surprisingly, associations are formed, dissolved, and modified on a regular basis. Therefore, it would not be terribly useful to
attempt a listing of current associations serving the field. Rather, it
might be helpful to distinguish associations according to the roles
they play and the *scope* of their concern (Brockett, 1989). For
instance, it can be argued that professional associations in adult education perform one of two roles: (1) to help unify divergent segments of the field or (2) to provide a "home" for specialized interests
(such as training and development, literacy, or continuing higher
education). Thus, some adult education associations serve an
umbrella function, while others target their membership to a more
specific segment of the field.

Associations are also defined by the geographical range of the
audiences they serve (in other words, their scope). Five such levels
include local, state-provincial, regional, national, and international.
Local associations, such as the Central New York Coalition for Adult
Continuing Education, provide a source of affiliation in one's home
community. Similarly, state or provincial associations provide a
resource for professional development that is typically attuned to
more local concerns and offers conferences and other professional
development opportunities at lower cost than those of national organizations. Regional associations are generally made up of members
from a group of contiguous states or provinces; three long-standing
examples are the Missouri Valley Adult Education Association, the
Mountain Plains Adult Education Association, and the Northwest
Adult Education Association. We already discussed national associations at some length earlier in this chapter. Finally, international
associations attempt to serve the needs of professionals across national
boundaries. While these groups are less common—probably because
they are so expensive to operate and because they are likelier than
other groups to be more removed from the concerns that educators

face in their daily practice—the International Council for Adult Education has long played an important role in global adult education, particularly in developing countries.

To summarize, most adult education professional associations view their role as either providing an "umbrella" designed to bring together divergent segments of the field into a unified entity, or serving the specific needs of a specialized segment of the field. Similarly, an association can strive to fulfill either of these roles at the local, state-provincial, regional, national, or international level. While there is no rule of thumb about how many or what types of associations an adult educator should join, it is common to belong to several associations that can help practitioners meet different sets of professional development needs.

Literature and Information Resources in Adult Education

A second force in the professionalization of any field is the development of a distinct literature base. To a large degree, the professional literature represents the formal body of knowledge in a field and is important "not only because it contains the information that makes the field unique—thus separating it from other disciplines—but also because it demonstrates what is known about the field of practice" (Imel, 1989, p. 134). More than twenty-five years ago, Dickinson and Rusnell (1971) identified the development of an organized body of knowledge as "one of the hallmarks of the emergence of adult education as a distinct profession" (p. 177).

Like professional associations, the literature of adult education began to emerge in this country during the 1920s. Prior to this, two seminal British publications were of particular note. A *History of the Origins and Progress of Adult Schools* (Pole, [1816] 1967), an account of adult schools in England during the late 1700s and early 1800s, is perhaps the first classic in the literature of adult education. A second classic from the British literature, a document commonly known as the "1919 Report" is the work of a committee "whose breadth of vision and earnest—sometimes impassioned—advocacy gave rise to adult education as it has been known ever since" (Houle, 1992, p. 17). During the 1950s, this report was reprinted simultaneously by the U.S., British, and Canadian national adult education associations under the title A Design for Democracy (1956).

In the United States, probably the first such classic in the literature is Eduard Lindeman's *The Meaning of Adult Education* [1926] 1989). By drawing largely from a perspective of Deweyan pragmatism, Lindeman provided insights into the vital links to experience and social change that survive to this day as cornerstones of contemporary practice. Other classic works from the early years of the adult education movement, as identified by Stubblefield (1991a), include James Harvey Robinson's *The Humanizing of Knowledge* (1924); William S. Learned's *The American Public Library and the Diffusion of Knowledge* (1924); Everett Dean Martin's *The Meaning of a Liberal Education* (1926); E. L. Thorndike's *Adult Learning* (1928) and *Adult Interests* (1935), which provided some of the earliest research findings on adult learners; Ruth Kotinsky's *Adult Education and the Social Scene* (1933); Lyman Bryson's *Adult Education* (1936), which was the first textbook in the field; Mortimer Adler's *How to Read a Book* (1940); and Harry Overstreet's *The Mature Mind* (1949).

One final important source of classic literature can be found in the series of "Handbooks" of adult education that include volumes from 1934, 1936, 1948, 1960, 1970, 1980 (an eight-volume series), and 1989. Wilson (1993a) analyzed how the handbooks have contributed to the formation of the professional knowledge base in adult education. Wilson concluded that these resources have been part of the official knowledge of adult education and, as such, have been tied to the technical rationality view of knowledge that Schön (1987) maintains is part of the public's lack of confidence in professions.

During the late 1920s, professional journals in adult education came into being. In 1929, the AAAE began publication of the *Journal of Adult Education*. During its twelve years of publication

(1929–1941), this periodical attracted writers representing a virtual Who's Who of intellectual and social leaders from the period, including Jane Addams, Charles Beard, Lyman Bryson, Nicholas Murray Butler, Eve Chappell, Eleanor G. Coit, Mary L. Ely (who served as editor of the journal), Dorothy Canfield Fisher, Abraham Flexner, Robert Maynard Hutchins, Alvin S. Johnson, William Heard Kilpatrick, Alain Locke, Everett Dean Martin, Bonaro Wilkinson Overstreet, Harry A. Overstreet, James Harvey Robinson, Theodore Roosevelt, James E. Russell, Hilda Worthington Smith, and Edward L. Thorndike.

Day (1981) developed a content analysis of the *Journal of Adult Education*, from which he concluded: "The underlying theme appears nestled in the conviction that adult education was vital to a democratic society. In support of a democratic society an enlightened citizenry was viewed essential" (Day, 1981, p. 182).

The *Journal of Adult Education* remains a valuable testimony to adult education's early development—and its response to a society that went from the end of the post–World War I era through the Great Depression and into World War II during the few years of the journal's existence. Its contents serve to illustrate the general tone of the field and, indeed, the nation during these years.

In 1941, with reduced funding from the Carnegie Corporation (and paralleling the United States' entry into World War II), the *Journal of Adult Education* ceased publication and was replaced in 1942 by the much smaller *Adult Education Journal*. During this same period, the NEA Department of Adult Education published the *Adult Education Bulletin*. When the NEA department and the AAAE merged, these two publications were replaced by *Adult Education*, which continues today as the *Adult Education Quarterly*. Shortly after its founding, the AEA/USA began publishing a second periodical, *Adult Leadership*. Unlike *Adult Education*, which was a more scholarly journal, *Adult Leadership* was presented in a magazine format designed specifically for teachers, administrators, and other practitioners in adult education. It continued publication through 1977, when it was replaced by *Lifelong Learning: The Adult Years* (which was, in turn, renamed *Lifelong Learning: An Omnibus of Practice and Research* in 1983). Today, *Adult Learning* is the practitioner-oriented magazine published by the AAACE.

Types of Resources

While books and journals remain central to the literature of the field, adult educators today have a much broader range of information resources on which to draw. We describe some of these briefly in the following paragraphs.

Books remain the most comprehensive knowledge source in adult education. Houle (1992) has identified and highlighted 1,241 books on the subject that have been published in the English language. This "bibliographic essay" is a thoroughly developed resource and is highly recommended for those who wish to become more fully acquainted with adult education books.

While books are generally the most comprehensive literature source in the field, *periodicals* (which include regularly published journals, magazines, and newsletters) usually provide more up-to-date material than is possible to find in books. Some of the current periodicals relevant to the field include *Adult Basic Education, Adult and Continuing Education Today, Adult Education Quarterly, Adult Learning, Canadian Journal for the Study of Adult Education, Continuing Higher Education Review, Educational Gerontology, International Journal of Lifelong Education, Journal of Continuing Higher Education, Journal of Continuing Education in Nursing, Journal of Extension, Mountain Plains Journal of Adult Education, New Horizons in Adult Education* (the first electronic journal in adult education), *Studies in the Education of Adults, Training and Development Journal,* and *Training/HRD*.

Monograph series have long been an important part of the adult education literature. In the 1930s, the American Association for Adult Education sponsored a twenty-seven-volume series, *Studies in the Social Significance of Adult Education*, that looked at a broad range of agencies and practices in adult education. The Center for the Study of Liberal Education for Adults (and subsequently Syracuse University Publications in Continuing Education) published more than 150 monographs between 1953 and 1976.

At present, three monograph series regularly serve the field. *New Directions for Adult and Continuing Education*, published quarterly by Jossey-Bass since 1979, includes issues on a wide range of current topics. More recently, Krieger Publishing has established a series titled *Professional Practices in Adult Education and Human Resource Development*, and the ERIC Clearinghouse has long published monographs that provide up-to-date material on current research-related areas in the field.

According to Brockett (1991a), "The Educational Resources Information Center (ERIC), established in 1966 and operated through funding by the U.S. Department of Education, comprises clearinghouses throughout the United States that specialize in the acquisition of materials from specific areas of education" (p. 125). *ERIC documents* are an invaluable resource for educators because they provide a comprehensive database on educational resources, as well as direct access to a wide range of hard-to-find publications in education. Included among these documents are a series of monographs that review literature (particularly ERIC documents) on a wide range of topics related to adult education. The ERIC Clearinghouse on Adult, Career, and Vocational Education is housed at Ohio State University.

Some of the most useful resources in adult education are documents such as project reports, brochures, regional or statewide publications, and conference proceedings. The term *fugitive literature* is sometimes used to describe such publications, because they may not be easily accessible beyond a limited scope. Through ERIC, many such documents are easier to find; however, there remain a great many resources that are not easy to locate.

During the past decade, with the emerging importance of the so-called information superhighway, *computer networks* and the World Wide Web have become particularly important sources of information for many educators. Several electronic-mail discussion groups, for example, have been established that will likely be of interest to adult educators. The first of these is AEDNET, the Adult Education Network. Developed at Syracuse University during the mid-1980s and currently operated by Nova Southeastern University, this network provides current information about events in adult education and discussions of current issues. Other discussion groups are devoted to distance education, training and development, literacy, and the activities of the Commission of Professors of Adult Education. Most of these groups are easy to join for those who have access to electronic mail.

The information superhighway will almost certainly continue to develop and expand, providing educators, learners, and society in general with an endless range of directions to pursue for information. An important role for educators during the next millennium will be to help learners develop skills in accessing information *and* to learn ways to critically assess the value of materials. So much information will be (and actually currently is) available that people will find it easy to become "lost on the highway" if they do not have the skills to focus their strategies for searching and assessing information.

Uses of the Literature

Different types of literature are designed to serve different purposes. While some resources are directed primarily to those directly practicing in the field, other publications strive to reach those concerned with the academic side of adult education.

Brockett (1991a) has developed a typology of potential uses of the knowledge base in adult education; four such uses are listed below.

1. *To share new information and ideas*. These publications include "how to" materials and typically describe the practices and experiences of others.

2. *To foster professional socialization and reaffirmation*. The knowledge base can "help to socialize new people in the field and to

strengthen the sense of professional identity" and commitment of those already practicing (Brockett, 1991a, p. 129).

3. *To promote critical thinking.* The knowledge base can help educators identify and challenge their assumptions and explore alternate ways to practice.

4. *To stimulate development of new knowledge.* Finally, the knowledge base is central to advancing the field. Without efforts to create new knowledge about the education of adults, practice is likely to stagnate.

It can be seen, then, that the knowledge base of adult education can serve many functions. With regard to professionalization, each of the uses can be of value. For instance, sharing new information and promoting critical thinking are uses that tie directly to professional practice in adult education. Fostering professional socialization and reaffirmation has a clear and obvious link to professionalization. And developing new knowledge involves the part of the profession concerned with advancing the knowledge base of the field. Clearly, knowledge is central to how we understand what we do, why we do it, and how we might do it differently.

Reading the professional literature can be an effective strategy for professional development. Similarly, joining professional associations, reading newsletters, and getting on publishers' mailing lists are three ways to keep abreast of current literature in the field. Stubblefield (1991a) stresses that reading the literature is a valuable part of professional development and that to get the most from professional reading, we must take a positive, proactive attitude and make reading an integral part of our professional lives—not merely an "add-on" to be fit in during spare moments.

Graduate Study in Adult Education

A third component of the professionalizing process with a long-standing tradition is the formal academic preparation of those who practice in the field. While some universities today offer undergraduate coursework in adult education, for the most part such preparation has been at the graduate level. As Cervero (1992) notes, the university-based model of research and training within most professions unites "the production of knowledge and the production of practitioners" into the same structure (p. 46). Unlike with many professions, however, formal study in adult education is not a necessary prerequisite for entry into the field. Indeed, the vast majority of people practicing in adult education do not have such formal preparation or a credential. Still, because much of adult education's knowledge base is produced in the university setting and because graduate programs typically provide a vehicle for socialization into the field, graduate study remains a mechanism by which the professionalization of adult education can be assessed.

According to Houle (1964), the first university course with "adult education" in the title was offered in 1922 at Teachers College, Columbia University. Two of the first programs to provide university training for adult education leaders were summer sessions also held at Teachers College and at the University of California, Berkeley (Brockett, 1990).

The first graduate program was established at Teachers College, Columbia University, in 1930, followed by one at Ohio State University in 1931. In 1935, programs were established at the University of Chicago (Houle, 1964) and New York University (New York University, 1935). The first doctoral degrees in adult education were awarded in 1935 to Wilbur C. Hallenbeck and William H. Stacy at Teachers College (Houle, 1964). By 1938, twenty-four institutions were offering courses in adult education ("Summer Courses," 1938); however, as late as 1962 only sixteen programs offered graduate degrees in North America (Houle, 1964).

In the opening session of the Commission of Professors of Adult Education's annual conference in 1987, Cyril Houle pointed out that graduate study in adult education began from a position of high prestige. This, he said, is a point well worth remembering when we look at the contemporary field and some of the concerns that graduate programs face—and have faced over the past several decades.

Almost from the beginning of university-level preparation for adult education leaders, several questions gave rise to tensions that still impact the field today. Three such questions can be summarized as follows (Brockett, 1990):

1. Should leadership in adult education be provided by "lay" leaders who are "attracted to the education of adults from outside of education, or by persons with professional training as educators?" (p. 72)

2. Should the preparation of leaders emphasize an experiential or academic focus?

3. Should the emphasis be on helping adult educators master their subject matter or on techniques of adult education (for example, teaching methods)?

These questions remain relevant to graduate study in adult education and are implicit in our discussion of graduate study in Chapter Eleven.

As of 1989, about four thousand doctoral degrees had been awarded in adult education (Peters and Kreitlow, 1991). However, in a combined analysis of two major dissertation databases—including adult education majors as well as those with majors in related areas—Lifvendahl reported in 1995 that more than eight thousand dissertations have been completed in the area of adult and continuing education. While it is difficult to know exactly how many graduate programs in adult education exist today, Peters and Kreitlow estimate that as of 1991, "66 doctoral programs (Ed.D. and Ph.D.) and 124 master's programs with majors in adult education, continuing education, or extension education operate in North America" (1991, p. 146). Over half of the institutions responding to a survey by Rose and Mason (1990) reported having three or fewer full-time faculty members in adult education, suggesting that "small" programs appear to be the mainstay of the field.

Exploring the value of graduate study in adult education as a professional development experience, Zeph (1991) makes the following observation: "To graduate from a degree program certifies that an individual has learned a body of knowledge, possesses certain skills, and is qualified to practice a chosen profession; completion of graduate school is often thought of as a major step in the professionalization process" (p. 79).

Various efforts have been made to identify the knowledge and skill areas most relevant to graduate study. For example, Knox (1979) has argued that successful adult education practitioners need to move beyond mere competency toward proficiency, which he describes as a desirable level that will allow them to perform well in a given situation. To support this idea, Knox identified the following proficiencies as important for adult education practitioners: (1) perspective on the field, "including an understanding of providers of programs, relations with parent organizations, societal influences, and awareness of resources" (p. 10); (2) an understanding of adults as learners, including adult development; and (3) personal qualities such as commitment, interpersonal skills, and an approach to practice that emphasizes "innovation and a sense of direction" (p. 19). In addition to these general proficiencies, Knox also identifies proficiencies specific to the roles of administrator, teacher and counselor, and policymaker.

Another attempt to identify core areas of necessary knowledge and skill is reflected in a set of standards developed by the Commission of Professors of Adult Education, or CPAE (1986). These standards, which were accepted by a majority of CPAE members, identify key areas of knowledge and skill and differentiate between master's and doctoral preparation. At the master's level, for instance, the core areas are

- Introduction to the fundamental nature, function, and scope of adult education
- Adult learning and development

- Adult education program processes—planning, delivery, and evaluation

- Historical, philosophical, and sociological foundations

- Overview of educational research [Commission of Professors of Adult Education, 1986, n.p.]

The doctoral level includes the areas listed above, as well as the following:

- Advanced study of adult learning (e.g., theory and research relating to specific issues)

- In-depth analysis of social, political, and economic forces that have shaped the historical and philosophical foundations of adult education

- Study of leadership, including theories of administration and management

- Study of issues that impinge on policy formation

- Advanced study of methods of inquiry, in order to conduct adult education research [Commission of Professors of Adult Education, 1986, n.p.]

Many questions have yet to be answered regarding the effectiveness, impact, and relevance of adult education graduate study. We address some of these concerns in Chapter Eleven.

Does Professionalization Make a Difference?

Like other professional fields that strive to serve individuals and society, adult education is ultimately concerned with practice. In addressing the question of whether professionalization makes a difference, then, our response must revolve around the extent to which it makes a difference *in our practice*.

In Chapter Eleven, we will return to the three components of professionalization discussed in this chapter in order to assess the impact of each, as filtered through an understanding of the "invisible" side of practice, which we present in the next chapter. However, we will bring this chapter to a close by looking briefly at the question of whether professionalization makes a difference, because it is the question that, more than any other, must drive future efforts to professionalize the field.

What professional associations, literature and resources, and graduate study in adult education share is that they all provide something of a gathering place for individuals with some degree of common identity in their view of adult education. These three elements provide a forum for such individuals to meet, share experiences, seek assistance, and learn from one another.

In adult education, professional associations provide benefits to individuals, the field, and society (Brockett, 1989). Regarding benefits to individuals, Darkenwald and Merriam (1982) have suggested that the most valuable function of adult education associations is in the arena of professional development. This is achieved through such activities as conferences and publications, as well as informal networking opportunities that evolve from involvement in the association. These activities also serve to acquaint new practitioners with the field's perspectives, philosophies, values, and mores—a socializing process common to all professional groups.

Adult education also benefits from its professional associations, which can play a key role in helping to shape the identity of the field and increase its visibility with important constituencies. By creating greater awareness about adult learning and the adult education field, professional associations can promote understanding of the field in the larger society, especially among those responsible for political processes and institutional policies that have an impact on adult education. For example, associations have played a role in promoting adult-literacy efforts during the Bush administration, and have contributed to workplace learning programs during the Clinton administration.

Similarly, while the large number of people who work with adult learners probably do not regularly keep up with the field's literature, those who do are in a position to look at their practice through a different lens. And the extremely small percentage of those working in the field who hold graduate degrees in adult education have had an opportunity to wrestle with ideas that can expand their repertoire of strategies, tools, and resources, as well as their worldview about the education of adults.

In attempting to assess the impact of professionalization in adult education, we believe that it is crucial to question the direction that this process will take in the future. We agree with Cervero (1992) that the professionalization of adult education is basically a nonissue; we should accept the professionalization process and "move on to the more important issue concerning our options in shaping the professionalization of the field" (p. 47). In the following chapter, we will present a very different vision of how the field has developed to date.

Summary

This chapter has presented an overview of the debate surrounding professionalization of adult education and has described some of the most common elements of professionalization. Such a discussion is grounded in three key questions: What does it mean to professionalize? How has the adult education field professionalized so far? And does professionalization make a difference?

While there has been considerable debate about the merits of professionalization in adult education, the fact remains that many elements often associated with professionalization have played an important role in the contemporary field and must be recognized. At various times professional associations, literature and resources, and graduate training and professional development in the field have each come under scrutiny and even attack. Yet they continue to serve as vital threads holding those who have made a professional commitment to adult education to their identities as professionals. We will highlight issues related to these and other areas of conflict in the next two chapters.

10

The Unacknowledged Side of Practice

In Chapter Nine, we discussed the mechanisms by which adult education has professionalized and explained how the intent of professionalization is to improve practice. This discussion included identifying a distinct knowledge base that has come to be associated with adult education, the fact that graduate degree programs are available that prepare people to be adult educators, the existence of research agendas that extend the knowledge base, and journals, conferences, and associations that function as forums, gatekeepers, and socializing agents for the profession.

The knowledge base is taught through graduate programs to new members, who then participate in professional activities, which in turn solidifies a sense of belonging to the profession. Those who identify themselves with the profession, or are seen by others as members, generally represent formal, institutionalized, mainstream adult education that for the most part we have described in this book.

There is another side to the field of adult education, however—one that challenges some of the assumptions underlying our description in the previous chapter of adult education as a professional field. This other side raises issues about the meaning of professionalism itself and its relationship to the world of practice—issues that we will discuss in more depth in Chapter Eleven.

The purpose of this chapter is to make visible those aspects of practice that have been marginalized as a result of the way the field has professionalized. Specifically, we will focus on those adult educators and adult learners who have not been acknowledged as part of mainstream adult education because of either who they are or what they do, or both. This segment of practice has been largely excluded in the professionalization of the field. In making this case, we realize the danger of oversimplifying the complex issue of who and what is counted and who and what is not. What constitutes the mainstream and the visible depends ultimately on where one is standing and which criteria one uses for inclusion. Nevertheless, as the field has professionalized, the contributions of some groups to the education of adults have been largely excluded.

Invisible by Who They Are

In fall 1990, Jane Hugo asked: "Why have women once visible and active in the formative years of the field become invisible in the histories of that period?. . . . Why have adult education historians continued to write women out of historical research and not questioned their absence?" (p. 6). In her analysis, she proposes that women have been left out because "official" knowledge of the field has been constructed by men, and is about men and the institutions they finance and manage. Women adult educators relegated to community and home spheres have not counted in shaping the field's history or practice.

Hugo's article was part of a wake-up call to mainstream adult educators that women—who constitute half the adult population—were being left out of the development of the professional field of practice. So too were African Americans, Native Americans, Hispanics, people with disabilities, gays and lesbians, older adults, working-class adults, and so on. Basically, the experiences and knowledge that counted most—those that found their way into histories and theories—were those of middle-class white males. Large numbers of adult educators and learners had therefore been rendered invisible to mainstream adult education by who they are.

Reasons for Exclusion

The exclusion of people from the mainstream, whether based on sex, race, class, sexual orientation, age, or other factors, permeates our society. Hayes and Colin (1994) write that racism and sexism "are part of the fabric of our society; they are reflected not only in individual actions but also in our institutions and even in the language that we use to understand and describe our world" (p. 6). Such views, they observe, are perpetuated through a number of mechanisms, including individual beliefs and behavior, educational institutions, and organizational policies and practices.

With regard to individual beliefs and behavior, Hayes and Colin note that discrimination can be both intentional, as in telling racist or sexist jokes, or unintentional, as when a person's unconscious assumptions lead to treating people differently. They point out that marginalized people themselves may be "socialized to stereotypes. . . . Accepting stereotypes can mean that they believe themselves to be inadequate or inferior, that they lower their aspirations, and even that they accept overtly discriminatory treatment" (p. 13). Educational institutions through both the formal and the informal curricula also perpetuate exclusionary and discriminatory practices. The absence of women in the field's history and in the curriculum materials of graduate adult education programs is a good example. Practices and policies of business and industry and other organizations—especially in hiring, firing, promotion, and benefits—continue to discriminate against women, minorities, and other groups.

The exclusion, oppression, and discrimination of certain groups from mainstream society is historically embedded in society's evolution. The situation comes to feel normal, so that "one group of people accept as normal, natural, and in need of no explanation, conditions that are in the interests of another group altogether." This phenomenon, termed *hegemony*, "refers to the standards, ideas, and modes of behaviour that come to pervade the institutions of a society, are accepted and lived by the population, and so become the media through which the population is controlled" (Newman, 1994, p. 85).

Central to the phenomenon of hegemony is the notion of power: who has it and how it is used to reinforce current structures of society, oppressive though they may be, so that those in power can remain there. Oppression can take many forms in contemporary society; it is less obvious and more subtle than traditional notions of Colonial domination, evil, and tyranny. Young (cited in McLaren and Lankshear, 1994) delineates five types of oppression "that affect groups in North America such as women, blacks, Chicanos, Puerto Ricans, most Spanish-speaking Americans, Native Americans, Jews, lesbians, gay men, Arabs, Asians, old people, working-class people, poor people, and physically and mentally impaired people" (pp. 4–5).

The first type of oppression that Young defines, *exploitation*, occurs in the labor force when groups such as women, ethnic and racial minorities, and the poor work at lower-paying, unskilled jobs "to benefit the wealthy, reproducing and causing class divisions and relations of inequality" (McLaren and Lankshear, 1994, p. 5). *Marginalization*, the second form of oppression, is the segmenting off of groups "who are positioned by the dominant culture in relations of dependency where they are excluded from equal citizenship rights" (p. 5). *Powerlessness* is related to social status, privilege, and autonomy and can be readily seen in the privilege given to professional groups over nonprofessionals. *Cultural imperialism* occurs when "the dominant cultural group exercises its power by bringing other groups under the measure of its domination" (p. 5). Consequently, the dominant groups construct the differences of subordinate groups as lack and negation in relation to their privileging norms. For instance, "the difference of women from men, Native Americans or Africans from Europeans, Jews from Christians, homosexuals from heterosexuals, or workers from professionals becomes reconstructed as deviance and inferiority" (p. 5). A case could be made that cultural imperialism is an apt description of this situation, in which learners are often positioned in terms of what they lack and what they need in terms of some social yardstick of the dominant group. "Cultural imperialism, Young notes, involves the paradoxical experience of being *invisible* while simultaneously being positioned as different" (McLaren and Lankshear, 1994, p. 6; emphasis added).

The last form of oppression in Young's model is *violence*. In our society, violence against "members of particular groups simply because they belong to those specific groups" is particularly evident with women, homosexuals, blacks, and Jews (p. 6).

Invisibility and Professionalization

The professionalism of adult education has been part of the same patterns of oppression, discrimination, and exclusion as have other aspects of society. As Bailey, Tisdell, and Cervero (1994) observe, "[P]rofessionalization is simply another mechanism by which social power is distributed in society, and all existing asymmetrical power relationships among different races and between men and women are reproduced (often in complex and subtle ways) through this process" (p. 65). Stalker (1996), for example, has recently analyzed how discourse and power relations in adult education have resulted in domination by the male agenda.

The professional field of adult education has developed without recognition of particular groups' contributions and without accounting for a large segment of practice: adult education for social action or social change. Through conscious or benign neglect, women, racial and ethnic minorities, homosexuals, older individuals, and so on have had little if any say in determining what counts as adult education. These voices have not been acknowledged in the construction of the official knowledge base, in the preparation of professionals, or in activities of the profession.

Since the beginnings of adult education as a profession in the 1920s, the knowledge base has focused on the growth of institutional sponsorship, the expanding participation of adults in formal programs, the development of a curriculum to meet the needs of adult learners, the training of educators, and the acquisition of methods for adding yet more knowledge to this field of study. Until most recently, then, the knowledge base has been about institutions and the white (usually male) middle-class who run programs that attract adults who are also generally white and middle-class. The methods used for planning programs and teaching adults, were in turn taught to other white middle-class adults in primarily white institutions of higher education, who then might contribute to the knowledge base. The result of this cycle is that the knowledge base reproduces itself.

With no way for the cycle to be broken, the participation, contributions, and knowledge of many groups have been absent from the official knowledge base of adult education. Cunningham (1989) identifies significant segments of practice that have been "lost" in the official knowledge: women educators in popular movements prior to the Civil War, farmers' movements against developing feudalism, the use of literature and the popular press to educate the masses, immigrant education, labor colleges, the Freedmen's Bureau, black colleges, the Marcus Garvey movement, workers' and union education, settlement houses, the Highlander Center, circles of culture. To underscore her point, Cunningham notes that "contributions of women and worker education itself tend to be the silent spaces in the graduate curricula of adult education today, when the education of workers from a corporate perspective (human resource development) appears to be one of the most well-studied areas" (p. 39).

The creation of the knowledge base has rested in part on the definition of what knowledge counts and how it is to be generated. Wilson (1993a) traces this theme and its relationship to professionalization through an analysis of the handbooks of adult and continuing education from 1934 to 1989. Knowledge that counted became associated with the positivist, scientific, technical-rational paradigm common to much of the twentieth century. Knowledge based on experience, intuition, and other alternative forms of understanding has not been valued; neither have alternatives to the scientific method of accessing knowledge.

An understanding of the nature and creation of the knowledge base of adult education is crucial to understanding the professionalization of the field. The voices of women, racial minorities, and other groups have not been heard largely because their knowledge and alternative means of accessing that knowledge have not been valued by those controlling the field.

Closely intertwined with the knowledge base is the training of professionals in adult education. This takes place mostly in graduate programs. As institutions of higher education mirror the power relationships of the larger society, it is not surprising that the vast majority of people being trained in these programs are white and middle-class—and, if they had trained for positions of authority and status in the early decades of graduate training—male.

Bailey, Tisdell, and Cervero (1994) analyze this phenomenon in terms of faculty, curriculum, and interactions among faculty and students. With regard to faculty in higher education, "those who have been given the power to produce and disseminate knowledge, are in 1993 still almost exclusively white" (p. 67), and about 32 percent are women. In terms of curriculum, "what gets taught and what has counted as true knowledge, throughout the entire educational system, has generally represented a white worldview" (pp. 68–69). Furthermore, the literature read in courses is predominantly produced by white males: "Much of the literature dealing with women that does exist tends to portray them in nonauthoritative roles (Collard and Stalker, 1991). In light of the overall lack of attention to feminist theory, the adult education literature and thus the adult education curriculum in higher education have inadvertently reinforced the subordination of women" (Bailey, Tisdell, and Cervero, 1994, p. 70).

Also, interactions among faculty and students in and out of the classroom setting tend to reinforce patterns of white male dominance. In a review of the higher education research focusing on issues of power and control, Tisdell (1995) writes that "these studies suggest that men receive far more attention than women, female professors encourage more classroom interaction, and the curricular materials reflect predominantly the white male experience" (p. 42).

In addition to development of the knowledge base and graduate training, a third mechanism for professionalization is active participation in activities sponsored by associations and other groups interested in continuing professional education. As might be expected, this arena exhibits the same exclusionary pattern as other facets of the field. Historically, leadership positions in the American Association for Adult and Continuing Education and the Commission of Professors of Adult Education have been held by white males. While this trend has begun to change recently, and while membership and attendance by women has increased over the years, racial minorities, gays, people with disabilities, community-based and working-class adult educators, and the like have been conspicuously absent. Nor have many nonwhites or women published in journals (Hayes and Smith, 1994) or in conference proceedings, or, until recently, presented at conferences.

Invisible by What They Do

Many people, perhaps the majority, who are engaged in the education of adults define themselves in relation to a content area, an institution, an educational method. Thus, rather than adult educators we have health educators, librarians, prison educators, religious educators, community developers, distance educators, and so on. Many who "do" adult education do not study the knowledge base, read the journals, attend the conferences, or join the associations. They are virtually invisible in any count of professionals in the field, yet their practice is often identical to that of adult educators, and they may be as mainstream as the local continuing educator in what they see as the purpose of their work. However, the defining of adult education as a profession has not been broad enough to include them.

The least visible of these educators of adults are those who work outside the mainstream. They are not typically found in formal institutions, and they align themselves with a social action or radical agenda, calling into question accepted norms, social structures, and educational practices. They go by a number of names, including community-based educators, popular educators, community activists, nonformal educators, social activists, and radicals. As M. K. Smith (1994) observes,

> Their main workplace is not the classroom. Shops, launderettes, streets, pubs, cafes, and people's front rooms are the settings for much of their work. Where they do appear in schools and colleges, it is in corridors, eating areas and student common rooms that they are most likely to be found. Their work is not organized by subject, syllabus or lessons. . . . They are not interested in possessing knowledge as one might own objects. Rather, they look to the way people are with themselves and the world. Such education is, as a result, unpredictable, risky and, hopefully, emancipatory [p. 1].

These educators are in the community, working with people on local issues and concerns. They are employed by social service agencies, governmental and nongovernmental bodies, and private and public organizations. Their numbers, and the numbers of people with whom they work, are unknown despite efforts to establish a worldwide databank of such information (Chu, 1994). Evidence of their presence can be found in the people with whom they work—in the form of personal testimonials, demonstrations, local initiatives, lobbying, and occasionally legislative reforms.

As we mentioned, this facet of adult education goes by a number of names. The terms *nonformal education* and *informal education* are used worldwide, *popular education* is common in Latin America, and *community-based education* or *community action* are familiar terms in

North America. Smith (1994) suggests using the term "local education," which "puts a proper emphasis on place . and brings out the
significance of local knowledge" (p. 21). In any case, finding the right
term to capture this element of practice is less important than understanding the basic perspective and its relationship to professionalism.

Adult Education for Social Change

The development of adult education as a field of practice has historically been linked to two very different movements—one focusing on social change or social action, and the other emphasizing
personal and economic development. We explored this tension in
Chapter Four, but it is worth reiterating here as a basis for understanding the more invisible or marginalized forms of community-
based adult education. North America, and to a large extent highly
industrialized nations in general, have trusted in education at all
levels to contribute to a strong economy by training citizens to be
more developed, skilled, or knowledgeable. Such a focus supports
the status quo, and sees those who don't buy into the paradigm as
marginal, deviant, or deficient. Educators are themselves "trained"
to be more efficient, skilled, and technologically adept in effecting
the desired outcomes. This is what much of mainstream professional
adult education is all about. While the economic force may be more
visible than ever before, it is not a new thrust (Cunningham, 1989;
Wilson, 1993a).

Concurrent with the "economic" agenda has been a focus on
social action. As Cunningham (1989) points out,

> A reading of history in which adult education is freed
> from the concept of schooling should also indicate its
> rich tradition in bringing about social change. The edu-
> cation of adults is a social activity, not a discipline, and
> can be seen as unique in that its history is not made
> behind the backs of people; it is made by people. And
> the history that is made can be influenced by the educa-

tional process; thus adult education has been, and is today, a contributor to social transformation, even if this fact has been largely ignored [p. 40].

Writers point to labor colleges, folk schools, settlement houses, land grant colleges, cooperatives, and so on as early examples of this orientation (Cunningham, 1989; Lovett, 1988; McLaren and Lankshear, 1994). Third World development projects, old and new social movements, community-action initiatives, and the Highlander Center for Research and Education are contemporary examples (Cunningham, 1989; Galbraith, 1990; Holford, 1995; McLaren and Lankshear, 1994; Newman, 1994; M. K. Smith, 1994).

Lovett (1988) believes that the "tradition of linking adult education to movements for social change is re-emerging as adult educators grapple with the social, economic, political and moral issues facing people in complex, violent, unequal and rapidly changing society" (p. xv). This reemergence, or perhaps growth, of adult education for social change—whether evolutionary or revolutionary (Hamilton and Cunningham, 1989)—challenges mainstream "economic" adult education on several fronts.

Major Concepts of Education for Social Change

Education that focuses on bringing about social change, whether in the form of community development, community education, or nonformal or popular education, holds in common certain beliefs or values. Some of these beliefs run counter to—and thus challenge the mechanisms of—mainstream professionalization, which we explored in Chapter Nine.

Collaborative Learning

Social-change education nearly always hinges on collaborative learning: it is *with* people, not *for* them, and it regards individual learning as a by-product of collective learning and not an end in itself. This collaborative type of learning is locally initiated and locally controlled, and to take place it requires space—both physical and psychological—for groups of people to create their own knowledge and examine the roles that power and oppression play in society. In his book *Local Education*, M. K. Smith (1994) gives a fair amount of attention to notions of space, time, and place. "Local educators," he writes, "have to co-ordinate activities with the rhythms and contours of the neighbourhood" (p. 87). The modes of work include being about, being there, working with individuals and groups, working on projects, doing administration and research, and reflecting on practice.

According to Smith, everyday conversations in everyday places within the community hold as much potential for change and learning as do more formal discussions and dialogues. Collaborative group exercises, discussions, and dialogues are all, of course, well-documented techniques in adult education literature, and Freire's problem-posing and dialogical method are often cited as appropriate strategies for collaborative learning. Educators working for social change warn, however, that merely appropriating these techniques is not the answer. Macedo (1994) proposes "an anti-method pedagogy that refuses the rigidity of models and methodological paradigms. The anti-method pedagogy forces us to view dialogue as a form of social praxis so that the sharing of experiences is informed by reflection and political action. . . . The anti-method pedagogy also frees us from the beaten path of certainties and specialisms" (p. xviii).

Collaborative learning comes up against mainstream professional practice when it runs counter to much of what is espoused about adult learning in North America. Andragogy, with its emphasis on the *individual* adult learner's characteristics and its humanistic ethos of personal development, has little to say about collaborative learning (see Chapter Six), critical thinking, and transformative learning—especially as characterized by Mezirow (1990, 1991a). And while collaborative learning, group interaction, and dialogical methods are espoused in the literature, actual practice in North America is more governed by competition, individual achievement, and didactic modes of instruction (Beder, 1987; Belenky, Clinchy, Goldberger, and Tarule, 1986; Tisdell, 1995).

Knowledge Production

A second defining factor of education for social action is the concept of *knowledge*. Knowledge, which is so fundamental to defining the profession of adult education (see Chapter Nine), is construed quite differently from a social-action perspective. Knowledge is more than what is produced by society's systems of government, business, and education and transmitted to the less knowledgeable. Legitimate knowledge can also be produced by the disenfranchised, those without degrees or certificates, and the uneducated. Social-action education "helps people to create their own knowledge, to celebrate their own culture, and to study their own history" (Hamilton and Cunningham, 1989, p. 443). Furthermore, this knowledge creation is a dialectic and dynamic process with no concluding, permanent, or objective end point. Knowledge is what is produced when people make sense out of their world, according to their experience in it. Knowledge is also what people construct to deal with the world as they experience it—the tools, approaches, and methods that work best in the particular situation.

In an interesting essay on the history of knowledge, R. Johnson (1988) traces what "really useful knowledge" has meant from a radical perspective. He concludes: "Who produces the knowledges and for what reasons was a central issue for nineteenth-century radicals. Their answer was very clear: in the end it is the people's knowledges that change the world. This means that self-education, or knowledge as self-production, is the only knowledge that really matters. Others may be resources here, but in the end you cannot be taught, you can only learn. Really useful knowledge occurs only in an active mood, and must have its active centre among subordinated social groups, the equivalents of 'the people'" (p. 29).

The starting point, then, for social change is the notion that people can create knowledge that is more relevant, useful, and empowering than knowledge brought in by outsiders.

Power

Knowledge creation is linked to the concept of power. The goal of popular education "is to transform social reality into a more democratic state by confronting dominant and dominating institutions through the creation of opposing knowledges—through the celebration of many indigenous cultures and the writing of many histories of and by the people" (Hamilton and Cunningham, 1989, p. 443). This is akin to what Smith (1994) refers to as "embedding practice" in the local social system and community. Understanding the networks of power relations and the boundaries of power leads to challenging inequalities and ultimately seeking to change the balance of power. Such work is, of course, highly political and sometimes dangerous. It involves making visible that which has been assumed to be true and which maintains control of the powerful over the powerless. An analysis of power from the standpoint of what people know, rather than what they are told, leads to the identification of forms of oppression. Some of these forms are subtle—"part of the basic fabric of social life" (McLaren and Lankshear, 1994, p. 4).

Equally important to studying forms of oppression through an analysis of power is that in doing so, individuals and groups become empowered. In Freire's words, people come out of a "culture of silence," "name their world," and realize that they can be actors in changing the world (1970). Newman (1994), in a provocative analysis of social-action adult education, writes that people not only need to name the world, but need to name the enemy as well: "When we ask who the enemies are we should try to prevent our learners [from] retreating into abstractions" and "depersonalised concepts such as society or hegemony or the unequal distribution of wealth. As far as possible we need to see these kinds of concepts as tools for analysis to be used in the search, not [as] the enemies themselves" (p. 149).

Analyzing power and oppression are only starting points, Newman suggests. "We and our learners need to find out more. . . . Who are the people, what are the organisations . . . [w]here do they operate? Can we name them and *do they have an address?* (1994, p. 149; emphasis in original). Once we identify them, there are other questions: "Are they really the enemy? Are they main players or bit players in the exercise of oppression? Are they beneficiaries of a hegemonic control or merely the foot soldiers?. . . . What kind of power do they wield?" (p. 149)

Empowerment allows individuals and communities "to control certain aspects of their lives" (Hamilton, 1992, p. 84). This notion of empowerment has three dimensions, according to Hamilton (1992). The first is a cognitive dimension in which group members understand "their history, social status, conditions of subordination, and the related reasons for current conditions" (p. 85). The psychological component, which is the second dimension, refers to the affective, feeling aspects of empowerment, including self-esteem and self-confidence. The third dimension, economic, "refers to the creation or development of productive activity that will enable citizens to improve their financial condition" (p. 85).

Praxis

Shared knowledge of oppression is aimed toward collective action to change that oppression. This leads to another important concept in social-action education: praxis—the interaction of reflection and action. Without the doing, without taking action, all of the analysis or reflection is disempowered. In the notion of praxis that Freire presented, "reflection and action are both contained in praxis and cannot be isolated one from the other. The two activities fuse into one dynamic process in which the learners act on themselves and on their world, bringing about a change in their own consciousness and in the way they engage with other people, organisations, institutions and objects around them" (Newman, 1994, p. 110).

The action component of education for social change takes many forms. It might be as individual as reporting sexual harassment or demanding access to a public official. It might be a collective protest, a mass demonstration, a concerted effort to expose inequities in power and control. Newman (1994) writes that taking action can include many strategies, including parleying with the other parties, consulting, and making a decision to collaborate. These strategies can be employed "guardedly" and "with one's own interests uppermost in one's mind" (p. 160).

Another set of strategies—negotiating, cooperating, or educating—assumes that learners have both common and conflicting interests. Lastly, if interests are predominantly in conflict, learners can disengage, defend, infiltrate, subvert, oppose, contest, challenge, or attack. Newman's strategies are defined less by the nature of the conflict than by the nature of the learning: "Learning by defining the enemy does not necessarily lead to open conflict or impossible divisions. On the contrary, unions develop modes of working with managements. Feminists have accepted the collaboration of men in the pursuit of the cause. And indigenous people can work towards reconciliation with their invaders. But if the focus in the learning is not on the learners' own condition so much as the condition, nature, and motives of their opponents, then the learning is likely to be clear-sighted, and the strategies realistic" (1994, p. 162).

The notion of praxis centers on a dialectic between reflection, or learning, and action; each informs the other, is defined by the other, and changes in relation to the other. This close connection between reflection and action is yet another way in which this "invisible" side of adult education challenges the mainstream. Because this dialectic is commonly couched in terms of the disjuncture between theory and practice—between the practical and the scientific—professional adult educators have found it difficult to wed the two concepts in any meaningful way. Practitioners complain that theories and research about adult education that make up the knowledge base have little relevance to their everyday practice; professionals, and in particular academicians, lament what they see as the aimlessness and atheoretical nature of practice.

While the schism between reflection and action—that is, between theory and practice—is recognized, mainstream adult educators do little about it. Newman (1994) poses a number of reasons for this, several of which reflect the disempowerment of professional adult educators themselves by their own rhetoric and forms of knowledge. For example, faith in human potential and the positive individual growth and development of learners has led adult educators to be too nice, "too understanding, too ready to hear the other point of view, too caring, too nurturing" (p. 19). This results in an inability to define the enemy in any realistic way. In the same manner, many adult educators focus on helping people function better in the existing system, never questioning whether the system itself is creating artificial learning needs in the first place.

Probably the most promising mainstream effort to link reflection and action in the service of a social-action agenda is in the area of critical theory and critical thinking. Both Mezirow (1985, 1991a, 1991b, 1994) and Brookfield (1987a) propose that adult learning should be about developing critical thinkers who examine assumptions and the world in which they live. Such learning can lead to empowerment, transformation, and emancipation—in short, social action. Both educators, however, have been criticized for emphasizing the internal and individual nature of the process, with few guidelines as to how it actually plays out in the community. Newman (1994) writes, "Neither [Brookfield nor Mezirow] satisfactorily describes how learning for perspective transformation or critical thinking might contribute in a political struggle when the battle lines are drawn and the parleying is over" (p. 47).

Thus, a large arena of practice in North American adult education is rarely if ever considered in descriptions of the field and in discussions about professionalization. Adult education that has an agenda of social action or social change works largely outside mainstream cultural, economic, political, and educational institutions.

Indeed, its very nature challenges mainstream philosophies, beliefs, and assumptions. Its emphasis on collaborative learning, its views of knowledge construction, its analysis of power, and its wedding of reflection and action in the notion of praxis are all factors foreign to or only partially acknowledged by mainstream adult education. Because of what social-action adult education tries to do, it is rendered invisible by the rest of the field.

This analysis of such invisibility is meant to raise questions (which we discuss in more depth in the next chapter) about the desirability of professionalizing the field of adult education. We do not mean to suggest that adult education should be only about social action or that adult education for social action does not have its own issues and tensions, some of which are shared by the mainstream field. R. Johnson (1988), for example, observes that the social movements of the 1970s were "strong precisely among those groups with the most extensive experience of formal education, especially in its more autonomous spaces in and around colleges and universities" (p. 27). Recently, Holford (1995) called for more study of the role of "movement intellectuals" who may hold ambivalent positions vis-à-vis the movement's interests (p. 108).

Further tensions are caused by an emphasis on individual versus collective empowerment, which according to Lovett (1988) is "the demand for access to educational institutions as opposed to the concern for local space for, and control over, their own educational resources; the tension between concern with method as against an emphasis on content" (p. xxii). Even more problematic, but rarely addressed in the literature, is the potential for social-action education to cause the substitution of one form of oppression and control with another. "How far . . . are radical adult educators prepared to engage in a fully democratic community education?" ask Taylor and Ward (1988, p. 251). "In a context where unemployed whites think that unemployment would be solved by 'repatriation' of black people and, generally, the adoption of National Front–type policies, are the facilitating roles of community education to be used? Obviously not: but how does this tally with community control?" (p. 251).

Toward a More Visible Presence

The voices of those who have been largely invisible to mainstream adult education because of who they are or what they do are beginning to be heard. This is partially due to changes in the larger society. The hegemony of white, middle-class males is harder to sustain in the face of growing numbers of ethnic and racial minorities.

> According to the U.S. Department of Commerce's Bureau of the Census (1991), in the United States between 1980 and '90, the Asian population more than doubled and the Latino/Latina population increased by more than 50 percent. Both the African American and Native American populations increased by approximately 30 percent each, while the Euro-American or white population increased by only 6 percent. This trend of increasing racial and ethnic diversity is projected to continue. Both within and across these ethnic boundaries, there are gender and economic class differences. In addition, roughly 10 percent of the total U.S. population is estimated to be gay, lesbian, or bisexual (Crooks and Baur, 1990), and a significant portion of our population has a physical or mental disability (Heward and Cavanaugh, 1993) [Tisdell, 1995, pp.3–4].

As a result of these changing demographics, North American society has become aware of issues of cultural and workplace diversity, bilingual schooling, diversity training, and so on. Policymakers, power brokers, and educators at all levels are grappling with the implications of ethnic and cultural diversity. These realities, coupled with an emergence of tools in the form of critical theory, postmodernism, and radical, feminist, and race theory, has at least increased awareness of the existence of previously marginalized, silenced, and unacknowledged people.

In adult education, Cunningham (1989) believes, "there is a nascent yet energetic stirring among many professional adult educators. . . . Professionals, who have heard themselves defined only in terms of what they do (that is, technology), are now beginning to wonder why they do it. As this critical reflection takes place, the ideology that supports the status quo is unmasked" (pp. 43–44). This "stirring" among adult educators involves not only critical reflection but also visible contributions to the knowledge base as well as activities in graduate programs and elsewhere that are designed to challenge the monopoly of mainstream adult education.

The literature of adult education is no longer exclusively institutionally based, technologically oriented, and white-male dominated. As we noted in Chapter Three, Stubblefield and Keane (1994) made a concerted effort to include voices not heard before in histories of adult education; there are also several recent publications on the history of African Americans in adult education (Neufeldt and McGee, 1990; E. A. Peterson, 1996). A number of books have been published that give some visibility to adult education outside the mainstream, including books on social action (Newman, 1994), radical adult education (Horton and Freire, 1990; Lovett, 1988; McLaren and Lankshear, 1994; Shor, 1992), and community-based adult education (Galbraith, 1990; Hamilton, 1992; M. K. Smith, 1994).

However, the major thrust in "alternative" literature has been in issues of race, sex, and multiculturalism. Prior to Hugo's article in 1990, few if any publications had presented a feminist analysis of adult education practice. Recent publications have focused on sex as well as race, economic class, lifestyle, and the interlocking systems of power and oppression in adult education (Hart, 1992; Hayes and Colin, 1994; R. J. Hill, 1995; Ross-Gordon, Martin, and Briscoe, 1990a; Tisdell, 1993a, 1993b, 1995). These and other publications offer more than a mere analysis of the phenomenon;

authors also suggest concrete strategies for including different voices in the practice of adult education. In addition, a book is in process that is endorsed by the Commission of Professors of Adult Education and is designed to provide a forum for people who have been excluded from the mainstream of adult education discourse.

Breaking the white, middle-class monopoly of adult education's "official" knowledge base is key to redefining the professional field of practice. Another key is to tap other modes of knowledge production, including the way in which research is conducted. In this area, too, there has been a growing awareness of paradigms other than the rational, scientific one for producing knowledge (Deshler and Hagan, 1989; Merriam, 1991). Interpretive, participatory, and critical frameworks are slowly making inroads. However, as Deshler (1991) points out, many questions remain unanswered regarding research and its relationship to professionalism:

> Does scholarship follow market demand, or does it have a life of its own independent from practice? Who should determine the focus and methodology of research? Should research be put to the task of social transformation or to the task of exploring whatever the individual researcher values? Who produces, controls, and benefits from research? Is participatory research legitimate for doctoral research? To whom is the researcher accountable—to academic colleagues in the field of study through peer review, to the institution of higher education, to external funders, to practitioners, to the demands of social and historical circumstances, or to himself or herself? [p. 413]

Changes in graduate training programs and in conference and association activities are other mechanisms for bringing the invisible side of adult education into the total picture. Diversifying faculties and student bodies by the systematic and relentless recruitment

of women, racial and ethnic minorities, and members of other marginalized groups is under way at some institutions, as is curriculum
reform (Bailey, Tisdell, and Cervero, 1994; Tisdell, 1995). Sessions
on diversity issues at conferences, as well as ongoing activities (such
as the African American Adult Education Research Pre-Conference,
and the international pre-conference associated with the American
Association for Adult and Continuing Education) are further examples of efforts to include heretofore marginalized adult educators and
learners.

Lastly, mainstream adult educators have been urged to develop a
personal agenda for change (Hayes, 1994; Tisdell, 1995). At the
very least, this involves becoming conscious of our own attitudes
and behaviors, how we have "all internalized to some degree the
values of the dominant culture in ways we are not fully conscious
[of]" (Tisdell, 1995, p. 66). Such an awareness must be followed by
conscious efforts to alter our behaviors at work, in the classroom,
and in the community so that they are more inclusive of the many
divergent voices that make up our society.

Summary

In this chapter, we have attempted to bring to light an unacknowledged side of adult education—one that has not been part of its
evolution as a professional field of practice. We described two
dimensions of this side: those who are unacknowledged because of
who they are, and those who are invisible because of what they do.
In reality, of course, there is much overlap between these two
groups, since the people and the practice are one and the same.
However, we believe that each component suggests different challenges to mainstream adult education, and so we discussed each one
separately.

The first dimension of invisibility is in the form of groups of people whose race or ethnicity, sex, economic class, sexual orientation,
able-bodiedness, or lifestyle have differed from mainstream adult

educators and learners, thus causing them to be marginalized or dis-empowered. These groups have challenged the very mechanisms by which the field has professionalized.

A second form, community-based adult education—especially with an agenda of social change or social action—has been largely ignored in histories, descriptions, and research in adult education. We proposed that characteristics of social-action adult education such as collaborative learning, indigenous knowledge production, empowering pedagogies, and the notion of praxis are largely incongruent with the values, practices, and assumptions of mainstream adult education—thus the resulting marginalization of this dimension of practice.

In the final section of the chapter, we addressed recent developments in the field that have opened the door to the possibility that adult education can begin to define itself more inclusively in relation to professional practice.

11

Reframing Practice
The Future of Adult Education

Throughout the previous chapters of this book, we have mapped the foundations and organization of the adult education field. The four chapters of Part One served as an overview of adult education by addressing the role and scope of the field, as well as its philosophical and historical foundations. In Part Two, our emphasis shifted more directly to the structure and practice of adult education. We outlined the range of providers, the nature of planning and administering programs, and ideas relative to working successfully with adult learners. And in Part Three, we have examined how adult education is developing as a professional field and have included chapters presenting two very different visions of adult education and those who practice in it.

This final chapter has a twofold purpose. First, we intend to identify several key areas of controversy pertaining to professionalization of adult education, and in so doing we will revisit the question "Does professionalization make a difference?" as it relates to the three elements we discussed in Chapter Nine. We will also illustrate how professionalization can be reframed in a way that is more inclusive than has traditionally been the case. In this way, the chapter serves to highlight key issues or tensions that we brought up in the chapters on professionalization—just as Chapters Four and Eight did for Parts One and Two, respectively. And second, the chapter is designed to bring closure to the book by offering some reflections and speculation about possible directions for the future of adult education.

Reframing the Professionalization of Adult Education

As can be seen from the previous two chapters, the question of professionalization is something of a paradox for the development of adult education. On one hand, there is a belief that professionalization is essential to moving the field from a marginal status (whether real or perceived) to one that wields more influence in society. At the same time, some very basic concerns must be addressed about adult education becoming so absorbed with the elements of professionalization that this process will ultimately produce a narrowly defined mainstream that excludes many of the diverse voices of those people who engage in its practice. Such an effort has the potential to widen the chasm that already exists between "professional" adult educators and others who work with adult learners.

Some would say that this has already happened. According to Heaney (1996), for example, "[S]o successful has the professionalization of adult education been that many . . . activists no longer think of themselves as adult educators. Hence the frustration of those who, marching to a different drummer, attempt to link learning with democratic social change and, without forsaking the status of their profession, forge a bond with social activists whose unacknowledged educational work challenges and illuminates the labor of mainstream adult education."

While the debate continues, some efforts have been made to move the discussion in a different direction. Indeed, Cervero (1992) believes that practitioners must turn their efforts toward determining how the field should professionalize. He argues that it is possible and desirable for adult education to avoid a more "traditional" model of professionalization, and instead move toward a view that questions authoritative assumptions about the field and reduces overdependence on professionals.

Looking at the issue from a different angle, Griffith (1989) makes a distinction between *adult educators* and *educators of adults*. According to Griffith, "Educators of adults have focused goals that typically address pressing problems in a single sector of the field of adult education, while adult educators have broad aspirations for the entire field. Adult educators have a high regard for professionalism, specialized academic preparation for their work, and a concern for the coordination of the field, while educators of adults mainly have practical concerns and less *grandiose ambitions*" (p. 5, emphasis added).

Although this distinction is generally helpful, it shares with the Houle pyramid (see Chapter Five) a pecking order that accords higher status to certain segments of the population who work with adult learners. Indeed, much of the debate and dissension found in the field today are tied to questions of elitism and gatekeeping. Historically, adult education in this country was grounded in the spirit of "friends teaching friends," where much of the joy was derived from a sense of informality and mutual sharing. Critics of professionalization often claim that this spirit is lost, and they blame this loss on the kind of hierarchical structure that professionalization can perpetuate.

Another way to capture the essence of Griffith's distinction is to differentiate between adult educators and those who "do adult education" (Brockett, 1991b, p. 11). This view differs from Griffith's distinction because in avoiding the temptation to compare or rank the importance of these two groups, the issue of elitism becomes moot, as is illustrated in the following description:

> One does not need to be a professional social worker in order to assist others in meeting certain social needs; however, such a person does not claim to *be* a social worker. Nor does one need to be a professional in order to share financial advice with another individual, as long as the adviser does not claim to be a "professional"

financial consultant. The same is true for adult education. One obviously does not need a graduate degree in
adult education to teach a personal interest course to a
group of adults, and such teachers, without claiming to
be "professional" adult educators, play an important role.
On the other hand, if we are to have a truly viable profession of adult and continuing education, we do need to
have some individuals who identify themselves as professionals and who engage in a professional socialization
process [Brockett, 1991b, p. 11].

The important point that Brockett makes is that both adult educators and those who "do" adult education play vital roles in the education of adults in our society, and that the relationship between
these two groups is more parallel than hierarchical. To try comparing or ranking the two categories becomes pointless because, while
the two groups are related, they can almost be seen to exist in parallel universes (Brockett, 1991b).

   In this section, we will revisit the three components of mainstream professionalization—associations, literature and information
resources, and graduate study—addressed in Chapter Nine. However,
this time we will take a broader look at each area and reframe the discussion by incorporating perspectives derived from the invisible side
of practice. As you read this chapter, we encourage you to bear in
mind the three questions posed at the beginning of Chapter Nine:
What does it mean to professionalize? How has adult education professionalized so far? And does professionalization make a difference?

Assessing the Impact of Professional Associations

In assessing the impact of professional associations as a component
of the professionalizing process, we can conclude that such associations have served as a major outlet for professional development
and socialization for thousands of adult educators over the years.

Most adult education conferences conducted since the 1920s have been under the sponsorship of one or more professional associations. Similarly, most of the past and current periodicals and a great many influential books about adult education would not have existed were it not for associations. Such associations have often worked with foundations and other funding sources to develop innovative experiential programs that serve adult learners in innovative ways. And finally, at various times and places, associations have been a force in helping to shape governmental policy on adult education.

At the same time, this success is not without its limits. As history has shown, efforts to establish and maintain a strong national umbrella association have been difficult. The history of such efforts, as we discussed in Chapter Nine, is a story of ebbs and flows, tensions, and divergent agendas. It is noteworthy that, according to the *Encyclopedia of Associations*, the national umbrella association in the United States—the American Association for Adult and Continuing Education—lists a membership of five thousand and an annual budget of $750,000 (Fischer and Schwartz, 1996, p. 974). By contrast, membership in the American Society for Training and Development, which serves a considerably more specialized audience, stands at about fifty-five thousand, with an annual budget of $15 million (Fischer and Schwartz, 1996, p. 957).

The point here is that the visibility and potential impact of an association that purports to represent such a diverse field must be called into question when its membership is so small. This is due, at least in part, to the fact that many people engaged in the education of adults either do not identify themselves with or are unaware of efforts to promote adult education broadly at the national level.

Another factor that needs to be considered relative to the impact of associations is the question of whose voices are reflected in the efforts of these groups. Historically, the American Association for Adult Education (AAAE) has been characterized in many circles as elitist. While this trait is often viewed in a negative light today, McClusky (1982) argues that in the early years of the movement, the adult education field "required the support of a prestigious foundation and the sponsorship and advocacy of the country's academic and intellectual elite to give it . . . instant prestige and respectability" so that the AAAE could come into existence (p. 9).

However, over time the need for this elitist stance faded. Subsequent national associations (for example, the Adult Education Association of the U.S.A. and the American Association for Adult and Continuing Education) have made active efforts to promote a more democratic structure within their policies and practices and have attempted to speak for divergent voices in the field. Clearly, many people in the field do not identify the national association as their voice. As was discussed in Chapter Ten, many of these educators practice outside the mainstream and thus may not be represented by the views and directions of a single national association.

All in all, professional associations have played an important role in the development of the adult education field. At the same time, these associations have probably been less influential in terms of providing a voice for adult educators nationwide than have associations in many other professions.

The Nature of Knowledge in Adult Education

The second theme we discussed in Chapter Nine was professional literature and information resources in the field. In this chapter, we expand the discussion to address the broader perspective of knowledge relative to adult education. Frequently, discussions of knowledge revolve around the role of research in a given field, but the range of knowledge that is relevant to adult education, as illustrated in Chapter Ten, clearly transcends the boundaries of traditional research and scholarship.

In examining the nature of knowledge in adult education, practitioners must continuously struggle with the question "What knowledge counts in adult education?" and with where the field's ideas should come from and how these ideas can be incorporated into the fabric of adult education. Chapters Nine and Ten presented very different responses to the question. While Chapter Nine emphasized knowledge derived from professional literature and information sources, Chapter Ten, in dealing with adult education's "invisible" side, shifts the emphasis to how knowledge that is not codified into the mainstream literature can help inform adult education. In a view of professionalization that stresses diversity and inclusiveness, both kinds of knowledge are valued.

The Formal Knowledge Base

During the 1920s and 1930s, when the adult education movement was first establishing a foothold in the United States, the individuals who provided leadership to the field came from a wide range of disciplines. A glance through the pages of the *Journal of Adult Education*, published between 1929 and 1941, reveals a virtual Who's Who of individuals from many corners of American intellectual and social life. Examples include historians Charles A. Beard and James Harvey Robinson, authors Dorothy Canfield Fisher and Bonaro Overstreet, social reformer Jane Addams, and former president Theodore Roosevelt. Since no "professional adult educators" were practicing during these early years, leadership and inspiration were brought to the budding field by people who saw the potential in serving adult learners.

As the professional tradition of adult education (Cotton, 1964) began to emerge during the 1930s, and as it became possible to earn graduate degrees in the field, a transition began to take place. During subsequent decades, the theories, practices, and ideals that drove adult education were increasingly those of individuals who identified themselves primarily as members of the adult education field. This transition is not unusual for an emerging field; indeed, today it is a sign that over the past six decades adult education has attracted large numbers of committed practitioners and has experienced a growth in both research and practice.

At the same time, however, this turning inward has led to a myopic view of whose knowledge counts and what kind of knowledge is considered "legitimate." Over the past three decades or so, this discussion has been rooted in a debate regarding the value of approaching adult education from an interdisciplinary perspective. A larger issue, though, is the question of what place informal knowledge and popular culture should play in informing adult education. The contributors to *Adult Education: Outlines of an Emerging Field of University Study* (Jensen, Liveright, and Hallenbeck, 1964)— commonly referred to as the "black book"—argued that while adult education had been establishing a unique perspective and body of knowledge on working with adult learners, it has also built its knowledge base by "borrowing and reformulating" knowledge from other disciplines for its own use (Jensen, 1964, p. 105). The black book, then, contains chapters that illustrate how adult education can adopt knowledge from sociology, social psychology, psychology, history, and organization and administration.

Taking a different perspective, Boyd and Apps (1980) argue that since "adult education has its own unique structure and function . . . it is an error to seek assistance from recognized disciplines until we have clearly understood the structure, function, problems, and purposes of adult education itself" (pp. 1–2). According to Boyd and Apps, by borrowing heavily from other disciplines, adult education is allowing itself to be defined by them. An alternative is to start by defining the field in terms of its "nature, function, methodology, setting, and audience" (p. 5); only then does it make sense to seek out other disciplines and to determine what they might contribute.

The Boyd-Apps model has provoked challenges from other adult educators. For instance, Carlson (1980) argues in the same volume that the model offers "the expression of only one philosophical approach—a utopian philosophy of adult education that posits the scientific use of institutions to create more perfect individuals and a more perfect society" (p. 174). His concern is that the view of adult education purported by the Boyd-Apps model overemphasizes professional practice at the expense of "independent, unorganized, and nonprofessional" activities in the field (p. 181). Cookson (1983) has also challenged the model on grounds that it fails to mention "any of the 'legitimate' contributions to the body of knowledge unique to adult education already made by other disciplines," such as self-actualization, reinforcement, social systems, job satisfaction, social class or socioeconomic status, and adult education participation as a subset of social participation (p. 48).

More recently, a follow-up volume to the so-called black book was published that emphasizes developments that have taken place in mainstream adult education since 1964 (Peters, Jarvis, and Associates, 1991). Like its predecessor, this volume addresses the link between adult education and several other disciplines—psychology, educational administration and leadership, sociology, philosophy, political science, and history. However, Jarvis points out that unlike the borrowing and reformulating perspective of the "black book," the newer volume stresses the examination of the disciplines "in terms of adult education, whereas adult education was examined in terms of the disciplines in the black book" (p. 3).

Sources of Informal Knowledge

In addition to formal knowledge, a second perspective on where adult education knowledge should come from is based on the belief—which we advocate—that practitioners need to cast the net much wider to ensure that such sources as general-trade books and biographies, popular culture, and informal knowledge are more fully incorporated into our vision of "legitimate" knowledge. For instance, many recent books written for a more general audience have much to say about the education of adults; examples include books by Cornel West (1993) and bell hooks (1994) on race and gender, Henry Giroux (1994) on learning about popular culture, Warren Bennis (1989) and Steven Covey (1989) on leadership, Peter Senge (1990) on the learning organization, Mihaly Csikszentmihalyi (1990) on the psychology of optimal experience, and Donald Schön (1983, 1987) on reflective practice. Similarly, biographies and autobiographies can offer valuable insights into the lives of others.

Another source of knowledge that lies outside the mainstream of adult education can be found in popular culture. In the 1930s, for instance, Leo Rosten (writing as Leonard Q. Ross, 1937) compiled a series of delightful short stories about Hyman Kaplan, a fictional adult student seeking to obtain citizenship. More recently, films such as *Philadelphia*, *Quiz Show*, *Dead Poets' Society*, *Renaissance Man*, *Educating Rita*, and *Higher Learning* can provide insights into various aspects of the human condition. So, too, do popular songs by artists such as Joan Baez, Harry Chapin, John Lennon and Paul McCartney, Pete Seeger, Bruce Springsteen, and many others.

In adult education, various writers have addressed the value of popular culture as a source of knowledge. For example, Ohliger (1985) developed a graduate course called "The Fictional Adult Educator" that looked at a wide range of films and plays, fictional stories, television shows, poems and songs, cartoons, and other sources of wit and humor. Merriam (1983) compiled a volume of readings that explored themes of adulthood through popular literature. E. A. Hill (1989) addressed the value of literary research in the study of reentry women and concluded that "from literary works, teachers can learn what kinds of things contribute to making adult students physically, mentally, and emotionally comfortable. And, unorthodox as it may seem, academicians would almost certainly profit from seeing themselves as their clients see them" (p. 10). Finally, Osborn (1990) discussed the value of learning through "classic" films, including *Apartment for Peggy*, *Joy in the Morning*, *Mother Is a Freshman*, and *Mr. Belvedere Goes to College*. Although Hill and Osborn stress the value of literature and film as topics for adult education research, the examples we have presented are intended to illustrate how popular culture can inform us about the human condition in ways rarely found in traditional adult education literature.

Yet another source of informal knowledge can be found in learning from ideas that are generated in actual practice. Traditionally, research on human behavior has been derived from the perspective of logical positivism. Essentially, this view "is con-

cerned only with knowledge of the world that is open to observation . . . anything that transcends the objective (physical) world is
not considered within the bounds of scientific investigation" (Garrison and Shale, 1994, p. 19). This line of thinking is the rationale
behind research studies based on observation, experimentation,
survey research, and the development and administration of standardized research instruments.

However, a very different approach—and one that is particularly
important in the arena of informal knowledge—is rooted in the
notion that there are individually constructed realities that can be
accessed only through qualitative methods of data collection.
Departing from positivism, this perspective holds that human
behavior can best be understood *within the context* of how and where
such behavior takes place. In other words, the most valuable
insights to be gained from research can be found when problems are
studied in the actual context in which they arise. This approach
emphasizes how the problems and perspectives are defined by those
being studied, and it employs methods such as participant observation, unstructured interviewing, and case studies (Bogdan and
Biklen, 1992; Merriam, 1988).

In adult education, some researchers have expanded on this perspective by advocating an approach to research that treats the participants as co-researchers. This approach, referred to variously as
participatory research, action research, and critical research, is based
on the idea that researchable problems begin with those who are
being studied; therefore, those who have the greatest stake in the
research should be active participants throughout the process. As
Merriam (1991) notes: "This type of research questions the origins
of the production of knowledge, who has access to knowledge, and
whose interests and ends [such] knowledge serves. It involves faith
in people's ability to produce their own knowledge through collective investigation of problems and issues, collective analysis of problems, and collective action to change the conditions that gave rise
to the problems in the first place. Participatory research is thus more

than a method of creating knowledge. It is also a process of education and consciousness-raising and 'of mobilization for action' (Gaventa, 1988, p. 19)" (p. 56).

Examples of participatory research can be found in a wide range of literature, including the journals *Convergence* (for example, Mellor, 1988; Foley and Flowers, 1992; Schmidt-Boshnick and Scott, 1995) and *Adult Education and Development;* in various research reports (for example, White and Merrifield, 1990; Merrifield, Norris, and White, 1991; Bingman, 1995); and publications from the Highlander Center in Tennessee and the Participatory Research Group in Toronto. More often, however, grassroots efforts to solve community problems are not formally documented but rather are passed on through informal networks of community-based educators and participatory researchers (Heaney, 1992).

Taken together, these sources of informal knowledge can help us reframe our understanding of knowledge about adult education and the adult learner. While the three approaches to informal knowledge we have discussed are different in many ways, they share at least two characteristics. First, they all emphasize socially constructed knowledge—that is, knowledge that is closely tied to the culture and social context in which it exists. Second, they are frequently located outside the realm of traditional adult education literature.

As attempts are made to reframe professionalization, it is important that informal knowledge sources play an increasingly vital role. Our view is that the entire realm of life experiences is a library of resources for the adult educator. To be sure, we believe that it is essential for adult educators to be conversant with and comfortable in their understanding of major concepts and literature produced from within the field. At the same time, to take a perspective that stresses the mastery of this rather specific body of knowledge *at the expense of* other kinds of knowledge is to greatly limit one's range of understanding. Sources of knowledge are limited only by our imaginations.

The Contributions of Graduate Study

A prime area of tension within adult education centers on the place of credentialing. In Chapter Nine, we addressed the impact of graduate study on the field. Similarly, in Chapter Ten we showed that some of the most important contributions to the education of adults have been made by individuals who have not been formally prepared in the field. The focus of this section, then, is on whether formal graduate study in adult education makes a difference.

One of the strongest indictments of graduate preparation in adult education was offered by Ingham and Hanks (1981), who argue that the "inability of the graduate programs in the field to clearly establish the superiority of the university-trained adult educator over the untrained one must be seen as a major failure of our graduate departments" (p. 21). As evidence of this point, Griffith (1989) points out that while nearly four thousand individuals in the United States and Canada have earned doctoral degrees in adult education, "most deans and directors of university extension divisions rarely seek out those with graduate preparation in this field when they hire new staff" (p. 8).

In an effort to address concerns about the lack of a common vision for adult education graduate study, the Commission of Professors of Adult Education (CPAE) adopted a set of standards in 1985. These standards address such areas as adult education curriculum, faculty qualifications, organization of graduate study, the nature of student programs, and resources and facilities. While there is no mechanism to enforce these standards, the document has served as a helpful planning tool for many graduate programs in the field. As such, the standards have the potential to increase the quality of graduate study in adult education and to create greater awareness of the existence and desirability of graduate study as a route to preparation in the field.

Documents such as the CPAE standards can prove useful in terms of helping to define what is valued by the field. At the same time, they can potentially reinforce the division between the mainstream and the invisible sides of the field by making operational and codifying practice in a way that promotes exclusion and gatekeeping. While we believe that there is value in developing and articulating a set of knowledge and skills that cuts across all areas of adult education, such a standard must be sensitive to the diversity of the field and to its potential to serve—intentionally or inadvertently—as a gatekeeping tool. If graduate study is to rise above the accusations that it is elitist and exclusionary, we will need to ask two questions: What does it mean to have a graduate degree in adult education? And can graduate study programs take steps to counter the elitism and gatekeeping that often occur in professional adult education?

Following are some questions that might be considered when exploring the future of graduate study.

- What unique qualities do graduate programs in adult education offer?

- Are there certain core proficiencies that all people who work with adult learners should possess?

- How can graduate study be structured to be more inclusive of all aspects of adult education practice?

- In what ways, other than through teaching in graduate programs, can adult education professors have an impact on greater numbers of people within the field?

- To what extent does the growth of graduate programs foster the potential for elitism in the professionalizing process?

- What roles might graduate study play in serving those whose practice lies outside the mainstream?

Other Issues Related to Professionalization

As we in adult education look to the future, the issues raised above will continue to provide the field with points of contention. In addition to these long-standing issues, however, many new concerns will arise to provoke potential controversy among those engaged in the education of adults. Some of these, such as divergent philosophies, new interpretations of adult education's past; the nature of adult education practice, and the increasing emphasis on a global perspective, have already been addressed in previous chapters. In this section, we would like to discuss two issues linked to professionalism that have been debated and will continue to grow in importance in the years ahead: *certification* and *ethics*.

Certification of Adult Educators

Closely related to the issue of graduate preparation in adult education is certification, which in recent years has emerged as a key issue throughout all spheres of education in the United States. In elementary and secondary schools, trends such as "career ladders" and competency testing are among the responses to certification, and adult education has not been exempt from the issue. For example, those who teach in adult basic education programs in most states are required to be certified. Usually, these teachers are required to be certified in elementary education; however, in several states, including Arkansas, Connecticut, Louisiana, Tennessee, and Virginia, various provisions exist that tie certification to coursework in adult education.

Over the years, graduate programs have been the major vehicle through which adult educators have been credentialed. However, there has been an ongoing dialogue about whether certification is a desirable avenue for practitioners to follow. Galbraith and Gilley (1985) define professional certification as "a voluntary process by which a professional association or organization measures the competencies of individual practitioners" (p. 12). Certification is different from both licensure, which is a mandatory legal requirement in some professions, and accreditation, which is based on an evaluation of instructional programs.

Since it serves as another form of credentialing, certification is often tied to professionalization of the field. Cameron (1981) notes that a link exists between certification and consumer protection.

She provides a rationale for certification based on several concerns: the changing nature of educational tasks that adult educators must address; a need for increased professional skills; and special competencies that adult educators need, such as knowledge in adult-learning principles, methods and materials for adult education, and program development. According to Cameron, certification for adult educators "should be voluntary, should designate quality, and should be accomplished by the profession itself" (p. 80). She goes on to conclude that "since the purpose of certification is to enhance quality, not simply to restrict professional entry [into the field], certification should be based on qualifications rather than simply on acquisition of credits in adult education" (p. 81).

Other positions in favor of certification have been presented by Galbraith and Gilley (1986) and B. A. White (1992). According to Galbraith and Gilley, certification should be a voluntary process regulated by a profession in order to determine the competencies that practitioners possess. White (1992) suggests that the process of certification "may serve to generate a customized career-long learning design or an individual curriculum for the highly motivated, self-directed learner" (p. 137). She goes on to note other benefits of certification, some of which include recognition for practitioners, greater clarity to the adult education field, added credibility to existing programs, and the opportunity to demonstrate a common core of knowledge and skills. Essentially, White's position illustrates how certification can serve as a component of professionalization.

Since certification can be viewed as one mechanism for professionalization, many of the arguments against it run parallel to the case against professionalization; charges of elitism and gatekeeping, reducing the essence of practice into identifiable "competencies," and questions about who would "own" such a process are common to the debates over both certification and professionalization. One of the most fully developed positions against certification has been presented by James (1981, 1992), who argues that certification is neither feasible nor necessary. She draws this conclusion by challenging five assumptions that certification advocates have presented. First, she questions whether "there is a core of knowledge and skills that can be identified as unique to adult education" (1981, p. 85). Second, she raises a concern about who will determine what level of competency should be used. Third, James challenges the assumption that a certification process could be designed; specifically she questions who would develop and oversee such a process. Fourth, she challenges the assumption that certification can provide recognition and protection for the field, because such efforts "may ultimately remove some effective but uncertified instructors from the teaching market" (p. 93). Finally, James wonders whether a relationship could ever be established between certification and effectiveness.

More recently, James (1992) has reflected on her earlier position and has reaffirmed this view. While she suggests that today, "certification is a possible benefit to professionalization," she believes that on a large-scale basis certification "is not only impractical but also unattainable for the entire field" (p. 130). The case against large-scale certification, according to James, is grounded in questions about the professional status of the field and its potential to develop, implement, maintain, and demonstrate success through such a process.

Another way to frame the issue might be to move away from an emphasis on grand-scale certification toward considering the potential of certification programs for specific segments of the field. Indeed, while James argues against large-scale certification, she believes that certification may be a possible direction for specific areas within the field. As was mentioned earlier, some states have established certification for teachers in adult basic education (ABE) programs. A rationale for certifying ABE teachers might be that traditionally such teachers had to be certified in elementary or secondary education. With the introduction of adult education certification, these teachers are assured of being exposed to adult education principles and practices before they can qualify for working with adult learners.

In thinking about the desirability and feasibility of certification for adult educators, then, it is important to consider questions related to who would develop and administer such programs, whether a core set of knowledge and skills can be identified that is relevant to all who work with adult learners regardless of the context or setting, whether "specialized" certification efforts (for instance, ABE and human resource development trainers) sufficiently overcome the major criticisms of large-scale certification programs, and whether certification is merely another way of excluding certain groups and individuals from functioning as educators of adults. To be sure, certification is an issue that will remain relevant to those involved with the adult education field for years to come.

Ethics and Adult Education

Few topics have received more attention throughout society in recent years than ethics. Much of this interest has been influenced by at least two factors: the increasing visibility of public scandals (beginning with Watergate in the 1970s), and an increased emphasis on consumer awareness at all levels of society. In any case, ethics is a topic that is pervasive throughout such realms as politics, business, medicine, science, journalism, and, yes, education. In the field of adult education, one response to the desire to promote ethical practice has been to raise the question of whether adult education should have a code of ethics.

Those who favor a code of ethics often stress such themes as consumer rights and professional responsibility and accountability. A code of ethics, it can be argued, can provide a clear set of guidelines to direct the conduct of those who practice in the field and to minimize the potential for abuse of clients. Sork and Welock (1992) argue that the field is obliged to develop a code and that such a code can offer several benefits:

1. A code is a tool that can steer educators away from "ethically hazardous practices" (p. 120).

2. A code can contribute to policymaking within adult education agencies.

3. A code "will provide limited protection from unethical practice for adult learners" (p. 120).

4. A code can be used in the professional preparation of adult
   educators by communicating shared values.

5. A code will make the moral dimension of practice more visible.

6. A code can be used by adult education agencies to differentiate
   them from those providers who do not subscribe to such a code.

In essence, the arguments on behalf of a code of ethics parallel those
in support of professionalization. As we noted in Chapter Nine,
Houle (1980) identified a code of ethics as an essential element of
the professionalizing process.

   Because codes of ethics are often tied to professionalization, critics of these codes typically use arguments such as those presented
against professionalization and certification; for example, they argue
that a code is likely to be overly prescriptive and thus out of touch
with the realities of day-to-day practice. In addition, there are questions about who would develop and enforce such a code and, indeed,
if it is even possible to have a single code that represents the diverse
interests of the contemporary adult education field. Cunningham
(1992) is more explicit in her criticism: "It is inappropriate because
codes are developed to privilege a group of persons who are either in
or working toward gaining positions of power. Further, written codes
are an ineffective means of preventing unfair, unequal, incompetent,
or negligent treatment of others. . . . Codes of ethics freeze the
oughts in time and space, tend to decontextualize normative behavior, privilege those in power positions, and inhibit the ability of
individuals or groups to reconstruct social reality" (pp. 107–108).

   In a similar vein, Carlson (1988) argues against professional
codes of ethics on political grounds: "The development of norms of
professional practice is not an ethical undertaking. It is a political

undertaking. Law and medicine may have reached the top of the professional ladder by dedication and hard work. But it was by dedication and hard work primarily in the political arena" (p. 167). According to Carlson, the case against a code of ethics is tied to the belief that attempting "to enforce any code of ethics on adult education would be falling into the professionalization trap and accepting the professional ethic, which is based on expertise, authority, monopoly, and mystification" (p. 169).

Another way to consider ethics in adult education is to look beyond the code-of-ethics question and instead focus on what constitutes ethical practice. Brockett (1988b, 1994) presented a model for ethical decision making that stresses the role of the individual making the decision. A response to an ethical dilemma involves the interaction of three key components: values, obligations, and consequences. *Values* center on the individual's basic belief system and commitment to it. Such beliefs address ideas about human nature, perceptions of adult learners, and views about the nature of ethics (for example, should ethical decisions be based on the consequences of such decisions, or on the fulfillment of a duty?). *Obligations* address the question of responsibilities. The obligations of adult educators lie in many different directions, and it is necessary to determine which obligations should take precedence in a given dilemma. *Consequences* refer to the realization that any dilemma will have more than one possible response. However, each decision will also have consequences. Thus, the educator needs to weigh options and consequences in relation to decisions about obligations and values.

Cervero and Wilson (1994a) also discuss the notion of responsibility in the context of program planning. They argue that in every planning activity, it is important to ask to whom the adult educator "is politically and ethically answerable" (p. 5). Their answer is that "the planner is responsible for negotiating the interests of all people who may be affected by the educational program" (p. 5).

This approach to ethical decision making is process-oriented, and as such it does not prescribe specific responses to specific dilemmas. It should be noted that this process does not satisfy the concerns of those who oppose individual approaches to making ethical decisions. However, it has direct relevance to practice since it is intended to help practitioners engage in a process of critical reflection on the ethical dilemmas they face.

Reflective Practice: An Emerging Perspective

Most of the chapters in this book have outlined the formal knowledge base of the field. But the actual practice of adult education involves much more than familiarity with the basic knowledge, skills, concepts, and theories of the field—or what Donald Schön (1987) calls "technical rationality." Rather, effective practice also involves being able to reflect critically upon our practice and as a result consider alternative ways of engaging in our work.

In laying a foundation for the idea of reflective practice, Schön (1987) has suggested that professional practice can be viewed as an art. He uses the term *professional artistry* to describe "the kinds of competence [that] practitioners sometimes display in unique, uncertain, and conflicted situations" (p. 22). Artistry, as Schön uses the term, involves the ability to perform in a situation without having to consciously think about it. Such artistry is often closely linked to what Polanyi (1967) called "tacit knowledge." If, for example, we see a familiar face in a crowd, we do not need to think about how we determine who the person is—we "just know." Similarly, when a jazz musician improvises a solo, he or she does not consciously think through each note to be played; and writers and painters might not be able to break down into identifiable components the specific process by which they create—they "just know."

In discussing the idea of reflection, Schön distinguishes between reflection on action and reflection in action. Certainly, it is possible to think back on one's actions to gain insights into what may have led to a particular outcome; this process is reflection on action. Brookfield (1986) emphasizes the role of critical thinking in this process. Critical thinking occurs when people question information, ideas, or behaviors. According to Brookfield, four components of critical thinking include (1) identifying and challenging assumptions; (2) recognizing how context influences thoughts and actions; (3) considering alternative ways of living and thinking; and (4) being unwilling to accept something just because "it's always been done that way" or because an "expert" says it is so. Brookfield suggests that a way to engage in critical thinking is to identify a critical incident or situation from practice that can be described and reflected upon using the four components listed above. Critical thinking goes hand in hand with critical reflection.

Suggesting that reflective practice involves both critical thinking and learning, Peters (1991b) has also identified a four-step model that can be used in the process of reflective practice. Peters's model involves reflecting on action and thus is a precursor to reflection in action. The DATA (Describe, Analyze, Theorize, Act) model can be summarized as follows:

1. Describe the problem, task, or incident that represents some critical aspect of practice needing examination and possible change.
2. Analyze the nature of what is described, including the assumptions that support the actions taken to solve the problem, task, or incident.
3. Theorize about alternative ways to approach the problem, task, or incident.
4. Act on the basis of the theory [Peters, 1991, p. 91; emphasis in original].

Peters's DATA model offers a useful way to introduce the process of reflection on action to those who may be unfamiliar with it. At the University of Tennessee, Knoxville, for example, a graduate course on reflective practice has become a core requirement for all candidates of master's degrees and doctorates in adult education, and the idea and spirit of reflective practice are promoted across the curriculum.

In contrast to reflection on action, Schön places greater emphasis on reflection in action, which occurs "in the midst of action [when] we can still make a difference to the situation at hand" (1987, p. 26). Just as most of the cases that a typical physician sees are not "in the book," so too is the educator faced with having to respond effectively to new and unique situations. On paper, a teacher may teach the same course time and again; however, because of the dynamics among class members; the physical, psychological, and social environment; the teacher's own changing perspectives; and so on, no two classes are quite alike. The teacher who engages in reflective practice is able to recognize subtleties that contribute to this uniqueness and, more important, can respond differently and effectively to each group.

However, reaching the point where one can "just know" what to do requires developing one's artistry to a level at which reflection in action becomes almost automatic. Educators need to develop a repertoire of knowledge, skills, and attitudes on which they can draw in an almost subconscious way.

What does reflective practice mean for adult education? It would appear that the model has potential to broaden the view of what it means to professionalize—primarily because it reframes the issue in a way that extends beyond the boundaries of technical rationality found in most traditional models of professionalization. Although the idea is relatively new, there is evidence that reflective practice holds promise as another way to think about professionalization in adult education.

Cervero (1988) for example, uses Schön's notion (1987) of reflection in action as a foundation for his approach to continuing professional education. He observes that "[m]ost of the spontaneous actions that professionals take do not stem from a rule or plan that was in the mind before acting. Professionals constantly make judgments and decisions, and cannot state the rules or theories on which they were based" (p. 43). This view is the antithesis of technical rationality and thus offers a whole new way of thinking about professional knowledge.

Reflective practice is perhaps one of the most exciting directions for the future of professional development in adult education. It moves us away from concern for the mere "application" of knowledge and skills toward a view that more fully interweaves theory and practice. Even more important, it is a process that can undergird practice in any context; therefore, it transcends the kinds of questions that have traditionally divided the mainstream and invisible sides of adult education.

Future of the Field

Throughout this book, we have attempted to address a wide range of ideas relative to the education of adults. We have presented different perspectives in the hope that you will think critically about where they fit into the big picture of the field. In essence, it has been our purpose to look at the past and present of adult education so that we could begin thinking about and acting in ways to create the kind of future we seek for the field (Hiemstra, 1988a).

Of course, a central issue in any effort to create the future means recognizing that there is no single, unified vision of adult education. Thus, when considering the future of the field, we need to return to some of the questions raised in earlier chapters:

- What counts as adult education?

- Is it possible to have a single, unified vision for the field?

- Does professionalization make a difference?

Griffith (1989) and Kett (1994) have offered some challenges by arguing, essentially, that the practice of adult education will continue to thrive with or without professional adult educators. Griffith, for example, writes that "as long as there is room for visionaries to try new ideas without first satisfying arbitrary criteria for their qualifications, the education of adults will remain a lively, responsive, and socially useful activity, with or without the maturation of the adult education profession" (1989, pp. 12–13). Similarly, in his historical analysis of the field, Kett concludes that while adult education today is thriving, professionals in the field "have become increasingly marginal to the education of adults" (p. xviii). If you are new to the field, these assessments of adult education may be somewhat disturbing, and rightly so. However, we suggest that you translate this concern into a challenge for the future.

Tough (1991), in a broad-ranging discussion of the future, suggests that the question we must be willing to ask about the future of society is *"What is most important of all?"* (p. 7, emphasis added). He suggests a process whereby we can arrive at an answer to this question. While Tough has designed this exercise as a way of examining the future of society in general, we as adult educators may find it helpful for asking what really matters to each of us in the field. If we substitute "adult education" for "the universe," Tough's first question can help us think through priorities for the future of adult education: "What is of supreme value? Of everything in the universe *[adult education]* (past, present, and future), what do you treasure and value beyond all else? What would you not want the universe *[adult education]* to lose or give up for the sake of anything else?" (p. 7). Ultimately, we must narrow our concerns in a way that is manageable to comprehend while not oversimplifying some very complex ideas.

We believe that regardless of our individual orientation to the education of adults, each of us must be willing to continuously ask ourselves two seminal questions that are clearly interrelated and have permeated our entire discussion throughout this book. First we must ask, *What do I believe should be the primary purpose of adult education?* This question is framed in an understanding that adult education serves myriad purposes in our society and that each of us needs to ask toward which purpose (or purposes) we wish to direct our energies and actions.

As we discussed in Chapter Four, this question is often played out in distinguishing between placing priority on individual growth (see, for example, Knowles, 1986; Beatty, 1992) or on social change (for example, Ilsley, 1992; Finger, 1995). It can also be reflected in the distinction between striving for the goal of "education for all" and directing limited financial and human resources toward those who, it is generally believed, will make the most of such opportunities; this is the equity-versus-elitism argument.

Although elitism would not have many proponents in contemporary adult education, William Henry III (1994) argues in a recent book that current efforts to promote inclusion across American society are a "brand of anti-intellectual populism" (p. 3), and that not all ideas or voices deserve equal consideration. Rather, he argues, we should be directing our energy and resources toward promoting the best of the best. While this case for elitism is likely to touch a nerve with many adult educators—particularly those with strong progressive, humanist, and critical influences—Henry's argument needs to be heard and understood, since it is not unlike the positions of many who seek to promote reform in education throughout society today.

The second question we must each ask ourselves—*Where do I stand on professionalization of the adult education field?*—is intimately related to the question of what we value as the primary purpose of adult education. Every one of us who makes a commitment to work with adult learners must come to terms with where we stand on such concerns as professional associations, the nature of knowledge in adult education, graduate study, certification of adult educators, and ethical practice. In the years ahead, it is doubtful that the tensions between those who favor further professionalization and those who practice beyond the mainstream will be easily resolved. However, if the education of adults is to thrive in the future, it will be crucial to find new ways of communicating what counts as adult education and who counts as an adult educator.

In closing, we believe that each of us must ultimately develop a vision for the field and be willing to commit to working toward that vision. By doing so, we are in a position to truly make a difference in the future of adult education. We hope that this book has helped you to take a critical look at your practice and that it will encourage you to tackle the difficult questions about how you wish to serve those whose lives you touch.

Epilogue: A Decade in Review and Trends for the Future

Adult education is a dynamic field of practice responsive to the context in which it takes place, at times adjusting tried and true ways of doing things to new circumstances, at other times challenging old ways of thinking and doing. What we wrote a decade ago was a snapshot of the field at that time, a view embedded in historical context. While that content is still a largely accurate portrayal of the field today, in the ten years since *The Profession and Practice of Adult Education* was first published, a number of trends have emerged that are currently shaping the field. For the most part, the trends per se are not new; rather it is the context of today's world that gives each issue a new perspective. We have identified five issues or trends that we believe will continue to engage practitioners and scholars in these early decades of the twenty-first century: (1) globalization, (2) workplace learning and human resource development, (3) holistic conceptions of learning, (4) critique and diversity, and (5) professionalization and practice.

Globalization

Many of us have had the experience of calling a catalogue company and having our order taken by someone answering the phone in India. Likewise, our television news might be reporting on an event in another part of the world *as it happens*. The world, as Friedman

(2005) points out, is now "flat." We are interconnected with the world in ways never before imagined. This interconnectedness, or globalization, has been defined as "a movement of economic integration, of cultural homogenization, and of technological uniformization" (Finger, 2005, p. 269).

Globalization is an enormously complex phenomenon, defined in various ways, and viewed as both a positive and negative force. Often associated with the outsourcing of manufacturing to low-wage, labor-intensive developing countries, and with transnational companies that operate across and outside the control of nation states, globalization is intricately interwoven with the "market economy." The change in how business is conducted has been dramatic. In just fifty years, business has moved from a domestic-focused enterprise where products were developed and marketed at home, to expanding to international markets to a multinational phase where firms organized "their multinational operations into highly integrated and standardized global lines of business" (Zieghan, 2000, p. 315). In the fourth and current "global" phase, companies have organized highly "flexible systems" that are "globally coordinated and that emphasize top quality, least cost, and state-of-the-art production and distribution" (p. 315). Friedman (2005) recounts a news report of this "global" phase in which some McDonald's restaurants are experimenting with using call centers to process drive-through orders. The order taker is in a call center "more than 900 miles, or 1,450 kilometers, away, connected to the customer and to the workers preparing the food by high-speed data lines." This system has had "lower costs, greater speed and fewer mistakes" (p. 40).

Even culture and education become commodities in the globalized market economy:

> In market terms, culture is an industry that involves producing and exchanging cultural goods and services for profit; education is an industry that involves producing and exchanging educational goods and services for

profit. . . . As societies integrate through globalization
there are both positive and negative outcomes. For
example, cultural integration brings down barriers among
people at the same time that its homogenization of traditions and customs can lead to loss of identity. Likewise,
educational integration provides a global market of ideas,
debate, and critical thought at the same time that it
moves education from a public good to private gain.
Thus, globalization and the market economy combine to
release forces that enslave and liberate alike [Merriam,
Courtenay, and Cervero, 2006, p. 2].

But globalization is not just about the market economy. It is also
about the movement of people, services, goods, and ideas across
national borders. Communication technology has enabled the flow
of information, ideas, and values. Nowhere is this more visible than
in mass media. "Because they are so pervasive, these global communication networks of the mass media in effect become systems of
informal adult education" (Guy, 2006, p. 64). While globalization
of mass media can be employed in positive ways as an informal adult
education system, Guy worries that the opposite is happening. Since
ownership of mass media is concentrated in the hands of a few,
these few "possess the capability to manipulate, enforce, and reinforce the messages they prefer for a large-scale audience on a global
level." The consequence of this power is to "steer consumers (learners) away from critical, socially conscious forms of learning and
social action" (p. 64). Guy also sees this globalized mass media as a
threat to diversity when only stereotypical images are presented,
and to democracy when only one perspective on a social issue is
advanced.

Technology is a major partner in the globalization process. Multinational companies rely on sophisticated communication technology
to run meetings, conduct business, and so on in an arena of collapsed
time and space. This wedding of globalization and technology is also

reshaping higher education. As Mason (2003) points out, media technologies "facilitate transnational circulation of text, images, and artifacts." Students in all parts of the world are demanding online courses from institutions all over the world, and there is a discernable "rise of international and virtual organizations offering Web-based education and training" to meet the demand (p. 744).

Globalization seems to benefit those countries that are already economically developed, while others "like Zambia are virtually excluded from the market" (Jarvis, 2004, p. 5). Furthermore, by exacerbating the gulf between rich and poor, some believe that globalization is destabilizing the world, creating factional and ideological conflicts. For example, the United States with only four percent of the world's population is "seen everywhere as the principal engine and principal beneficiary of global capitalism. We are also seen as 'almighty,' 'exploitative,' and 'able to control the world'" (Chua, 2003, p. 16), generating resentment, often with deadly consequences. Even within our own North American borders, globalization has had an impact. Hill and Moore (2000), for example, explain how global trends are disadvantaging rural economies:

> Small-scale fishing, logging, mining, and farming are in decline, which is connected to the loss of productive work from local economies. . . . The disintegration of rural economies can be connected to the evolution of large North American companies into giant multinational corporations with huge investments around the world (Fellegri, 1997; Theobald, 1996). In a nonsustainable economy, based on technology and manufacturing, jobs are often exported overseas where labor costs are lower. As adult educators, our ability to be effective in the rural community is compromised by decisions made far from home (Hall, 1996), yet the marginalization of rural people associated with the global economy remains unaddressed [p. 349].

Clearly, globalization challenges both our practice and our philosophy as adult educators. Adult educators from around the world are asking us to examine globalization and its various manifestations with a critical eye (Fiallos, 2006; Finger, 2005; Goerne, 2006; Groener, 2006; Guy, 2006; Holst, 2006; Schied, 2006). Folkman (2006) for example, suggests that we need to facilitate cognitive development in our learners in order for them to mentally cope with the pace and level of globalization. Are we as adult educators just to respond by preparing and training workers for the global workplace? Certainly we need to consider what literacy and job skills are needed in today's market. Friedman (2005) writes that "there is only one message: You have to constantly upgrade your skills" (p. 237) and that we need to make ourselves "untouchable" by preparing for jobs that cannot be outsourced. But what of the social and not just economic aspects of our practice? As Cunningham (2000, p. 577) has so astutely observed, "the question that currently divides many adult educators is whether to locate their practice in civil society or the economic sector." She believes that it is not necessarily an either-or choice. We can all participate in "the realignment of the state, the market, and civil society" through working critically in each sector: "Within civil society adult educators have the greatest challenge in building democratizing structures to confront unchecked economic forces. Within the state, linkages could be built in building transnational structures from below and a legal and policy environment fostering social demand from civil society. Finally, within the economic sphere, those in HRD could reconceptualize their work by framing a critique from a societal demand analysis rather than the almost universal single 'bottom line' criterion of economic profits" (Cunningham, 2000, p. 579).

Globalization is an extremely complex phenomenon, a phenomenon that is defining the world in which we live. We have been able to present only some of its broad outlines—a canvas of sorts upon which we place the following discussions of the workplace and human resource development, learning, diversity, and the profession of adult education. These topics are integrally connected to each other and to globalization.

Workplace Learning, Human Resource Development, and Adult Education

Few areas of practice are more directly associated with contemporary adult education than the workplace. As we noted in Chapter Five, Rachal (1989) described the workplace as "the engine that is changing the nature of adult education" (p. 7). Rachal's metaphor has, indeed, come to pass over the last decade. Although this is not a new development per se, it nonetheless is worthy of discussion because in addition to being the most prevalent site for adult learning, the workplace has often been a source of contention in terms of who *owns* the domain of workplace learning and what *counts* as learning in the workplace context. Learning in the workplace, or training, is often claimed by both the human resource development (HRD), and adult education fields, as well as several other fields, perhaps most notably industrial psychology. Historically, the dynamic between HRD and adult education relative to workplace learning has been interesting and has at times been a source of contested territory.

Briefly stated, one view emphasizes the connections between adult education and HRD while another view emphasizes the differences between the fields and questions the desirability of building connections between them. In the following discussion, we share several perspectives that illustrate this tension.

Adult educators who have been critical of the HRD field have often done so on the belief that HRD emphasizes learning as a means to helping organizations increase profits while ignoring the historic role of adult education as a means of promoting social change and social justice. Cunningham (1996) illustrates this point in a discussion of "learning for earning," which she describes as "putting the entire educational system to work for the market to make the rich richer and the poor poorer" (n.p.). In a similar vein, Baptiste (2001) has examined the implications of human capital theory for the education of adults. In his analysis, Baptiste argues that human capital theorists "construe social inequalities not as injustices, the result of exploitation and oppression, but rather as the natural and inevitable outcomes of a competitive free market" (p. 195). Although Cunningham and Baptiste are not writing solely about the workplace context, the implications for HRD and the workplace are clear. The argument here is that since HRD is designed to help businesses increase profitability, it is not truly committed to helping bring about social change by empowering learners and workers.

Like Baptiste, Schied (2001) raises concerns about what he sees as the human capital emphasis of HRD. Drawing from the historical development of workers' education and labor education, through the emergence of personnel and HRD departments, Schied illustrates how the control of workplace learning has shifted over time from the learner to the organization. He concludes that "if adult education is to be concerned with the democratic possibilities within the workplace, then a first step needs to be an unmasking of the psychological forms of control within the humanistic language of HRD" (p. 134).

Approaching the HRD/adult education divide from a different perspective, Bierma, Cseh, Ellinger, Ruona, and Watkins (2001) discuss how HRD is often marginalized within the adult education field. They state that "there is little space on the agenda for HRD at adult education research conferences" and that sessions about HRD at these meetings "tend to be less constructive than combative" (p. 51). Because of this dynamic, Bierma et al. state that "many adult educators who are interested in HRD have moved to circles that are more hospitable" (p. 51). As a result, the influence of adult educators on HRD is diminishing. In an attempt to address this problem, Bierma et al. have identified ten myths often associated with HRD that have contributed to criticism from the adult education field. These are:

1. HRD Professionals Are Capitalist Sympathizers
2. HRD Professionals Embrace Pavlovian Behaviorism
3. HRD Has No Ethics
4. HRD Professionals Do Not Deeply Reflect on Practice, Theory, or Philosophy
5. The Critiques Represent the Majority of HRD Practice
6. HRD Cannot Influence the System
7. HRD Lacks an International Perspective
8. The Primary Role of HRD Professionals Is Educating Adults
9. HRD Exploits the Disenfranchised According to Race, Gender and Class
10. HRD is a Subset of Adult Education [pp. 52–57]

The authors offer evidence to refute each of the above myths. In an epilogue to this paper, Karen Watkins observed that as one who participates in both the adult education and HRD worlds, she felt as if she were "bicultural" and, in fact, marginalized in both arenas.

The last myth is of particular interest to adult educators. In a *New Directions for Adult and Continuing Education* sourcebook on workplace learning (Rowden, 1996), one of the critical questions debated is whether HRD is a "part" of adult education. Dirkx (1996) answers in the affirmative arguing that "HRD continues to be influenced by an ideology of scientific management and reflects a view of education where the power and control over what is learned, how, and why is located in the organizational leadership, corporate structure, and HRD staff" (p. 42). He contends that HRD needs to move away from its market-driven focus toward a more democratic ideal that reflects the adult education tradition. By contrast, Willis (1996) points out that HRD draws from a wide range of fields and adult education is but one of these. She states that it is important for HRD professionals to draw from whatever resources inform practice. In this view, HRD is hardly a subset of adult education; instead, adult education is only one of many fields that contribute to informing HRD.

Several authors have written about the value of integrating concepts and practices of adult education and HRD. When Malcolm Knowles died in 1997, Elwood F. Holton III and Richard A. Swanson updated and expanded Knowles's classic work *The Adult Learner.* In the most recent edition, these authors continue to seek common ground between adult education and HRD. However, they also emphasize a fundamental difference in perspectives on adult learning. They point out that the "goals and purposes for which adult learning is employed" (Knowles, Holton, and Swanson, 2005, p. 165) emphasize individual control in adult education and organizational control in HRD. From an HRD perspective, then, learning is viewed as a means of enhancing performance within an organization in order to help the organization to thrive.

Bierema (2000) also lends a voice to the potential of building stronger connections between HRD and adult education when she suggests that bringing these fields together "seems a much simpler task than changing the global economy" (p. 290). She goes on to state that the two fields have potential to complement each other; however, failing "to work together may result in HRD swallowing adult education, at least in U.S. higher education settings" (p. 291).

Akdere and Conceicao (2006) suggest that the traditional emphasis in HRD on behaviorism and performance needs to be broadened in order to deal with current workplace learning concerns. They conclude that while there are clear differences between the two fields, "a complementary relationship between the two professions has been emerging to cope with the changes that affect individuals and organizations as the line distinguishing them blurs and their applications are becoming increasingly integrated" (p. 300).

Another example of how potential exists for bringing adult education and HRD into closer alignment is offered by Smith (2006), who, while pointing out that some in the business world look askance at adult education because of an "ivory tower" perception, believes that there is much potential for forging partnerships between the two fields.

Yet another perspective on the HRD/adult education link is offered by Fenwick (2004), who advocates a critical theory of HRD. She suggests that adult education theorists who have "taken up an antagonistic position to the HRD field" based on various critical perspectives would be better served "if these energies were diverted to support a space *within* HRD to nurture critical questions about power, interests, and equity" (p. 193).

Finally, in an editorial published in the *Human Resource Development Quarterly*, Hatcher (2006) identified several challenges to HRD, which include efforts to redefine HRD, expand theory and research by drawing from a wide range of perspectives and research approaches, create a long-term vision that, among other things, addresses the responsibilities of HRD professionals and the need to act with integrity, and finally, continue working toward becoming a recognized profession. Like Fenwick, Hatcher identifies the need for HRD to consider the role of critical and feminist theories and to address "important questions about workplace democracy, social justice, the environment, and equality" (p. 2). Although Hatcher is writing primarily to an HRD audience, his thoughtful commentary reflects a clear link to concerns that are relevant to adult educators and, more important, toward addressing some of the common ground between the fields.

The question of how adult education and HRD should or should not interface has been around for a long time, and we anticipate that it is not going to go away any time soon. Based on our understanding of the issues, we believe that it is crucial to listen carefully to the critical concerns raised by some adult educators. At the same time, we believe that adult education and HRD have much to gain by exchanging ideas and perspectives and seeking out common ground. And there is much to be lost by not doing so.

Holistic Conceptions of Adult Learning

Adult educators can be found in all of society's institutions including hospitals, prisons, museums, businesses, schools, churches, colleges and universities, community organizations, and online. What unites such a diverse field of practice is a focus on the adult learner. The more we know about who our adult learners are, about the social context in which they learn, and about *how* adults learn, the more effective our practice.

In this book, Chapter Six on adult learning introduced the reader to participation and characteristics of adult learners, and several models, concepts, and theories relevant to the process of learning in adulthood. Much of what we wrote in 1997 is still descriptive of adult learners and learning today. For example, the profile of the typical participant in adult education has remained the same through the most recent National Center for Education Statistics study conducted in 2001 (Merriam, Caffarella, and Baumgartner, 2007). Further, andragogy, self-directed learning, transformational learning, and knowledge of adult development are still foundational to understanding adult learning.

Some of the "emerging concepts" that we identified in Chapter Six have become major areas of research and writing. Two of those areas, training and development and critical and feminist pedagogy, are discussed in other sections of this Epilogue. Experiential learning and the context of adult learning (which includes two other of our emerging concepts—learning environment and situated cognition) have also received much attention in the last decade. What we did not attend to in 1997, but has become a prominent trend in the work on adult learning, is a more holistic understanding of learning; that is, how our bodies, our emotions, and our spirits are connected to knowing.

For centuries, our Western heritage has defined learning as a cognitive process located in the brain. The mind-body split is so ingrained in our notions of learning that until recently, investigations into learning have focused on how information is processed in the brain, and how knowledge is constructed through cognitive reflection on experience. By the time we are adults, learning that is valued, formal, and systematic is devoid of anything emotional or physical. However, most adults will acknowledge that we come to "know" through other means, perhaps through a "gut" reaction, a contemplative moment, a dream. Some of the most recent research and theory building in adult learning are based on the premise that knowledge construction and learning can be through pathways *other* than those that depend on the mind. Scholars are now trying to explain and legitimize the role played by emotions, the body, and the spirit in learning.

Knowledge construction is more than a cognitive process of meaning-making. We "know" through our emotions and our physical body. Dirkx (2001) argues that learning itself is inherently an imaginative, emotional act and that significant learning is inconceivable without emotion and feelings. It is through emotions that deeply personal, meaningful connections are made so that significant learning can take place. These connections are of two kinds. First, there is the connection to one's own inner experiences; "emotions are gateways to the unconscious and our emotional, feeling selves" (p. 69); second, "emotions and feelings can connect to the shared ideas within the world as well and are reflected in big words or concepts, such as Truth, Power, Justice, and Love" (p. 69). Through engagement with these emotions and the images they evoke, we can deepen "both the meaning of what we are studying and what it means to us in the course of our lives" (Dirkx, 2006a, p. 24).

Somatic or embodied learning is closely related to emotional responses in learning. In somatic knowing, we can learn through our bodies, as we do when we attribute physical, bodily responses to the psychological "stress" in our lives. Pert (1997) in fact argues that since receptors are found throughout the body's nerves, it would then follow that emotions could be stored and mediated by parts of the body other than just the brain. "These recent discoveries are important for appreciating how memories are stored not only in the brain, but in a *psychosomatic network* extending into the body" (p. 141). These very connections between the brain and aspects of our learning are also the subject of much recent scholarship in the neuroscience of learning (see Johnson and Taylor, 2006).

Although feminist scholars have for some time recognized the body as central to their analysis of female oppression (Chapman, 2002; Somerville, 2004), adult educators have only recently attended to how we learn through and in our bodies. Amann (2003) has proposed a four-part model of somatic knowing that may prove helpful for guiding inquiry into this dimension of knowing. *Kinesthetic* learning is familiar to athletes, artists, and dancers who learn in the movement of the body. *Sensory* learning is how we access information through our senses and is thus highly "embodied." *Affective* learning is the emotional or feeling dimension to embodied learning. Finally, *spiritual* learning is meaning-making through artistic expression, symbols, and rituals and intersects with the other three dimensions.

It is clear that a false dichotomy has been created by the Western philosophical bias that dissects the whole person into mind and body, limiting knowledge construction to what goes on in one's mind. Even physiologically, the mind, body, and emotions cannot be separated. And certainly in our own experiences of living and learning, we involve our emotions and our body at least as much as our intellect.

In addition to the mind and the body, a third dimension of a holistic perspective on learning is one's "spirit." Part of the difficulty in considering spirituality in learning has been definitional. There is little consensus about the boundaries of its meaning; the most writers can do is to define it as they are using the term. Nearly all agree that spirituality is not the same as religion which is an organized community of faith; rather, spirituality is more about one's own beliefs and experience of a higher power or higher purpose. Spirituality is "about how we construct meaning, and what we individually and communally experience and attend to and honor as sacred in our lives" (Tisdell, 2003, p. 29). It is, as Tolliver and Tisdell (2006, p. 38) write, "about meaning making and a sense of wholeness, healing, and the interconnectedness of all things."

Those who write about spirituality connect it with adult learning through meaning-making. As learners and as human beings we are inveterate meaning-makers. Tisdell (1999) makes several points about the relationship between spirituality, meaning-making, and adult learning. First, educators should recognize that a search for or an acknowledgment of the spiritual in the lives of adult learners "is connected to how we create meaning in our relationships with others. It is in our living and loving. It is also connected with how we understand a higher power or a transcendent being" (p. 93). Second, adults come into our classroom with this agenda (meaning-making), whether or not it is articulated. And third, meaning-making is knowledge construction that uses images and symbols "which often emanate from the deepest core of our being and can be accessed and manifested through art, music, or other creative work" (p. 93). Tolliver and Tisdell (2006) recognize that adult educators are not about promoting a particular type of spirituality, in fact may never use the word in the classroom. Rather, they are "committed to learning that makes a difference in learners' lives and increases their sense of knowing the content of the course in their heads, their hearts, their souls, and their entire being—that has meaning to them and makes a difference in the world" (p. 45).

There is a growing body of literature about *how* to facilitate learning from a holistic perspective, learning that involves not just the mind, but the body, emotions, and the spirit (English, Fenwick and Parsons, 2003; Tisdell, 2003; Vella, 2000). Journal writing, poetry, storytelling, myths, symbols, images, even dreams can be used in an adult learning environment to foster a more holistic learning experience. Indeed, an entire volume of *New Directions for Adult and Continuing Education* is devoted to *Artistic Ways of Knowing* (Lawrence, 2005). In this volume, authors speak to the use of art, music, poetry, photography, and drama to "extend the boundaries of how we come to know. . . . Making space for creative expression in the adult education classroom and other learning communities helps learners uncover hidden knowledge that cannot easily be expressed in words. It opens up opportunities for adult learners to explore phenomena holistically, naturally, and creatively, thus deepening understanding of self and the world" (Lawrence, 2005, p. 3).

Finally, we can make the case that a more holistic perspective on learning includes recognizing how culture shapes notions of learning and knowing. Tisdell's research positions spirituality in a cultural context wherein the meaning of spiritual experiences differs by culture as does "further expression" of those experiences "in art, music, or ritual" (2003, p. 86). Not only does culture structure how and what we know, it appears that many non-Western systems of knowing and learning are more holistic in what counts as learning. Two recent publications featuring non-Western epistemologies with regard to learning and the workplace (McLean and Johansen, 2006) and learning and knowing (Merriam, 2007) underscore the holism of other systems such as Buddhist, Maori, Native American, Hindu, African, and so on. Lifelong learning from a non-Western perspective is truly lifelong, seamless, and without institutional, age, or formal boundaries. The goals of this lifelong journey also vary from the typical Western goals of independence and personal and economic success. Rather, learning is to lead to enlightenment, to becoming "fully human," and to being an ethical, informed, and caring citizen in the community. The learning itself involves the mind, the body, and one's spirit in honoring indigenous myths, folklore, symbols, and a multitude of artistic forms of expression.

In summary, while there are currently a number of areas in adult learning receiving attention from both scholars and practitioners, it seems that many are writing about some aspect of learning beyond our historical emphasis on cognition and information processing. What we are calling holistic learning includes examining the interconnections among the body, emotions, and the spirit, and their relation to the mind. These connections are clearly visible in non-Western systems of knowing and learning.

Critique and Diversity

Adults have always learned and how they have learned—through informal self-study, experience, from others, or in the classroom—has constituted the practice of adult education. With the growth of more formal educational programs for adults has evolved the profession of adult education (see Chapters One and Nine). Dating from the 1920s when the first professional association (the American Association for Adult Education) was formed, the field has passed through several stages of development. We propose that in the decade since the publication of this book we have entered a phase of growing critique and attention to diversity. By critique we refer to the recognition and analysis of taken-for-granted worldviews and assumptions about all aspects of our practice. The "tools" for such analysis come from critical theory, Marxist philosophy, feminist theory, critical race theory, postcolonialism, queer theory, and multiculturalism. At the heart of these perspectives is a concern with social justice and emancipation. Attention to diversity is intertwined with this critical perspective for, as we analyze power and oppression as part of the critical debate, we become aware of who is marginalized and not in the mainstream of our practice.

A quick review of the handbooks of adult education reveals different phases of the field's development. The handbooks originated in 1934 and are overviews of the field of adult education at that point in time. After publications in 1934, 1936, and 1948, handbooks have been published each decade including 1960, 1970, 1980, 1989, and 2000 (and one is commissioned for 2010). The earliest handbooks were more or less directories of organizations, programs, and key providers of adult education. The 1948 handbook continued the directory format but added a few research studies and a section on professional common concerns such as the preparation of adult educators and leaders, and coordination and collaboration.

Beginning with the 1960 handbook, the format changed to chapters on aspects of the field but with more attention to what the literature (research and theoretical) had to say. From the 1960 edition through the 2000 handbook, the emphasis has been on "identifying, organizing, and prescribing the organization of the knowledge and practice of adult education as a professional and scientific endeavor" (Wilson and Hayes, 2000b, p. 11). But the 2000 handbook did something different from the earlier handbooks—overlaying the description of the field at this point in time is a stance of *reflection and critique*. Authors of the 2000 handbook were challenged by the editors "to rethink how we think and act, to question how we have continued to insist on what we think is the proper (scientific) relation between knowledge and practice, to open up for debate and change the very nature of how we understand the world of adult and continuing education and our ways of acting in it" (Wilson and Hayes, 2000b, p. 12). In addition to all chapter authors taking a critical perspective, there are specific chapters exploring these issues such as "The Concept of Critically Reflective Practice," "Different Perspectives on Teaching for Critical Consciousness," "The Invisible Politics of Race in Adult Education," "Cultures of Transformation," "The Politics of Knowledge Construction," and so on.

While adult educators have been writing from a critical perspective since the 1980s and certainly this perspective can be traced to earlier writings by Freire in particular (see Chapter Two), the 2000 handbook validated this critically reflective perspective as mainstream in the scholarship of the field. In the trends that we have discussed so far in this chapter, we can see how a critical perspective adds depth to our understanding of the impact of these forces. Adult educators writing about globalization, for example, question whose interests it serves, who stands to gain by companies becoming transnational, and what the "downside" of global media is when ownership is in the hands of a few. Neither is technology an "equalizer" for access to education. In the United States, "high-income households are twenty times more likely to have access to the Internet than low-income families," and "two-thirds of college-educated people have access to the Internet and only 6% of those with primary or elementary education" (Moore, 2001, ¶25). With regard to the workplace and human resource development, writers like Fenwick (2005) and Bierema (2000) are challenging the "bottom line" mentality of corporate HRD: "The work to make HRD more socially responsible in a globalizing context demands that the performance-based assumptions of performativity, discourse, credibility, and power be questioned. This challenge calls for both adult educators and HRD professionals to critically assess how HRD knowledge is created and identify constructive measures that can be taken to provide a more balanced perspective for HRD research, theory, and practice" (Bierema, 2000, p. 286).

A critical perspective is permeating other areas of adult education practice. Mezirow's (2000) theory of transformational learning, which is currently receiving more attention than any other area of adult learning, is firmly based in a critical theory foundation. Drawing from Habermas's critical theory philosophy, transformational learning is about critically examining our underlying assumptions regarding how we see the world. It is through this critical reflection on assumptions, reflective discourse, and action that we become freed or emancipated from uncritical acceptance of others' purposes, values, and beliefs. However, as we noted in Chapter Six, not all writers agree that transformational learning truly reflects a critical viewpoint (Collard and Law, 1989).

Through the work of Cervero and Wilson (1994, 2005), a critical perspective is being applied to program development. They maintain that planning an adult education program is much more than a simple technical process. All stakeholders, such as sponsors, learners, and the community, have interests that shape their participation in the process. These interests are negotiated in the context of power—who has what power to effect which changes. Cervero and Wilson (2005) explain their perspective: "In the face of power, we continually argue for the ethical commitment to nurture a substantively democratic process when planning programs. This understanding of people acting in context not only accounts for planners' experiences but also provides the best opportunity to produce educational programs that enlarge people's life chances in the real world" (p. 102).

Another recent work from a general critical perspective is Brookfield's *The Power of Critical Theory: Liberating Adult Learning and Teaching* (2005). Here Brookfield proposes a critical theory framework for a theory of adult learning. The core of this theory is that adult learners must recognize how thoughts and actions are governed by unexamined beliefs. To enable adult learners to do this, there are seven "learning tasks": challenging ideology, contesting hegemony, unmasking power, overcoming alienation, learning liberation, reclaiming reason, and practicing democracy (Brookfield, 2005). He also answers the question of why engage in critically reflective practice:

> For most of us, critical reflection is premised on the idea that change for the better is, in spite of all the contradictory complications of the postmodern condition, still a real possibility. . . . We do our work as adult educators because we believe that through our practice we can help ourselves and others lead more authentic and compassionate lives in a world organized according to the ideals of fairness and social justice. A critically reflective pose increases our chance of taking informed actions in pursuit of this project. . .
>
> But, more fundamentally, it is clear to me that taking a critically reflective stance towards practice usually

encourages more inclusive, collaborative, and democratic forms of adult education [Brookfield, 2000, p. 47].

Linked to a critical stance on adult education is a more inclusive view of who is included in practice, what needs and interests different groups of people may have, how institutions and social forces have marginalized many, and how what we do as adult educators can address these inequities. As St. Clair and Sandlin, editors of a volume on *Promoting Critical Practice in Adult Education* (2004) point out, educators who espouse a critical perspective "are all concerned on some level with real material inequity and seek to link critique to action (praxis) by pursuing social change as a major goal of education" (2004, p. 1). Indeed, a critical perspective has moved into the mainstream discussions about race (Lee and Johnson-Bailey, 2004; McDowell, 2003), class (Nesbit, 2005, 2006), gender (English, 2006; Tisdell, 1995), disability (Rocco, 2006) multiculturalism (Guy, 2005), homophobia and heterosexism (Hill, 2006), the "margins" of adult education (Wise and Glowacki-Dudka, 2004), the environment (Hill and Clover, 2003), and non-Western perspectives on work and learning (McLean and Johansen, 2006; Merriam, 2007) .

These writings and many others have helped to make visible the inequities, the imbalances of power and privilege, the contested nature of what we believe to be "true" of adult education. Practitioners, however, unless they have been trained in adult education, may have little awareness of this perspective. Those who are aware and "critical" in their perspective find it a challenge to implement their views in practice. How do we handle power relations in our classroom, for example? What of the institutions in which we work and their practices that privilege some and marginalize others? How do we address the structural inequities of our society that reinforce racism, classism, heterosexism, ageism, and so on? What we can do is learn from others' experiences in this effort, experiences that involve action and even "defiance," a stance Newman (2006)

defines as "taking control of our moment" (p. xi); it is rebellious-
ness instilled with "purpose" (p. 61).

The Profession and Practice Revisited

Many changes have taken place in adult education, both in terms
of the profession and practice, over the past decade. Clearly, trends
such as globalization and the changing workplace have had a
tremendous impact on the very nature of adult education practice.
Likewise, holistic conceptions of learning have fueled the development of new research and innovative practices centering on understanding and working with adult learners. Overall, there has been
much to be excited about in the world of adult education.

At the same time, there is room for concern, particularly in
issues related to the professionalization of adult education. In Chapter Eleven, we addressed questions related to the future of the field.
Here we presented challenges to the profession offered by Griffith
(1989) and Kett (1994) who each said, in essence, that the practice
of adult education will continue to thrive regardless of whether the
profession plays an important role in the future of adult education.
Ten years later, we believe that in some ways, this scenario has been
borne out. At the same time, there is evidence that major growth
has taken place in some areas related to professionalization. Taken
together, we believe that the advancement of professional adult education in the past decade has been a mixed bag. Revisiting the areas
of the knowledge base, graduate study, and professional associations
can shed light on some of the major developments and concerns
that characterize the adult education profession at the beginning of
the twenty-first century.

In terms of the knowledge base, what stands out clearly is that,
as is the case with most other fields, there has been an explosion in
the availability of information. We discussed the formal and informal sources of knowledge in Chapter Eleven. Clearly, the Internet
has played a vital role in helping to expand the informal knowledge

base by providing access to Web sites of individuals and organizations, online periodicals that can be accessed from virtually any location, and the availability of information relative to elements of popular culture, such as film, music, literature, and cultural institutions like museums and libraries. It almost seems trite to say but in today's world, information is more readily available than at any other time. No longer is the issue about having or gaining access to information; rather it is about being able to sort out and assess such resources for accuracy and credibility.

When attempting to assess the knowledge base, it is important to examine the perspectives that are represented and the voices that are heard (Imel, Brockett, and James, 2000). In a content analysis of *Adult Education Quarterly* submissions between 1989 and 1999, Taylor (2001) concluded that while academic, male, single-author submissions were predominant during this time period, there had been an increase in the number of submissions by women authors, as well as an increase in the use of qualitative research designs and the addressing of issues of gender and diversity.

Research in adult education and adult learning has employed a wide range of designs drawing from different epistemological orientations. We believe that this has had a tremendous impact on strengthening the knowledge base of adult education. However, this methodological diversity has come under scrutiny with the rise in emphasis on evidence-based research (EBR). Evidence-based, or scientifically based, research has emerged recently in an effort, which actually has been implemented as policy by the U.S. Department of Education, to support experimental, quasi-experimental, and regression designs for evaluating the effectiveness of funded projects (U.S. Government, 2005). St. Pierre (2006) has argued that an exclusive focus on evidence-based research is "a hot, almost blistering" issue "because the very nature of science and scientific evidence and therefore the nature of knowledge itself is being contested" by those who work from different epistemological and methodological positions (p. 239). Dirkx (2006b) states that EBR "can play an important role in helping to inform and shape policy" (p. 286). However, he argues that this approach is not sufficient to truly understand problems of practice. Dirkx advocates the use of an "insider" research approach emphasizing "systematic approaches to the use of reflection and narrative with one's own practice" (p. 287). This insider approach, Dirkx suggests, can help adult education researchers understand what works. Clearly, the controversy surrounding evidence-based research will have an impact on the knowledge base in the coming years, especially if support for government-funded research is tied to this paradigm.

Over the past decade, numerous books have been published that have given voice to perspectives traditionally outside the mainstream. For example, the 2000 *Handbook of Adult and Continuing Education* (Wilson and Hayes, 2000a) was organized around the concept of "critically reflective practice" (p. xvi). Other books that have addressed perspectives from what we refer to in Chapter Ten as the "invisible side of practice" include *Making Space* (Sheared and Sissel, 2001), *Freedom Road* (Second Edition, Peterson, 2002), *Teaching Defiance* (Newman, 2006), and *The Power of Critical Theory* (Brookfield, 2005). Several other books dealing with giving voice were mentioned earlier in this Epilogue. Imel, Brockett, and James (2000) concluded that while "the growing number of voices critical of the current knowledge base is a healthy development" (p. 632), there is a need to expand this work. Books such as those listed above, as well as periodicals such as *Adult Education Quarterly*, the *International Journal of Lifelong Education*, and the *Canadian Journal for the Study of Adult Education*, along with the annual proceedings of the Adult Education Research Conference (AERC) offer evidence that the knowledge base is increasingly reflective of a more inclusive vision of adult education.

With regard to graduate study, many of the trends reported by Imel, Brockett, and James (2000) are still accurate. Most programs are small, with two or three full-time faculty, and most are housed in departments with other programs. In addition, the "ebb and flow of program closings and openings" that has characterized the history of adult education graduate study continues (p. 633). Among the concerns facing graduate programs in adult education, as identified by Imel, Brockett, and James, are the following:

- Most people who engage in the education of adults do not actually hold a graduate degree in adult education, do not see the value of the degree, and quite frequently are not even aware that such programs exist.

- Some people hold the perception that graduate preparation in adult education "does not make a difference in terms of effective performance" (p. 634).

- Graduate programs are sometimes considered to be elitist by serving a gatekeeping function.

- Graduate programs are often marginalized within their institutions and because most programs are small, they can be vulnerable to cuts and even closure.

- Adult education graduate programs can sometimes offer a "chilly climate" for students, particularly those who are minorities in terms of gender, race, class, sexual orientation, and disability.

Regarding institutional factors affecting graduate programs in adult education, Milton, Watkins, Studdard, and Burch (2003) used a mixed-method design to determine which factors contributed to changes in the program over the previous five years and how these changes impacted program size. The authors found that increasing enrollment in a program did not ensure additional faculty. In addition, they found that integration with other departments or program areas had a strong connection to changes in program size, but also "had the potential to diffuse or dilute the strengths of the program" (p. 39).

As for the "chilly climate" issue, Chapman and Sork (2001) described their relationship as "feminist graduate student and non-feminist male supervisor" (p. 94) and how their working relationship evolved over time with discussions of issues such as power, gender, expectations for each other, and differing views on research. They encourage other students and professors to engage in this kind of dialogue.

In assessing the changing landscape of adult education, Brockett (2000) concluded that the adult education professorate and population of graduate students has never been more diverse, but instead of celebrating how the field is becoming increasingly informed by perspectives such as feminist pedagogy, postmodernism, critical theory, Afrocentrism, and queer theory, we often find ourselves entrenched within our own paradigms. He suggests that only through dialogue, debate, and reflection will it be possible to create the kind of cross-fertilization needed for a truly inclusive spirit.

Professional associations are perhaps where the most visible challenges to the adult education profession have been found in recent years. And nowhere is this more clearly apparent than in efforts to maintain an all-encompassing "umbrella" adult education association. After several years of fiscal and management crisis in the American Association for Adult and Continuing Education (AAACE) in the 1990s, the Commission on Adult Basic Education (COABE) voted to end its affiliation with AAACE. As probably the largest group within AAACE, the decision of COABE to become an independent association has allowed it to thrive with its own identity as an association of adult basic educators. At the same time, AAACE has downsized to the point where on more than one occasion since 1999, there have been discussions about whether to dissolve the association. Today, AAACE has about 500 members (personal communication between C. Anderson and J. Taylor, February, 2007), which is a far cry from the 5,000 members reported when this book was originally published. It continues to hold an annual conference and to publish two periodicals, *Adult Education*

Quarterly and *Adult Learning*. AAACE membership consists pre-dominantly of two groups: (1) professors and graduate students and (2) military adult educators. Both hold preconferences in conjunction with the annual AAACE conference.

The reasons for the diminished presence and influence of the AAACE are complex and beyond the scope of this discussion. However, we believe that the main issue is a longstanding concern that because there is no holistic conception of an adult education field, educators of adults tend to cluster around associations that meet the needs of their specific areas of practice (for example, continuing higher education, literacy, extension). With tight travel budgets, adult educators may not have the resources to attend a conference within their specialty area *and* an umbrella organization. Nor can they often afford to join both kinds of associations. Given that associations such as COABE, the Association for Continuing Higher Education, the University Continuing Education Association, and the Academy of Human Resource Development are thriving today, perhaps the future of professional associations in adult education lies in these more clearly targeted organizations, rather than in broad-based associations such as AAACE. Thus, in response to the question "Is it possible to have a single, unified vision for the field?" which we asked in Chapter Eleven, our answer at present would have to be "no." At the same time, the many clusters where adult education can be found are quite strong and we believe will continue to thrive with or without a vision for a single, unified field.

Conclusion

In this Epilogue, it has been our intent to offer a brief update on several areas that have emerged since *The Profession and Practice of Adult Education* was originally published. Although we addressed international perspectives on adult education, the workplace as a setting for learning, concepts of learning, and diversity, changes over the past decade have reframed the discussion. Here, we have presented these issues as globalization, the workplace, holistic learning, diversity and critique, and an update on the professionalization of the field. This Epilogue is in no way a comprehensive look at developments in adult education over the past decade. Instead, we have presented it as a way of illustrating the need to continuously stay abreast of the rapid change that has characterized adult education as a field of study and practice. We hope that *The Profession and Practice of Adult Education* has helped to introduce you to the world of adult education. But we also encourage you to think of the book as a starting point. By supplementing the book with current literature from the field, such as the kinds of sources we have cited in this Epilogue, you should have a good map of the territory of this exciting, challenging, and ever-changing field of study and practice.

References

The 1919 report: The final and interim reports of the Adult Education Committee of the Ministry of Reconstruction, 1918–1919 (1980). Nottingham, UK: Department of Adult Education, University of Nottingham. (Original work published in 1919.)

A design for democracy (1956). New York: Association Press.

Adams, F. (1975). *Unearthing seeds of fire: The idea of Highlander.* Winston-Salem, NC: John F. Blair.

Adams, J. T. (1944). *Frontiers of American culture.* New York: Charles Scribner's Sons.

Adler, M. J. (1940). *How to read a book: The art of getting a liberal education.* New York: Simon & Schuster.

Adler, M. J. (1982). *The paideia proposal.* New York: Macmillan.

Akdere, M., and Conceicao, S. (2006). Integration of human resource development and adult education theories and practices: Implications for organizational learning. *Proceedings of the Academy of Human Resource Development International Conference.* Columbus, OH: Academy of Human Resource Development. (ERIC Document Reproduction Services No. ED492681).

Allison, C. B. (1995). *Past and present: Essays for teachers in the history of education.* New York: Peter Lang.

Amidon, B. (1933). Sacrificed to schooling: A layman points out dangers to adult educators. *Journal of Adult Education, 5*(2), 384–387.

Amann, T. (2003). Creating space for somatic ways of knowing within transformative learning theory. In C. A. Wiessner, S. R. Meyer, N. L. Pfhal, and P. G. Neaman (Eds.), *Proceedings of the Fifth International Conference on Transformative Learning* (pp. 26–32). New York: Teacher's College, Columbia University.

Anderson, M. L., and Lindeman, E. C. (1927). *Education through experience*. New York: Workers Education Bureau.

Anderson, R. E., Lundmark, V., Harris, L., and Magnan, S. (1994). Equity in computing. In C. Huff and T. Finholt (Eds.), *Social issues in computing* (pp. 352–385). New York: McGraw-Hill.

Apple, M. (1993). *Official knowledge: Democratic education in a conservative age*. New York: Routledge.

Apps, J. W. (1973). *Toward a working philosophy of adult education*. Syracuse, NY: Syracuse University Publications in Continuing Education.

Apps, J. W. (1979). *Problems in continuing education*. New York: McGraw-Hill.

Apps, J. W. (1985). *Improving practice in continuing education*. San Francisco: Jossey-Bass.

Apps, J. W. (1987). Adult education and the learning society. *Educational Considerations, 14*(2–3), 14–18.

Apps, J. W. (1988). *Higher education in a learning society*. San Francisco: Jossey-Bass.

Apps, J. W. (1989a). Providers of adult and continuing education: A framework. In S. B. Merriam and P. M. Cunningham (Eds.), *Handbook of adult and continuing education* (pp. 275–286). San Francisco: Jossey-Bass.

Apps, J. W. (1989b). What should the future focus be for adult and continuing education? In B. A. Quigley (Ed.), *Fulfilling the promise of adult and continuing education*. New Directions for Continuing Education, No. 44. San Francisco: Jossey-Bass.

Apps, J. W. (1994). *Leadership for the emerging age: Transforming practice in adult and continuing education*. San Francisco: Jossey-Bass.

Aslanian, C. B., and Brickell, H. M. (1980). *Americans in transition: Life changes as reasons for adult learning*. New York: College Entrance Examination Board.

Atlanta Journal/Atlanta Constitution. (1994, June 9), p. D7.

Bailey, J. J., Tisdell, E. J., and Cervero, R. M. (1994). Race, gender, and the politics of professionalism. In E. Hayes and S.A.J. Colin III (Eds.), *Confronting racism and sexism* (pp. 63–76). New Directions for Adult and Continuing Education, No. 61. San Francisco: Jossey-Bass.

Bailyn, B. (1960). *Education in the forming of American society*. Chapel Hill: The University of North Carolina Press.

Baptiste, I. (2001). Educating lone wolves: Pedagogical implications of human capital theory. *Adult Education Quarterly, 51*(3), 184–201.

Baritz, L. (1962). The historian as playwright. *The Nation, 195*(17), 340–343.

Bassett, D. S., and Jackson, L. (1994). Applying the model to a variety of adult learning situations. In L. Jackson and R. S. Caffarella (Eds.), *Experiential learning: A new approach* (pp. 73–86). New Directions for Adult and Continuing Education, No. 62. San Francisco: Jossey-Bass.

Bates, A. W. (1995). Educational technology in distance education. In T. Husen and T. N. Postlethwaite (Eds.), *The international encyclopedia of education* (2nd ed., Vol. 3, pp. 1573–1580). New York: Pergamon Press.

Bathory, Z. (1994). Hungary: System of education. In T. Husen and T. N. Postlethwaite (Eds.), *The international encyclopedia of education* (2nd ed., Vol. 1, pp. 2697–2707). New York: Pergamon Press.

Beatty, P. T. (1992). The undeniable link: Adult and continuing education and individual change. In M. W. Galbraith and B. Sisco (Eds.), *Confronting controversies in challenging times: A call for action*. New Directions for Adult and Continuing Education, No. 54. San Francisco: Jossey-Bass.

Beder, H. (1987). Dominant paradigms, adult education, and social justice. *Adult Education Quarterly, 37*(2), 105–113.

Beder, H. (1989). Purposes and philosophies of adult education. In S. B. Merriam and P. M. Cunningham (Eds.), *Handbook of adult and continuing education* (pp. 37–50). San Francisco: Jossey-Bass.

Beder, H. (1992). Adult and continuing education should not be market driven. In M. W. Galbraith and B. Sisco (Eds.), *Confronting controversies in challenging times: A call for action*. New Directions for Adult and Continuing Education, No. 54. San Francisco: Jossey-Bass.

Bee, H. L. (1995). *The journey of adulthood* (3rd ed.). New York: Macmillan.

Belanger, P. (1995). Adult education and the changing role of UNESCO and of the UN organizations. In B. B. Cassara (Ed.), *Adult education through world collaboration* (pp. 3–22). Malabar, FL: Krieger.

Belenky, M. F., Clinchy, B. M., Goldberger, N. R., and Tarule, J. (1986). *Women's ways of knowing: The development of self, voice, and mind*. New York: Basic Books.

Bennis, W. (1989). *On becoming a leader*. Reading, MA: Addison-Wesley.

Bergevin, P. (1967). *A philosophy for adult education*. New York: Seabury.

Bierema, L. L. (2000). Moving beyond performance paradigms in human resource development. In A. L. Wilson and E. R. Hayes (Eds.), *Handbook of adult and continuing education* (pp. 278–293). San Francisco: Jossey-Bass.

Bierema, L. L., Cseh, M., Ellinger, A., Ruona, W., and Watkins, K. (2001). HRD on the margins: Exploring resistance to HRD in adult education. In R. O. Smith, J. M. Dirkx, P. L. Eddy, P. L. Farrell, and M. Polzin (Eds.), *Proceedings of the 42nd Annual Adult Education Research Conference* (pp. 51–62). E. Lansing: Michigan State University.

Bingman, M. B. (1995). *Appalachian women learning in community*. Unpublished doctoral dissertation, University of Tennessee, Knoxville.

Birren, J. E., and Schaie, K. W. (1990). *Handbook of the psychology of aging* (3rd ed.). San Diego, CA: Academic Press.

Blackburn, D. J. (Ed.). (1988). *Foundations and changing practices in extension.* Toronto: Thompson Educational Publishing.

Bloom, A. (1987). *The closing of the American mind.* New York: Simon & Schuster.

Blundell, S. (1992). Gender and the curriculum of adult education. *International Journal of Lifelong Education, 1*(3), 199–216.

Bock, J. C., and Bock, C. M. (1989). Nonformal education policy: Developing countries. In C. J. Titmus (Ed.), *Lifelong learning for adults: An international handbook* (pp. 64–69). New York: Pergamon Press.

Bogdan, R. C., and Biklen, S. K. (1992). *Qualitative research for education* (3rd ed.). Needham Heights, MA: Allyn & Bacon.

Boggs, D. L. (1991). *Adult civic education.* Springfield, IL: Thomas.

Boshier, R. (1971). Motivational orientations of adult education participants: A factor analytic exploration of Houle's typology. *Adult Education, 21*(2), 3–26.

Boshier, R. (1989). Participant motivation. In C. J. Titmus (Ed.), *Lifelong education for adults: An international handbook* (pp. 147–150). New York: Pergamon Press.

Boshier, R., and Collins, J. B. (1985). The Houle topology after twenty-two years: A large-scale empirical test. *Adult Education Quarterly, 35*(3), 113–130.

Boucouvalas, M. (1994). Cooperation, collaboration and networking. In C. J. Polson and F. M. Schied (Eds.), *Challenge and change: Proceedings of the 1994 Annual Conference of the Commission of Professors of Adult Education* (pp. 120–123). College of Education, Kansas State University, Manhattan, KS.

Boud, D. (1994). Conceptualising learning from experience: Developing a model for facilitation. In M. Hyams, J. Armstrong, and E. Anderson (compilers), *Proceedings of the 35th Annual Adult Education Research Conference* (pp. 49–54). Knoxville: University of Tennessee.

Boud, D., Cohen, R., and Walker, D. (Eds.). (1993). *Using experience for learning.* Buckingham, UK: Open University Press. Distributed by Taylor and Francis, Bristol, PA.

Boud, D., and Walker, D. (1991). *Experience and learning: Reflection at work.* Geelong, Australia: Deakin University Press.

Boyd, R. D., and Apps, J. W. (1980). A conceptual model for adult education. In R. D. Boyd, J. W. Apps, and Associates (Eds.), *Redefining the discipline of adult education* (pp. 1–13). San Francisco: Jossey-Bass.

Bridges, W. (1980). *Transitions.* Reading, MA: Addison-Wesley.

Briscoe, D. B. (1990). Community education: A culturally responsive approach to learning. In J. M. Ross-Gordon, L. G. Martin, and D. B. Briscoe (Eds.), *Serving culturally diverse populations*. New Directions for Adult and Continuing Education, No. 49. San Francisco: Jossey-Bass.

Brockett, R. G. (Ed.). (1988a). *Ethical issues in adult education*. New York: Teachers College Press.

Brockett, R. G. (1988b). Ethics and the adult educator. In R. G. Brockett (Ed.), *Ethical issues in adult education* (pp. 1–16). New York: Teachers College Press.

Brockett, R. G. (1989). Professional associations for adult and continuing education. In S. B. Merriam and P. M. Cunningham (Eds.), *Handbook of adult and continuing education* (pp. 112–123). San Francisco: Jossey-Bass.

Brockett, R. G. (1990). Early ideas on the training of leaders for adult education. In R. W. Rohfeld (Ed.), *Breaking new ground: The development of adult and workers' education in North America. Proceedings from the Syracuse University Kellogg Project's First Visiting Scholar Conference in the History of Adult Education* (pp. 64–82). Syracuse, NY: Syracuse University Kellogg Project.

Brockett, R. G. (1991a). Disseminating and using adult education knowledge. In J. M. Peters, P. Jarvis, and Associates (Eds.), *Adult education: Evolution and achievements in a developing field of study* (pp. 121–144). San Francisco: Jossey-Bass.

Brockett, R. G. (1991b). Professional development, artistry, and style. In R. G. Brockett (Ed.), *Professional development for educators of adults*. New Directions for Adult and Continuing Education, No. 51. San Francisco: Jossey-Bass.

Brockett, R. G. (Ed.) (1991c). *Professional development for educators of adults*. New Directions for Adult and Continuing Education, No. 51. San Francisco: Jossey-Bass.

Brockett, R. G. (1992). Do we really need mandatory continuing education? In M. W. Galbraith and B. Sisco (Eds.), *Confronting controversies in challenging times: A call for action*. New Directions for Adult and Continuing Education, No. 54. San Francisco: Jossey-Bass.

Brockett, R. G. (1994, July). *Ethical decision-making: A cornerstone for effective leadership*. Opening keynote address at the Nova Southeastern University Programs for Higher Education Summer Institute, Scottsdale, AZ.

Brockett, R. G. (2000). The changing landscape of graduate study in adult education: Reflections from mid-career. *The Jackson Hole proceedings: Symposium for the discussion of graduate study in adult learning and technology*. Laramie, WY: Department of Adult Learning and Technology, University of Wyoming.

Brockett, R. G., and Hiemstra, R. (1991). Self-direction in adult learning: Perspectives on theory, research, and practice. London and New York: Routledge.

Brookfield, S. D. (1985). Analyzing a critical paradigm of self-directed learning: A response. *Adult Education Quarterly, 36*(1), 60–64.

Brookfield, S. D. (1986). *Understanding and facilitating adult learning*. San Francisco: Jossey-Bass.

Brookfield, S. D. (1987a). *Developing critical thinkers: Challenging adults to explore alternative ways of thinking and acting*. San Francisco: Jossey-Bass.

Brookfield, S. D. (Ed.). (1987b). *Learning democracy: Eduard Lindeman on adult education and social change*. London: Croom Helm.

Brookfield, S. D. (1989). The epistemology of adult education in the United States and Great Britain: A cross-cultural analysis. In B. P. Bright (Ed.), *Theory and practice in the study of adult education: The epistemological debate* (pp. 141–173). London: Routledge.

Brookfield, S. D. (1992). Learning in communities. In L. E. Burton (Ed.), *Developing resourceful humans* (pp. 144–160). London: Routledge.

Brookfield, S. D. (1994). Adult learning. In T. Husen and T. N. Postlethwaite (Eds.)., *The international encyclopedia of educators* (2nd ed., Vol 1, pp. 163–168). New York: Pergamon Press.

Brookfield, S. (2000). The concept of critically reflective practice. In A. L. Wilson and E. R. Hayes (Eds.), *Handbook of adult and continuing education* (pp. 33–50). San Francisco: Jossey-Bass.

Brookfield, S. (2005). *The power of critical theory: Liberating adult learning and teaching*. San Francisco: Jossey-Bass.

Brooks, A., and Watkins, K. E. (Eds.). (1994a). *The emerging power of action inquiry technologies*. New Directions for Adult and Continuing Education, No. 63. San Francisco: Jossey-Bass.

Brooks, A., and Watkins, K. E. (1994b). A new era for action technologies: A look at the issues. In A. Brooks and K. E. Watkins (Eds.), *The emerging power of action inquiry technologies*. New Directions for Adult and Continuing Education, No. 63. San Francisco: Jossey-Bass.

Brown, C. S. (Ed.). (1981). *Alexander Meiklejohn: Teacher of freedom*. Berkeley, CA: Meiklejohn Civil Liberties Institute.

Brown, C. S. (Ed.). (1990). *Ready from within: Septima Clark and the civil rights movement*. Trenton, NJ: Africa World Press.

Brunner, E. deS (1936). Placement possibilities. *Journal of Adult Education, 8*(4), 455–459.

Bryson, L. L. (1936). *Adult education*. New York: American Book Company.

Burnham, B. R. (1989). Marginality thirty years later. *Conference proceedings from the 30th Annual Adult Education Research Conference, April 27–29, 1989* (pp. 49–54). Madison: University of Wisconsin.

Caffarella, R. S. (1993). Self-directed learning. In S. B. Merriam (Ed.), *An update on adult learning theory*. New Directions for Adult and Continuing Education, No. 57. San Francisco: Jossey-Bass.

Caffarella, R. S. (1994). Planning programs for adult learners: A practical guide for educators, trainers, and staff developers. San Francisco: Jossey-Bass.

Caffarella, R. S., and Olson, S. K. (1993). The psychosocial development of women. *Adult Education Quarterly, 43*(3), 125–151.

Cameron, C. R. (1981). Certification should be established. In B. W. Kreitlow and Associates (Eds.), *Examining controversies in adult education* (pp. 72–83). San Francisco: Jossey-Bass.

Candy, P. C. (1991). *Self-direction for lifelong learning: A comprehensive guide to theory and practice*. San Francisco: Jossey-Bass.

Carlson, R. A. (1970). Americanization as an early twentieth-century adult education movement. *History of Education Quarterly, 10*(4), 440–464.

Carlson, R. A. (1977). Professionalization of adult education: An historical-philosophical analysis. *Adult Education, 28*(1), 53–63.

Carlson, R. A. (1980). The foundation of adult education: Analyzing the Boyd-Apps model. In R. D. Boyd, J. W. Apps, and Associates (Eds.), *Redefining the discipline of adult education* (pp. 174–189). San Francisco: Jossey-Bass.

Carlson, R. A. (1987). *The Americanization syndrome: A quest for conformity.* New York: St. Martin's Press.

Carlson, R. A. (1988). A code of ethics for adult educators? In R. G. Brockett (Ed.), *Ethical issues in adult education* (pp. 162–177). New York: Teachers College Press.

Carnevale, A., Gainer, L., and Villet, J. (1990). *Training in America: The organization and strategic role of training*. San Francisco: Jossey-Bass.

Carp, A., Peterson, R., and Roelfs, P. (1974). Adult learning interests and experiences. In K. P. Cross, J. R. Valley, and Associates (Eds.), *Planning nontraditional programs: An analysis of the issues for postsecondary education* (pp. 11–52). San Francisco: Jossey-Bass.

Cartwright, M. A. (1935). *Ten years of adult education*. New York: Macmillan.

Cassara, B. B. (1993). *Adult educators with a global perspective*. Paper presented at the annual meeting of the Association for Continuing Higher Education, Jackson, MS. (ED 363 771)

Cassara, B. B. (1994). Women, literacy, and development: Challenges for the 21st century. A report on the Fifth World Assembly of the International Council for Adult Education, Cairo, Egypt, September 15–23, 1994 (attachment). In C. J. Polson and F. Schied (Eds.), *Challenge and change: Proceedings of the 1994 Annual Conference of the Commission of Professors of Adult Education* (pp. 112–116). College of Education, Kansas State University, Manhattan, KS.

Cassara, B. B. (Ed.). (1995). *Adult education through world collaboration*. Malabar, FL: Krieger.

Cattell, R. B. (1963). Theory of fluid and crystallized intelligence. *Journal of Educational Psychology, 54*(1), 1–22.

Cervero, R. M. (1988). *Effective continuing education for professionals*. San Francisco: Jossey-Bass.

Cervero, R. M. (1991). Changing relationships between theory and practice. In J. M. Peters, P. Jarvis, and Associates (Eds.), *Adult Education: Evolution and achievements in a developing field of study* (pp. 19–41). San Francisco: Jossey-Bass.

Cervero, R. M. (1992). Adult education should strive for professionalization. In M. W. Galbraith and B. Sisco (Eds.), *Confronting controversies in challenging times: A call for action*. New Directions for Adult and Continuing Education, No. 54. San Francisco: Jossey-Bass.

Cervero, R. M., and Wilson, A. L. (1994a). *Planning responsibly for adult education: A guide to negotiating power and interests*. San Francisco: Jossey-Bass.

Cervero, R. M., and Wilson, A. L. (1994b). The politics of responsibility: A theory of program planning practice for adult education. *Adult Education Quarterly, 45*(1), 249–268.

Cervero, R. M., and Wilson, A. L. (2005). *Working the planning table: Negotiating democratically for adult, continuing and workplace education*. San Francisco: Jossey-Bass.

Chapman, S. W. (1990). The marginality of adult education units within three types of organizations: Development and application of an index. Unpublished doctoral dissertation, University of Georgia, Athens.

Chapman, V. (2002). "Knowing one's self": Selfwriting, power and ethical practice. In J. M. Pettitt (Ed.), *Proceedings of the 43rd Annual Adult Education Research Conference* (pp. 73–78). Raleigh: North Carolina State University.

Chapman, V-L, and Sork, T. J. (2001). Confessing regulation or telling secrets? Opening up the conversation on graduate supervision. *Adult Education Quarterly, 51*(2), 94–107.

Charters, A. N., and Associates (1981). *Comparing adult education worldwide*. San Francisco: Jossey-Bass.

Charters, A. N., and Hilton, R. J. (Eds.). (1989). *Landmarks in international adult education: A comparative analysis*. London: Routledge.

Choi, J., and Hannafin, M. (1995). Situated cognition and learning environments: Roles, structures, and implications for design. *Educational Technology Research and Development, 43*(2), 53–69.

Chu, S. K. (1994). Adult and nonformal education: Statistics. In T. Husen and T. N. Postlethwaite (Eds.), *International encyclopedia of education* (2nd ed., Vol. 1, pp. 94–100). New York: Pergamon Press.

Chua, A. (2003). Globalization and ethnic hatred. *Phi Kappa Phi Forum, 83*(4), 13–16.

Clark, B. R. (1956). *Adult education in transition: A study of institutional insecurity.* Berkeley: University of California Press.

Clark, B. R. (1958). *The marginality of adult education.* Brookline: MA: Center for the Study of Liberal Education for Adults.

Clark, M. C. (1993). Transformational learning. In S. B. Merriam (Ed.), *An update on adult learning theory.* New Directions for Adult and Continuing Education, No. 57. San Francisco: Jossey-Bass.

Clark, M. C., and Wilson, A. W. (1991). Context and rationality in Mezirow's theory of transformational learning. *Adult Education Quarterly, 41*(2), 75–91.

Cochrane, N. J., and others (1986). *J. R. Kidd: An international legacy of learning.* Monographs on Comparative and Area Studies in Adult Education. Vancouver: Centre for Continuing Education, University of British Columbia.

Colin, S.A.J., III, and Preciphs, T. K. (1991). Perceptual patterns and the learning environment: Confronting white racism. In R. Hiemstra (Ed.), *Creating environments for effective adult learning.* New Directions for Adult and Continuing Education, No. 50. San Francisco: Jossey-Bass.

Collard, S., and Law, M. (1989). The limits of perspective transformation: A critique of Mezirow's theory. *Adult Education Quarterly, 39*(2), 99–107.

Collard, S., and Stalker, J. (1991). Women's trouble: Women, gender, and the learning environment. In R. Hiemstra (Ed.), *Creating environments for effective adult learning.* New Directions for Adult and Continuing Education, No. 50. San Francisco: Jossey-Bass.

Colletta, N. J. (1996). Formal, nonformal, and informal education. In A. C. Tuijnman (Ed.), *International encyclopedia of adult education and training* (2nd ed.). New York: Pergamon Press.

Collins, M. (1983). A critical analysis of competency-based systems in adult education. *Adult Education Quarterly, 33*(3), 174–183.

Collins, M. (1991). *Adult education as vocation: A critical role for the adult educator.* New York: Routledge.

Collins, M. (1992). Adult education should resist further professionalization. In M. W. Galbraith and B. Sisco (Eds.), *Confronting controversies in challenging times: A call for action.* New Directions for Adult and Continuing Education, No. 54. San Francisco: Jossey-Bass.

Collins, M., and Long, H. B. (1989). Federal and provincial adult education agencies in the United States and Canada. In S. B. Merriam and P. M. Cunningham (Eds.), *Handbook of adult and continuing education* (pp. 384–396). San Francisco: Jossey-Bass.

Comings, J. P. (1995). The United States: Adult education within the Foreign Aid Program. In B. B. Cassara (Ed.), *Adult education through world collaboration* (pp. 171–184). Malabar, FL: Krieger.

Commission of Professors of Adult Education (1986). *Standards for graduate programs in adult education.* Washington, DC: Commission of Professors of Adult Education and the American Association for Adult and Continuing Education.

Cookson, P. S. (1983). The Boyd and Apps conceptual model of adult education: A critical examination. *Adult Education Quarterly, 34*(1), 48–53.

Cookson, P. S. (1989). International and comparative adult education. In S. B. Merriam and P. M. Cunningham (Eds.), *Handbook of adult and continuing education* (pp. 70–83). San Francisco: Jossey-Bass.

Cookson, P. S. (1994). International adult education cooperation and exchange revisited. In C. J. Polson and F. M. Schied (Eds.), *Challenge and change: Proceedings of the 1994 Annual Conference of the Commission of Professors of Adult Education* (pp. 105–111). College of Education, Kansas State University, Manhattan, KS.

Coombs, P. H. (1985). *The world crisis in education: The view from the eighties.* New York: Oxford University Press.

Coombs, P. H. (1989). Formal and nonformal education: Future strategies. In C. J. Titmus (Ed.), *Lifelong education for adults: An international handbook* (pp. 57–60). New York: Pergamon Press.

Coombs, P. H., with Prosser, R. C., and Ahmed, M. (1973). *New paths to learning for children and youth.* New York: International Council for Educational Development.

Cotton, W. E. (1964). The challenge confronting American adult education. *Adult Education, 14*(2), 80–88.

Cotton, W. E. (1968). *On behalf of adult education: A historical examination of the supporting literature.* Boston: Center for the Study of Liberal Education for Adults.

Counter, J. E. (1992a). A community building process: An investigation of the Montana Study. In A. Blunt (Ed.), *Proceedings of the 33rd Annual Adult Education Research Conference* (pp. 37–42). Saskatoon, Canada: University of Saskatchewan.

Counter, J. E. (1992b). The Montana Study: Idealistic failure or innovative success? (Doctoral dissertation, Montana State University, 1991). *Dissertation Abstracts International, 52,* 3154A.

Courtenay, B. C. (1989). Education for older adults. In S. B. Merriam and P. M. Cunningham (Eds.), *Handbook of adult and continuing education* (pp. 525–536). San Francisco: Jossey-Bass.

Courtenay, B. C. (1990). An analysis of adult education administration literature, l936–l989. *Adult Education Quarterly, 40*(2), 63–77.

Courtenay, B. C. (1994). Are psychological models of adult development still important for the practice of adult education? *Adult Education Quarterly, 44*(3), 145–153.

Courtney, S. (1989). Defining adult and continuing education. In S. B. Merriam and P. M. Cunningham (Eds.), *Handbook of adult and continuing education* (pp. 15–25). San Francisco: Jossey-Bass.

Courtney, S. (1991). *Why adults learn: Toward a theory of participation.* London and New York: Routledge.

Covey, S. R. (1989). *The 7 habits of highly effective people.* New York: Fireside.

Cranton, P. (1994). *Understanding and promoting transformative learning: A guide for educators of adults.* San Francisco: Jossey-Bass.

Cremin, L. A. (1965). *The transformation of the school: Progressivism in American education, 1876–1957.* New York: Vintage Books.

Cremin, L. (1970). *American education: The Colonial experience, 1607–1783.* New York: HarperCollins.

Cremin, L. (1977). *American education: The national experience, 1783–1876.* New York: HarperCollins.

Cremin, L. (1988). *American education: The metropolitan experience, 1876–1980.* New York: HarperCollins.

Cropley, A. J. (1989). Factors in participation. In C. J. Titmus (Ed.), *Lifelong education for adults: An international handbook* (pp. 145–147). New York: Pergamon Press.

Cross, K. P. (1981). *Adults as learners.* San Francisco: Jossey-Bass.

Csikszentmihalyi, M. (1990). *Flow: The psychology of optimal experience.* New York: HarperCollins.

Cunningham, P. M. (1989). Making a more significant impact on society. In B. A. Quigley (Ed.), *Fulfilling the promise of adult and continuing education.* New Directions for Continuing Education, No. 44. San Francisco: Jossey-Bass.

Cunningham, P. M. (1990). Own your advocacy. *Adult Learning, 2*(3), 15, 18–19, 27.

Cunningham, P. M. (1991). International influences on the development of knowledge. In J. M. Peters and P. Jarvis (Eds.), *Adult education: Evolution and achievements in a developing field of study* (pp. 347–380). San Francisco: Jossey-Bass.

Cunningham, P. M. (1992). Adult and continuing education does not need a code of ethics. In M. W. Galbraith and B. Sisco (Eds.), *Confronting controversies in challenging times: A call for action*. New Directions for Adult and Continuing Education, No. 54. San Francisco: Jossey-Bass.

Cunningham, P. M. (1993). The politics of workers' education: Preparing workers to sleep with the enemy. *Adult Learning, 5*(1), 13–14, 24.

Cunningham, P. M. (1995). U.S. educational policy and adult education: Social control; social demand; and professional adult educator participation. *Conference proceedings of the 36th Annual Adult Education Research Conference* (pp. 83–90). Edmonton, Alberta, Canada: University of Alberta.

Cunningham, P. M. (1996). *Conceptualizing our work as adult educators in a socially responsible way*. (ERIC Document Reproduction Service No. ED401410).

Cunningham, P. M. (2000). A sociology of adult education. In A. L. Wilson and E. R. Hayes (Eds.), *Handbook of adult and continuing education* (pp. 573–591). San Francisco: Jossey-Bass.

Daloz, L. A. (1986). *Effective teaching and mentoring: Realizing the transformational power of adult learning*. San Francisco: Jossey-Bass.

Darkenwald, G. G., and Merriam, S. B. (1982). *Adult education: Foundations of practice*. New York: HarperCollins.

Darkenwald, G. G., and Valentine, T. (1985). Factor structure of deterrents to public participation in adult education. *Adult Education Quarterly, 35*(4), 177–193.

Davenport, J., and Davenport, J. A. (1985). A chronology of the andragogy debate. *Adult Education Quarterly, 35*(3), 152–159.

Day, M. (1981). Adult education as a new educational frontier: Review of the Journal of Adult Education 1929–1941. Unpublished doctoral dissertation, University of Michigan, Ann Arbor.

Day, M., and Seckinger, D. (1989). Everett Dean Martin: Liberal in adult education. *Journal of Thought, 12*(1–2), 26–40.

deMarrais, K. (1991). John's story: An exploration into critical theory in education. *Adult Learning, 2*(8), 9–10.

de Sola Pool, I. (1990). *Technologies without boundaries: On telecommunications in a global age*. Cambridge, MA: Harvard University Press.

Denton, V. L. (1993). *Booker T. Washington and the adult education movement*. Gainesville: University of Florida Press.

Deshler, D. (1991). Social, professional, and academic issues. In J. M. Peters and P. Jarvis (Eds.), *Adult education: Evolution and achievements in a developing field of study* (pp. 384–420). San Francisco: Jossey-Bass.

Deshler, D., and Hagan, N. (1989). Adult education research: Issues and directions. In S. B. Merriam and P. M. Cunningham (Eds.), *Handbook of adult and continuing education* (pp. 147–167). San Francisco: Jossey-Bass.

Dewey, J. (1938). *Education and experience*. New York: Collier Books.

Dickinson, G., and Rusnell, D. (1971). A content analysis of adult education. *Adult Education, 21*(3), 177–185.

Dirkx, J. M. (1996). Human resource development as adult education: Fostering the educative workplace. In R. W. Rowden (Ed.), *Workplace learning: Debating five critical questions of theory and practice* (pp. 41–47). New Directions for Adult and Continuing Education, No. 72. San Francisco: Jossey-Bass.

Dirkx, J. (2001). The power of feelings: Emotion, imagination, and the construction of meaning in adult learning. In S. B. Merriam (Ed.), *The new update on adult learning theory* (pp. 63–72). New Directions for Adult and Continuing Education, No. 89. San Francisco: Jossey-Bass.

Dirkx, J. (2006a). Engaging emotions in adult learning: A Jungian perspective on emotion and transformative learning. In E. W. Taylor (Ed.), *Teaching for change: Fostering transformative learning in the classroom* (pp.15–26). New Directions for Adult and Continuing Education, No. 109. San Francisco: Jossey-Bass.

Dirkx, J. M. (2006b). Studying the complicated matter of what works: Evidence-based research and the problem of practice. *Adult Education Quarterly, 56*(4), 273–290.

Draper, J. A. (1992). The dynamic mandala of adult education. *Convergence, 25*(4), 73–82.

Duke, C. (1994a). International adult education. In T. Husen and T. N. Postlethwaite (Eds.), *The international encyclopedia of education* (2nd ed., Vol. 5, pp. 2945–2951). New York: Pergamon Press.

Duke, C. (1994b). Trends in the development of adult education as a profession. *Adult Education and Development, 43*, 305–317.

Edelson, P. J. (Ed.) (1992). *Rethinking leadership in adult and continuing education*. New Directions for Adult and Continuing Education, No. 56. San Francisco: Jossey-Bass.

Egan, J. (Ed.). (2005). *HIV/Aids education for adults*. New Directions for Adult and Continuing Education, No. 105. San Francisco: Jossey-Bass.

Elias, J. L. (1979). Andragogy revisited. *Adult Education, 29*(4), 252–256.

Elias, J. L., and Merriam, S. B. (1994). *Philosophical foundations of adult education* (2nd ed.). Malabar, FL: Krieger.

Ely, M. L. (Ed.). (1948). *Handbook of adult education in the United States*. New York: Institute of Adult Education, Teachers College, Columbia University.

English, L. M. (2006). A Foucauldian reading of learning in feminist, nonprofit organizations. *Adult Education Quarterly, 56*(2), 85–101.

English, L. M., Fenwick, T. J., and Parsons, J. (2003). *Spirituality of adult education and training.* Malabar, FL: Krieger.

Epskamp, K. P. (1995). The Netherlands: Dutch viewpoints on adult education in developing countries. In B. B. Cassara (Ed.), *Adult education through world collaboration* (pp. 147–170). Malabar, FL: Krieger.

Erikson, E. H. (1963). *Childhood and society* (2nd ed.). New York: W. W. Norton.

Eurich, N. (1985). *Corporate classrooms: The learning business.* Princeton, NJ: The Carnegie Foundation for the Advancement of Teaching.

Ewert, D. M. (1989). Adult education and international development. In S. B. Merriam and P. M. Cunningham (Eds.), *Handbook of adult and continuing education* (pp. 84–98). San Francisco: Jossey-Bass.

Fansler, T. L. (1931). In defense of the expert. *Journal of Adult Education, 3*(1), 57–61.

Fellenz, R. A., and Conti, G. J. (Eds.). (1990). *Social environment and adult learning.* Bozeman: Center for Adult Learning Research, Montana State University.

Fenwick, T. (2005). Conceptions of critical HRD: Dilemmas for theory and practice. *Human Resource Development International, 8*(2), 225–238).

Fenwick, T. (2004). Toward a critical HRD in theory and practice. *Adult Education Quarterly, 54*(3), 193–209.

Fiallos, C. A. (2006). Adult education and the empowerment of the individual in a global society. In S. B. Merriam, B. C. Courtenay, and R. M. Cervero (Eds.), *Global issues and adult education: Perspectives from Latin America, Southern Africa, and the United States* (pp. 15–29). San Francisco: Jossey-Bass.

Finger, M. (1995). Adult education and society today. *International Journal of Lifelong Education, 14*(2), 110–119.

Finger, M. (2005). Globalization. In L. M. English (Ed.), *International encyclopedia of adult education* (pp. 269–273). London: Palgrave Macmillan.

Fischer, C. A., and Schwartz, C. A. (Eds.). (1996). *National organizations of the U.S.,* Vol. 1, *Encyclopedia of associations.* Detroit: Gale Research.

Fischer, D. H. (1970). *Historians' fallacies: Toward a logic of historical thought.* New York: HarperCollins.

Fisher, D. C. (1930). *Learn or perish.* New York: Horace Liveright.

Fisher, J.C. (1986). Participation in educational activities by active older adults. *Adult Education Quarterly, 36*(4), 202–210.

Fiske, M., and Chiriboga, D. A. (1990). *Change and continuity in adult life.* San Francisco: Jossey-Bass.

Flexner, A. (1915). Is social work a profession? *School and Society, 1,* 901–911.

Folkman, D. V. (2006). Framing a critical discourse on globalization. In S. B. Merriam, B. C. Courtenay, and R. M. Cervero (Eds.), *Global issues and adult education: Perspectives from Latin America, Southern Africa, and the United States* (pp. 78–89). San Francisco: Jossey-Bass.

Foley, G., and Flowers, R. (1992). Knowledge and power in Aboriginal adult education. *Convergence, 25,* 61–74.

Forest, L. B. (1989). The cooperative extension service. In S. B. Merriam and P. M. Cunningham (Eds.), *Handbook of adult and continuing education* (pp. 332–343). San Francisco: Jossey-Bass.

Fowler, J. (1981). *Stages of faith: The psychology of human development and the quest for meaning.* New York: HarperCollins.

Frederick, H. (1994). Computer networks and the emergence of global civil society. In L. M. Harasim (Ed.), *Global networks: Computers and international communication* (pp. 283–95). Cambridge, MA: MIT Press.

Freire, P. (1970). *Pedagogy of the oppressed.* New York: Herder and Herder.

Freire, P. (1973). *Education for critical consciousness.* New York: Seabury.

Freire, P. (1985). *The politics of education: Culture, power, and liberation.* South Hadley, MA: Bergin & Garvin.

Freire, P., and Faundez, A. (1989). *Learning to question: A pedagogy of liberation.* New York: Continuum.

Friedman, T. L (2005). *The world is flat: A brief history of the twenty-first century.* New York: Farrar, Straus and Giroux.

Fulton, R. D. (1991). A conceptual model for understanding the physical attributes of learning environments. In R. Hiemstra (Ed.), *Creating environments for effective adult learning.* New Directions for Adult and Continuing Education, No. 50. San Francisco: Jossey-Bass.

Galbraith, M. W. (Ed.). (1990). *Education through community organizations.* New Directions for Adult and Continuing Education, No. 47. San Francisco: Jossey-Bass.

Galbraith, M. W., and Gilley, J. W. (1985). An examination of professional certification. *Lifelong Learning: An Omnibus of Practice and Research, 9*(2), 12–15.

Galbraith, M. W., and Gilley, J. W. (1986). *Professional certification: Implications for adult educators.* Columbus, OH: ERIC Clearinghouse on Adult, Career, and Vocational Education.

Galbraith, M. W., and Sisco, B. (Eds.). (1992). *Confronting controversies in challenging times: A call for action.* New Directions for Adult and Continuing Education, No. 54. San Francisco: Jossey-Bass.

Gardner, H. (1983). *Frames of mind.* New York: Basic Books.

Garrison, D. R., and Shale, D. (1994). Methodological issues: Philosophical differences and complementary methodologies. In D. R. Garrison (Ed.), *Research Perspectives in Adult Education* (pp. 17–37). Malabar, FL: Krieger.

Gaventa, J. (1988). Participatory research in North America. *Convergence*, *21*(2/3), 19–28.

Gelpi, E. (1985). *Lifelong education and international relations*. London: Croom Helm.

Gerver, E. (1992). Commentary: Wilted flowers—the demographic imperative: Contrasts and connections. In L. E. Burton (Ed.), *Developing resourceful humans: Adult education within the economic context*. London: Routledge.

Gessner, R. (Ed.). (1956). *The democratic man: Selected writings of Eduard C. Lindeman*. Boston: Beacon Press.

Gibbons, M., and others (1980). Toward a theory of self-directed learning: A study of experts without formal training. *Journal of Humanistic Psychology*, *20*(2), 41–56.

Gilley, J. W., and Galbraith, M. W. (1986). Examining professional certification. *Training and Development Journal*, *40*(6), 60–61.

Gilligan, C. (1982). *In a different voice: Psychological theory and women's development*. Cambridge, MA: Harvard University Press.

Giroux, H. A. (1994). *Disturbing pleasures: Learning popular culture*. London and New York: Routledge.

Glen, J. M. (1988). *Highlander: No ordinary school, 1932–1962*. Lexington: University Press of Kentucky.

Goerne, J.J.M. (2006). Development of educators in relation to globalization in Latin America. In S. B. Merriam, B. C. Courtenay, and R. M. Cervero (Eds.), *Global issues and adult education: Perspectives from Latin America, Southern Africa, and the United States* (pp. 30–40). San Francisco: Jossey-Bass.

Grattan, C. H. (1955). *In quest of knowledge: A historical perspective on adult education*. New York: Association Press.

Griffin, C. (1983). *Curriculum theory in adult and lifelong learning*. New York: Nickols Publishing.

Griffin, C. (1987). *Adult education as social policy*. London: Croom Helm.

Griffin, C. (1991). A critical perspective on sociology and adult education. In J. M. Peters, P. Jarvis, and Associates (Eds.), *Adult education: Evolution and achievements in a developing field of study* (pp. 259–281). San Francisco: Jossey-Bass.

Griffith, W. S. (1989). Has adult and continuing education fulfilled its early promise? In B. A. Quigley (Ed.), *Fulfilling the promise of adult and continu-*

ing education. New Directions for Continuing Education, No. 44. San Francisco: Jossey-Bass.

Griffith, W. S., with Fujita-Starck, P. J. (1989). Public policy and the financing of adult education. In S. B. Merriam and P. M. Cunningham (Eds.), *Handbook of adult and continuing education* (pp. 168–180). San Francisco: Jossey-Bass.

Groener, Z. (2006). Adult education and social transformation. In S. B. Merriam, B. C. Courtenay, and R. M. Cervero (Eds.), *Global issues and adult education: Perspectives from Latin America, Southern Africa, and the United States* (pp. 5–14). San Francisco: Jossey-Bass.

Groennings, S. (1986). *The new south and innovation in international education*. Paper presented at the University of Georgia, Athens.

Grow, G. O. (1991). Teaching learners to be self-directed. *Adult Education Quarterly, 41*(3), 125–149.

Guglielmino, L. M. (1978). Development of the Self-Directed Learning Readiness Scale. *Dissertation Abstracts International, 38*, 6467A.

Guy, T. C. (1994). Prophecy from the periphery: Alain Locke's philosophy of cultural pluralism and adult education. In M. Hyams, J. Armstrong, and E. Anderson (compilers), *Proceedings of the 35th Annual Adult Education Research Conference* (pp. 175–180). Knoxville: University of Tennessee.

Guy, T. C. (2005). Culturally relevant adult education. In L. M. English (Ed.), *International encyclopedia of adult education* (pp. 180–184). London: Palgrave Macmillan.

Guy, T. C. (2006). Adult education and the mass media in the age of globalization. In S. B. Merriam, B. C. Courtenay, and R. M. Cervero (Eds.), *Global issues and adult education: Perspectives from Latin America, Southern Africa, and the United States* (pp. 53–63). San Francisco: Jossey-Bass.

Hall, B. L., and Kassam, Y. (1989). Participatory research. In C. J. Titmus (Ed.), *Lifelong education for adults: An international handbook* (pp. 536–540). New York: Pergamon Press.

Hamilton, E. (1992). *Adult education for community development*. New York: Greenwood Press.

Hamilton, E., and Cunningham, P. M. (1989). Community-based adult education. In S. B. Merriam and P. M. Cunningham (Eds.), *Handbook of adult and continuing education* (pp. 439–450). San Francisco: Jossey-Bass.

Hareven, T. K. (1978). The last stage: Historical adulthood and old age. In E. H. Erikson (Ed.), *Adulthood* (pp. 201–208). New York: W. W. Norton.

Hart, M. U. (1992). *Working and educating for life: Feminist and international perspectives on adult education*. London: Routledge.

Hatcher, T. (2006). An editor's challenge to human resource development. *Human Resource Development Quarterly, 17*(1), 1–4.

Hayes, E. (1988). A typology of low-literate adults based on perceptions of deterrents to participation in adult basic education. *Adult Education Quarterly, 39*(1), 1–10.

Hayes, E. (1989). Insights from women's experiences for teaching and learning. In E. R. Hayes (Ed.), *Effective teaching styles.* New Directions for Continuing Education, No. 43. San Francisco: Jossey-Bass.

Hayes, E. (1994). Developing a personal and professional agenda for change. In E. Hayes and S.A.J. Colin III (Eds.), *Confronting racism and sexism.* New Directions for Adult and Continuing Education, No. 61. San Francisco: Jossey-Bass.

Hayes, E., and Colin, S.A.J., III (Eds.). (1994). *Confronting racism and sexism.* New Directions for Adult and Continuing Education, No. 61. San Francisco: Jossey-Bass.

Hayes, E., and Smith, L. (1994). Women and adult education: An analysis of perspectives in major journals. *Adult Education Quarterly, 44*(4), 201–221.

Hayslip, B., and Panek, P. (1989). *Adult development and aging.* New York: HarperCollins.

Heaney, T. W. (1992). Resources for popular education. *Adult Learning, 3*(5), 10–11, 25.

Heaney, T. W. (1993). Identifying and dealing with educational, social, and political issues. In P. Mulcrone (Ed.), *Current perspectives on administration of adult education programs.* New Directions for Adult and Continuing Education, No. 60. San Francisco: Jossey-Bass.

Heaney, T. W. (1996). *Adult education: From center stage to the wings and back again.* Columbus, OH: ERIC Clearinghouse on Adult, Career, and Vocational Education, Information Series No. 365.

Heller, J. (1975). *Something happened.* New York: Ballantine Books.

Hellyer, M. R., and Schulman, B. (1989). Workers' education. In S. B. Merriam and P. M. Cunningham (Eds.), *Handbook of adult and continuing education* (pp. 569–582). San Francisco: Jossey-Bass.

Henry, W. A., III. (1994). *In defense of elitism.* New York: Doubleday.

Hiemstra, R. (1980). Howard Yale McClusky: Adult education pioneer and statesman. *Lifelong Learning: The Adult Years, 4*(2), 5–7, 25.

Hiemstra, R. (1988a). Creating the future. In R. G. Brockett (Ed.), *Continuing education in the year 2000.* New Directions for Continuing Education, No. 36. San Francisco: Jossey-Bass.

Hiemstra, R. (1988b). Translating personal values and philosophy into practical action. In R. G. Brockett (Ed.), *Ethical issues in adult education* (pp. 178–194). New York: Teachers College Press.

Hiemstra, R. (1991). Toward building more effective learning environments. In R. Hiemstra (Ed.), *Creating environments for effective adult learning.* New Directions for Adult and Continuing Education, No. 50. San Francisco: Jossey-Bass.

Hiemstra, R., and Brockett, R. G. (Eds.). (1994). *Overcoming resistance to self-direction in adult learning.* New Directions for Adult and Continuing Education, No. 64. San Francisco: Jossey-Bass.

Hiemstra, R., and Sisco, B. (1990). *Individualizing instruction: Making learning personal, empowering, and successful.* San Francisco: Jossey-Bass.

Hill, E. A. (1989). Literary research and the study of reentry women. *Journal of Continuing Higher Education, 37*(2), 7–10.

Hill, L. H., and Clover, D. E. (2003). *Environmental adult education: Ecological learning, theory, and practice for socioenvironmental change.* New Directions for Adult and Continuing Education, No. 99. San Francisco: Jossey-Bass.

Hill, L. H., and Moore, A. B. (2000). Adult education in the rural community development. In A. L. Wilson and E. R. Hayes (Eds.), *Handbook of adult and continuing education* (pp.344–359). San Francisco: Jossey-Bass.

Hill, R. J. (1995). Gay discourse in adult education: A critical review. *Adult Education Quarterly, 45*(3), 142–158.

Hill, R. J. (Ed.). (2006). *Challenging homophobia and heterosexism: Lesbian, gay, bisexual, transgender and queer issues in organizational settings.* New Directions for Adult and Continuing Education, No. 112. San Francisco: Jossey-Bass.

Hill, S. T. (n.d.). *Trends in adult education: 1969–1984.* Washington, DC: Center for Educational Statistics, Office of Educational Research and Improvement, U.S. Department of Education.

Hilton, R. J. (1981). *The short happy life of a learning society: Adult education in America 1930–39.* Unpublished doctoral dissertation, Syracuse University, Syracuse, NY.

Hilton, R. J. (1982). *Humanizing adult education research: Five stories from the 1930s.* Syracuse, NY: Syracuse University Publications in Continuing Education.

Hinzen, H. (1994). Policy and practice of literacy: Experiments and interpretations. *Adult Education and Development, 43,* 213–232.

Hirsch, E. D., Kett, J. F., and Trefil, J. (1987). *Cultural literacy: What every American needs to know.* Boston: Houghton Mifflin.

Holden, J. B., and Dorland, J. R. (1995). Adult education and the World Bank. In B. B. Cassara (Ed.), *Adult education through world collaboration* (pp. 23–38). Malabar, FL: Krieger.

Holford, J. (1995). Why social movements matter: Adult education theory, cognitive praxis, and the creation of knowledge. *Adult Education Quarterly, 45*(2), 63–78.

Holst, J. D. (2006). Globalization and the future of critical adult education. In S. B. Merriam, B. C. Courtenay, and R. M. Cervero (Eds.), *Global issues and adult education: Perspectives from Latin America, Southern Africa, and the United States* (pp. 41–52). San Francisco: Jossey-Bass.

hooks, b. (1994). *Teaching to transgress: Education as the practice of freedom.* London and New York: Routledge.

Horton, A. I. (1989). *The Highlander Folk School: A history of its major programs, 1932–1961.* Brooklyn, NY: Carlson.

Horton, M., and Freire, P. (1990). *We make the road by walking.* Philadelphia: Temple University Press.

Horton, M., Kohl, J., and Kohl, H. (1990). *The long haul: An autobiography.* New York: Doubleday.

Houle, C. O. (1964). The emergence of graduate study in adult education. In G. Jensen, A. A. Liveright, and W. Hallenbeck (Eds.), *Adult education: Outlines of an emerging field of university study* (pp. 69–83). Washington, DC: Adult Education Association of the U.S.A.

Houle, C. O. (1969). Adult education. In R. Ebel (Ed.), *Encyclopedia of educational research* (4th ed., pp. 51–55). New York: Macmillan.

Houle, C. O. (1970). The educators of adults. In R. M. Smith, G. F. Aker, and J. R. Kidd (Eds.), *Handbook of adult education* (pp. 109–120). New York: Macmillan.

Houle, C. O. (1972). *The design of education.* San Francisco: Jossey-Bass.

Houle, C. O. (1980). *Continuing learning in the professions.* San Francisco: Jossey-Bass.

Houle, C.O. (1988) *The inquiring mind.* Norman, OK: Oklahoma Research Center for Continuin Professional and Higher Education, University of Oklahoma. (Original work published in 1961.)

Houle, C. O. (1992). *The literature of adult education: A bibliographic essay.* San Francisco: Jossey-Bass.

Hugo, J. M. (1990). Adult education history and the issue of gender: Toward a different history of adult education in America. *Adult Education Quarterly, 41*(1), 1–16.

Illich, I. (1970). *Deschooling society.* New York: HarperCollins.

Ilsley, P. J. (1992). The undeniable link: Adult and continuing education and social change. In M. W. Galbraith and B. Sisco (Eds.), *Confronting controversies in challenging times: A call for action.* New Directions for Adult and Continuing Education, No. 54. San Francisco: Jossey-Bass.

Imel, S. (1989). The field's literature and information sources. In S. B. Merriam and P. M. Cunningham (Eds.), *Handbook of adult and continuing education* (pp. 134–146). San Francisco: Jossey-Bass.

Imel, S., Brockett, R. G., and James, W. B. (2000). Defining the profession: A critical appraisal. In A. L. Wilson and E. R. Hayes (Eds.), *Handbook of adult and continuing education* (pp. 628–642). San Francisco: Jossey-Bass.

Ingham, R. J., and Hanks, G. (1981). Graduate degree programs for professional adult educators. In S. M. Grabowski and Associates (Eds.), *Preparing educators of adults* (pp. 17–38). San Francisco: Jossey-Bass.

Inkster, I. (Ed.) (1985). *The steam intellect societies: Essay on culture, education and industry circa 1820–1914.* Derby, UK: Saxon Printing. International handbook of adult education (1929). London: World Association for Adult Education.

Jackson, L., and Caffarella, R. S. (Eds.). (1994). *Experiential learning: A new approach.* New Directions for Adult and Continuing Education, No. 62. San Francisco.

Jackson, L., and MacIsaac, D. (1994). Introduction to a new approach to experiential learning. In L. Jackson and R. S. Caffarella (Eds.), *Experiential learning: A new approach.* New Directions for Adult and Continuing Education, No. 62. San Francisco: Jossey-Bass.

Jacobs, R. (1987). *Human performance technology: A systems-based field for the training and development profession.* Columbus, OH: ERIC Clearinghouse on Adult, Career, and Vocational Education, Information Series No. 326.

James, W. B. (1981). Certification is unfeasible and unnecessary. In B. W. Kreitlow and Associates (Eds.), *Examining controversies in adult education* (pp. 84–95). San Francisco: Jossey-Bass.

James, W. B. (1992). Professional certification is not needed in adult and continuing education. In M. W. Galbraith and B. Sisco (Eds.), *Confronting controversies in challenging times: A call for action.* New Directions for Adult and Continuing Education, No. 54. San Francisco: Jossey-Bass.

Jarvis, P. (1985). *The sociology of adult and continuing education.* London: Croom Helm.

Jarvis, P. (1987a). *Adult learning in the social context.* London: Croom Helm.

Jarvis, P. (Ed.). (1987b). *Twentieth century thinkers in adult education.* London: Croom Helm.

Jarvis, P. (Ed.). (1990). *An international dictionary of adult and continuing education*. London and New York: Routledge.

Jarvis, P. (1991). Growth and challenges in the study of adult education. In J. M. Peters, P. Jarvis, and Associates (Eds.), *Adult education: Evolution and achievements in a developing field of study* (pp. 1–13). San Francisco: Jossey-Bass.

Jarvis, P. (1992). *Paradoxes of learning: On becoming an individual in society*. San Francisco: Jossey-Bass.

Jarvis, P. (1993). *Adult education and the state*. London: Routledge.

Jarvis, P. (2004). *Adult education and lifelong learning: Theory and practice* (3rd ed.). London and New York: Routledge/Falmer Press.

Jensen, G. (1964). How adult education borrows and reformulates knowledge of other disciplines. In G. Jensen, A. A. Liveright, and W. Hallenbeck (Eds.), *Adult education: Outlines of an emerging field of university study* (pp. 105–111). Washington, DC: Adult Education Association of the U.S.A.

Jensen, G., Liveright, A. A., and Hallenbeck, W. (Eds.). (1964). *Adult education: Outlines of an emerging field of university study*. Washington, DC: Adult Education Association of the U.S.A.

Jimmerson, R. M., Hastay, L. W., and Long, J. S. (1989). Public affairs education. In S. B. Merriam and P. M. Cunningham (Eds.), *Handbook of adult and continuing education* (pp. 451–464). San Francisco: Jossey-Bass.

Johnson, A. (1952). *Pioneer's progress*. New York: Viking Penguin.

Johnson, M. (1995). Drucker speaks his mind. *Management Review*, 84 (10), 10–14.

Johnson, R. (1988). "Really useful knowledge" 1790–1850: Memories for education in the 1980s. In T. Lovett (Ed.), *Radical approaches to adult education: A reader* (pp. 3–34). London: Routledge.

Johnson, S. and Taylor, K. (Eds.). (2006) *The neuroscience of adult learning*. New Directions for Adult and Continuing Education, No. 110, San Francisco: Jossey-Bass.

Johnstone, J.W.C., and Rivera, R. (1965). *Volunteers for learning: A study of the educational pursuits of adults*. Hawthorne, NY: Aldine.

Jordan, W. D. (1978). Searching for adulthood in America. In E. H. Erikson (Ed.), *Adulthood* (pp. 189–199). New York: W. W. Norton.

Kasworm, C. E. (1983). An examination of self-directed learning contracts as an instructional strategy. *Innovative Higher Education*, 8(1), 45–54.

Kegan, R. (1994). *In over our heads: The mental demands of modern life*. Cambridge, MA: Harvard University Press.

Kett, J. F. (1994). *The pursuit of knowledge under difficulties: From self-improvement to adult education in America, 1750–1990*. Stanford, CA: Stanford University Press.

Kidd, J. R. (1981). Research. In A. N. Charters and Associates (Eds.), *Comparing adult education worldwide* (pp. 218–239). San Francisco: Jossey-Bass.

Kim, K., Collins, M., Stowe, P., and Chandler, K. (1995). *Forty percent of adults participate in adult education activities: 1994–95*. Washington, DC: National Center for Educational Statistics, Office of Educational Research and Improvement, U.S. Department of Education.

Kimmel, D. C. (1990). *Adulthood and aging* (3rd ed.). New York: Wiley.

Knowles, M. S. (1962). *The adult education movement in the United States*. Austin, TX: Holt, Rinehart and Winston.

Knowles, M. S. (1964). The field of operations in adult education. In G. Jensen, A. A. Liveright, and W. Hallenbeck (Eds.), *Adult education: Outlines of an emerging field of university study* (pp. 41–67). Washington, DC: Adult Education Association of the U.S.A.

Knowles, M. S. (1968). Andragogy, not pedagogy. *Adult Leadership, 16*, 350–352, 386.

Knowles, M. S. (1970). *The modern practice of adult education: Andragogy vs. pedagogy*. New York: Association Press.

Knowles, M. S. (1975). *Self-directed learning*. New York: Association Press.

Knowles, M. S. (1977). *A history of the adult education movement in the United States* (Rev. ed.), original work published as *The adult education movement in the United States, 1962*. Malabar, FL: Krieger.

Knowles, M. S. (1980a). The growth and development of adult education. In J. M. Peters and Associates, (Eds.), *Building an effective adult education enterprise* (pp. 12–40). San Francisco: Jossey-Bass.

Knowles, M. S. (1980b). *The modern practice of adult education: From pedagogy to andragogy* (Rev. ed.). New York: Association Press.

Knowles, M. S. (1986). *The adult learner: A neglected species* (3rd ed.). Houston: Gulf.

Knowles, M. S. (1989). *The making of an adult educator: An autobiographical journey*. San Francisco: Jossey-Bass.

Knowles, M. S., Holton, E. F. III, and Swanson, R. A. (2005). *The adult learner: The definitive classic in adult education and human resource development* (6th ed.). Burlington, MA and London: Elsevier.

Knox, A. B. (Ed.). (1979). *Enhancing proficiencies of continuing educators*. New Directions for Continuing Education, No. 1. San Francisco: Jossey-Bass.

Knox, A. B. (1991). Educational leadership and program administration. In J. M. Peters, P. Jarvis, and Associates (Eds.), *Adult education: Evolution and achievements in a developing field of study* (pp. 217–258). San Francisco: Jossey-Bass.

Knox, A. B. (1993). *Strengthening adult and continuing education: A global perspective on synergistic leadership.* San Francisco: Jossey-Bass.

Kohlberg, L. (1969). Stage and sequence: The cognitive-developmental approach to socialization. In D. A. Goslin (Ed.), *Handbook of socialization theory and research* (pp. 347–480). Skokie, IL: Rand McNally.

Kolb, D. A. (1984). *Experiential learning: Experience as the source of learning and development.* Englewood Cliffs, NJ: Prentice-Hall.

Koloski, J. A. (1989). Enhancing the field's image through professionalism and practice. In B. A. Quigley (Ed.), *Fulfilling the promise of adult and continuing education.* New Directions for Continuing Education, No. 44. San Francisco: Jossey-Bass.

Konopka, G. (1958). *Eduard C. Lindeman and social work philosophy.* Minneapolis: University of Minnesota Press.

Kopka, T.L.C., and Peng, S. S. (1993). *Adult education: Main reasons for participating.* Washington, DC: National Center for Educational Statistics, Office of Educational Research and Improvement, U.S. Department of Education.

Kornbluh, J. L., and Frederickson, M. (Eds.). (1984). *Sisterhood and solidarity: Workers' education for women, 1914–1984.* Philadelphia: Temple University Press.

Kotinsky, R. (1933). *Adult education and the social scene.* East Norwalk, CT: Appleton & Lange.

Kowalski, T. J. (1988). *The organization and planning of adult education.* Albany: State University of New York Press.

Kulich, J. (1970). *An historical overview of the adult self-learner.* Paper presented at the Northwest Institute Conference on Independent Study: The adult as a self-learner. University of British Columbia, Vancouver.

Larson, M. S. (1977). *The rise of professionalism.* Berkeley: University of California Press.

Laubach, F. C. (1970). *Forty years with the silent billion: Adventuring in literacy.* Old Tappan, NJ: Revell.

Lawler, P. (1991). *The challenges of the future: Ethical issues in a changing student population.* (ED 340 305)

Lawrence, R. L. (Ed.). (2005). *Artistic ways of knowing: Expanded opportunities for teaching and learning.* New Directions for Adult and Continuing Education, No. 107. San Francisco: Jossey-Bass.

Lawson, K. H. (1975). *Philosophical concepts and values in adult education.* Nottingham, UK: Barnes & Humby.

Lawson, K. H. (1982). *Analysis and ideology: Conceptual essays on the education of adults.* Nottingham, UK: University of Nottingham.

Lawson, K. H. (1991). Philosophical foundations. In J. M. Peters and P. Jarvis (Eds.), *Adult education: Evolution and achievements in a developing field of study* (pp. 282–300). San Francisco: Jossey-Bass.

Learned, W. S. (1924). *The American public library and the diffusion of knowledge*. Orlando, FL.: Harcourt Brace Jovanovich.

Lee, M. and Johnson-Bailey, J. (2004). Challenges to the classroom authority of women of color. In R. St. Clair and J. A. Sandlin (Eds.), *Promoting critical practice in adult Education* (pp. 55–64). New Directions for Adult and Continuing Education, No. 102. San Francisco: Jossey-Bass.

LeGrand, B. F. (1992). A change of heart: Continuing professional education should be mandatory. In M. W. Galbraith and B. Sisco (Eds.), *Confronting controversies in challenging times: A call for action*. New Directions for Adult and Continuing Education, No. 54. San Francisco: Jossey-Bass.

Leonard, E. L. (1991). *Friendly rebel: A personal and social history of Eduard C. Lindeman*. Adamant, VT: Adamant Press.

Leumer, W. (1994). Migrants and ethnic minorities: A European challenge to adult education. *Adult Education and Development, 43,* 233–245.

Levison, A. (1995, July 2). Computers may widen social-class gap. *Atlanta Journal/Atlanta Constitution,* B5.

Levinson, D. J., and others (1978). *The seasons of a man's life*. New York: Knopf.

Lewis, L. H. (1989). New educational technologies for the future. In S. B. Merriam and P. M. Cunningham (Eds.), *Handbook of adult and continuing education* (pp. 613–627). San Francisco: Jossey-Bass.

Lewis, L. H., and Williams, C. J. (1994). Experiential learning: Past and present. In L. Jackson and R. S. Caffarella (Eds.), *Experiential learning: A new approach* (pp. 5–16). New Directions for Adult and Continuing Education, No. 62. San Francisco: Jossey-Bass.

Lifvendahl, T. A. (1995). An analysis of the dissertation trends of adult education: Perceptions resulting from the creation of a dissertation registry. Unpublished doctoral dissertation, Northern Illinois University, De Kalb.

Lindeman, E. C. (1989). *The meaning of adult education*. Norman: Oklahoma Research Center for Continuing Professional and Higher Education, University of Oklahoma. (Original work published in 1926.)

Liveright, A. A. (1968). *A study of adult education in the United States*. Boston: Center for the Study of Liberal Education for Adults.

Loevinger, J. (1976). *Ego development: Conceptions and theories*. San Francisco: Jossey-Bass.

London, J. (1973). Adult education for the 1970s: Promise or illusion? *Adult Education, 24*(1), 60–70.

Long, H. B. (1976). *Continuing education of adults in Colonial America* (Occasional Papers No. 45). Syracuse, NY: Syracuse University Publications in Continuing Education.

Long, H. B. (1987). *New perspectives on the education of adults in the United States.* London: Croom Helm.

Long, H. B. (1990). History: Its place in the study of adult education. *Historical Foundations of Adult Education, 4*(3–4), 1–10.

Lovett, T. (Ed.). (1988). *Radical approaches to adult education: A reader.* London: Routledge.

Lowe, J. (1975). *The education of adults: A world perspective.* Paris: UNESCO.

Lowenthal, M. F., Thurnher, M., Chiriboga, D. A., and Associates (1975). *Four stages of life: A comparative study of women and men facing transitions.* San Francisco: Jossey-Bass.

Luke, R. A. (1992). *The NEA and adult education, a historical review: 1921–1972.* N.p.: R. A. Luke.

Macedo, D. (1994). Preface. In P. L. McLaren and C. Lankshear (Eds.), *Politics of liberation* (pp. xiii–xviii). London: Routledge.

MacKaye, D. L. (1931). Tactical training for teaching adults. *Journal of Adult Education, 3*(3), 290–294.

MacKenzie, L. (1993). On our feet: Taking steps to challenge women's oppression. *Supplement to Adult Education and Development, 41.*

Martin, E. D. (1926). *The meaning of a liberal education.* New York: W. W. Norton.

Mason, R. (2003). Global education: Out of the ivory tower. In M. G. Moore and W. G. Anderson (Eds.), *Handbook of distance education* (pp. 743–752). Hillsdale, NJ: Erlbaum.

McCarten, A. M. (1987). Statewide planning for adult learning services. In W. M. Rivera (Ed.), *Planning adult learning: Issues, practices and directions* (pp. 127–141). London: Croom Helm.

McClusky, H. Y. (1982). The legacy of the AEA/USA with implications for the future of adult and continuing education. *Lifelong Learning: The Adult Years, 6*(1), 8–10.

McCullough, K. O. (1980). Analyzing the evolving structure of adult education. In J. M. Peters and Associates (Eds.), *Building an effective adult education enterprise* (pp. 158–163). San Francisco: Jossey-Bass.

McDonald, K. S., and Wood, G. S., Jr. (1993). Surveying adult education practitioners about ethical issues. *Adult Education Quarterly, 43*(4), 243–257.

McDowell, T. (2003). Answering the call for anti-racist praxis in adult education. *Proceedings of the 44th Annual Adult Education Research Conference* (pp. 279 283). San Francisco: San Francisco State University.

McKenzie, L. (1978). *Adult education and the burden of the future*. Washington, DC: University Press of America.

McKenzie, L. (1991). *Adult education and worldview construction*. Malabar, FL: Krieger.

McLaren, P. L., and Lankshear, C. (1994). Introduction. In P. L. McLaren and C. Lankshear (Eds.), *Politics of liberation* (pp. 1–11). London: Routledge.

McLean, G. N. and Johansen, B. P. (Eds.) (2006). Worldviews of adult learning in the workplace. *Advances in Developing Human Resources, 8*(3).

Mellor, M. (1988). Ethics and accountability: Participatory research in a worker co-operative. *Convergence, 21*(2/3), 73–84.

Merriam, S. B. (1979). Ben Franklin's Junto revisited. *Lifelong Learning: The Adult Years, 2,* 18–19.

Merriam, S. B. (1984). *Adult development: Implications for adult education*. Columbus, OH: ERIC Clearinghouse on Adult, Career, and Vocational Education.

Merriam, S. B. (1988). *Case study research in education: A qualitative approach*. San Francisco: Jossey-Bass.

Merriam, S. B. (1991). How research produces knowledge. In J. M. Peters and P. Jarvis (Eds.), *Adult education: Evolution and achievements in a developing field of study* (pp. 42–65). San Francisco: Jossey-Bass.

Merriam, S. B. (Ed.). (1993). *Themes of adulthood through literature*. New York: Teachers College Press.

Merriam, S. B. (2007). *Non-western perspectives on learning and knowing*. Malabar, FL: Krieger.

Merriam, S. B., and Caffarella, R. S. (1991). *Learning in adulthood*. San Francisco: Jossey-Bass.

Merriam, S. B., Caffarella, R. S., and Baumgartner, L. M. (2007). *Learning in adulthood* (3rd ed.). San Francisco: Jossey-Bass.

Merriam, S. B., Courtenay, B. C., and Cervero, R. M. (2006). Globalization and the market economy. In S. B. Merriam, B. C. Courtenay, and R. M. Cervero (Eds.), *Global issues and adult education: Perspectives from Latin America, Southern Africa, and the United States* (pp. 1–4). San Francisco: Jossey-Bass.

Merriam, S. B., and Cunningham, P. M. (Eds.). (1989). *Handbook of adult and continuing education*. San Francisco: Jossey-Bass.

Merriam, S. B., Mott, V., and Lee, M. (1996). Learning that comes from the negative interpretation of life experiences. *Studies in Continuing Education*.

Merriam, S. B., and Yang, B. (1996). A longitudinal study of adult life experiences and development outcomes. *Adult Education Quarterly, 46*(2), 62–81.

Merrifield, J., Norris, L., and White, L. (1991). *I'm not a quitter! Job training and basic education for women textile workers*. Knoxville: Center for Literacy Studies, University of Tennessee.

Mezirow, J. (1975). *Education for perspective transformation: Women's reentry programs in community colleges*. New York: Center for Adult Education, Teachers College, Columbia University.

Mezirow, J. (1978). Perspective transformation. *Adult Education, 28*(2), 100–110.

Mezirow, J. (1981). A critical theory of adult learning and education. *Adult Education, 32*(1), 3–24.

Mezirow, J. (1985). Concept and action in adult education. *Adult Education Quarterly, 35*(3), 142–151.

Mezirow, J. (1989). Transformation theory and social action: A reply to Collard and Law. *Adult Education Quarterly, 39*(2), 170–176.

Mezirow, J. (1990). Conclusion: Toward transformative learning and emancipatory education. In J. Mezirow and Associates (Eds.), *Fostering critical reflection in adulthood: A guide to transformative and emancipatory learning* (pp. 354–376). San Francisco: Jossey-Bass.

Mezirow, J. (1991a). *Transformative dimensions of adult learning*. San Francisco: Jossey-Bass.

Mezirow, J. (1991b). Transformation theory and cultural context: A reply to Clark and Wilson. *Adult Education Quarterly, 41*(3), 188–192.

Mezirow, J. (1994). Understanding transformation theory. *Adult Education Quarterly, 44*(4), 222–232.

Mezirow, J., and Associates. (1990). *Fostering critical reflection in adulthood: A guide to transformative and emancipatory learning*. San Francisco: Jossey-Bass.

Mezirow, J., and Associates. (2000). *Learning as transformation: Critical perspectives on a theory in progress*. San Francisco: Jossey-Bass.

Miller, P. A. (1995). Adult education's mislaid mission. *Adult Education Quarterly, 46*(1), 43–52.

Miller, V. (1985). *Between struggle and hope: The Nicaraguan literacy crusade*. Boulder, CO: Westview Press.

Milton, J., Watkins, K. E., Studdard, S. S., and Burch, M. (2003). The ever widening gyre: Factors affecting change in adult education graduate programs in the United States. *Adult Education Quarterly, 54*(1), 23–41.

Minnis, J. R. (1993). Adult education and the African state in the post Cold War era. *Convergence, 26*(2), 11–19.

Moore, M. G. (1994). Distance education at the school level. In T. Husen and T. N. Postlethwaite (Eds.), *The international encyclopedia of education* (2nd ed., Vol. 3, pp. 1563–1567). New York: Pergamon Press.

Moore, M. G. (2001). *Distance education in the United States: The state of the art*. Series of lectures on the education use of ICT and virtual education by UOC. http:www.uoc.edu/web/eng/art/uoc/moore/moore.html. Accessed July 1, 2004.

Moreland, W. D., and Goldenstein, E. H. (1985). *Pioneers in adult education*. Chicago: Nelson-Hall.

Morgan, C. T. (1982). Finding a way out: Adult education in Harlem during the Great Depression. *Proceedings of the Lifelong Learning Research Conference* (pp. 172–176). College Park: Department of Agricultural Extension Education, University of Maryland.

Morrison, J. (1989). Canada: Frontier college. In A. N. Charters and R. J. Hilton (Eds.), *Landmarks in international adult education: A comparative analysis* (pp. 96–113). London: Routledge.

Morrison, T. (1974). *Chautauqua: A center for education, religion, and the arts in America*. Chicago: University of Chicago Press.

Morstain, B. R., and Smart, J. C. (1974). Reasons for participation in adult education courses: A multivariate analysis of group differences. *Adult Education, 24*(2), 83–98.

Mulcrone, P. (Ed.). (1993). *Current perspectives on administration of adult education programs*. New Directions for Adult and Continuing Education, No. 60. San Francisco: Jossey-Bass.

Nadler, L., and Nadler, Z. (1989). *Developing human resources* (3rd ed.). San Francisco: Jossey-Bass.

Naisbitt, J. (1996). *Megatrends—Asia*. New York: Simon & Schuster.

Nardine, F. E. (1990). The changing role of low-income minority parents in their children's schooling. In J. M. Ross-Gordon, L. G. Martin, and D. B. Briscoe (Eds.), *Serving culturally diverse populations*. New Directions for Adult and Continuing Education, No. 48. San Francisco: Jossey-Bass.

Nesbit, T. (Ed.). (2005). *Class concerns: Adult education and social class*. New Directions for Adult and Continuing Education, No. 106. San Francisco: Jossey- Bass.

Nesbit, T. (2006). What's the matter with social class? *Adult Education Quarterly, 56* (3), 171–187.

Neufeldt, H. G., and McGee, L. (Eds.). (1990). *Education of the African American adult*. Westport, CT: Greenwood Press.

Neustadt, R. E., and May, E. R. (1986). *Thinking in time: The uses of history for decision makers*. New York: Free Press.

New York University. (1935). *Journal of Adult Education, 7*(2), 216.

Newman, M. (1994). *Defining the enemy: Adult education in social action*. Sydney: Stewart Victor.

Newman, M. (2006). *Teaching defiance*. San Francisco: Jossey-Bass.

Nordhaug, O. (1986). Adult education in the welfare state: Institutionalization of social commitment. *International Journal of Lifelong Education*, 5(1), 45–57.

Norris, J. A., and Rennington, P. (1992). *Developing literacy programs for homeless adults*. Malabar, FL: Kreiger.

Nottingham Andragogy Group. (1983). *Towards a developmental theory of andragogy*. Nottingham, UK: University of Nottingham, Department of Adult Education.

Oglesby, K. L., and Bax, W. (1993). The new Europe: Challenges for European adult education. *Convergence*, 26(1), 51–58.

Oglesby, K. L., Krajnc, A., and Mbilinyi, M. (1989). Adult education for women. In C. J. Titmus (Ed.), *Lifelong education for adults: An international handbook* (pp. 322–334). New York: Pergamon Press.

Ohliger, J. (1985). *The fictional adult educator*. Unpublished course syllabus. Madison, WI: Basic Choices.

Oliver, L. P. (1987). Study circles: Coming together for personal growth and social change. Washington, DC: Seven Locks Press.

O'Neil, W. F. (1981). Educational ideologies: Contemporary expressions of educational philosophy. Dubuque, IA: Kendall/Hunt. (Reprinted 1990.)

Organization for Economic Co-operation and Development. (1973). *Recurrent education: A strategy for lifelong learning*. Paris: Organization for Economic Co-operation and Development.

Osborn, R. (1990). Adult college students in American films: An untapped resource for research in adult and continuing education. *Journal of Continuing Higher Education*, 38(2), 25–28.

Overstreet, H. A. (1949). *The mature mind*. New York: W. W. Norton.

Pace, R. W., Smith, D. C., and Mills, G. E. (1991). *HRD: The field*. Englewood Cliffs, NJ: Prentice-Hall.

Paterson, R.W.K. (1979). *Values, education and the adult*. London: Routledge and Kegan Paul.

Paterson, R.W.K. (1984). Objectivity as an educational imperative. *International Journal of Lifelong Education*, 3(1), 17–29.

Paulston, R., and Altenbaugh, R. (1988). Adult education in radical U.S. social and ethnic movements. In T. Lovett (Ed.), *Radical approaches to adult education: A reader* (pp. 114–137). London: Routledge.

Pennington, F., and Green, J. (1976). Comparative analysis of program development in six professions. *Adult Education*, 28,(1) 13–23.

Perelman, L. J. (1984). *The learning enterprise: Adult learning, human capital, and economic development*. Washington, DC: Council of State Policy and Planning Agencies Publications. (ED 317 784)

Perry, W. (1970). *Forms of intellectual and ethical development in the college years*. New York: Holt, Rinehart and Winston.

Pert, C. B. (1997). *Molecules of emotion: Why you feel the way you feel*. New York: Scribner.

Peters, J. M. (1991a). Advancing the study of adult education: A summary perspective. In J. M. Peters, P. Jarvis, and Associates (Eds.), *Adult education: Evolution and achievements in a developing field of study* (pp. 421–446). San Francisco: Jossey-Bass.

Peters, J. M. (1991b). Strategies for reflective practice. In R. G. Brockett (Ed.), *Professional development for educators of adults*. New Directions for Adult and Continuing Education, No. 51. San Francisco: Jossey-Bass.

Peters, J. M., Jarvis, P., and Associates (Eds.). (1991). *Adult education: Evolution and achievements in a developing field of study*. San Francisco: Jossey-Bass.

Peters, J. M., and Kreitlow, B. W. (1991). Growth and future of graduate programs. In J. M. Peters, P. Jarvis, and Associates (Eds.), *Adult education: Evolution and achievements in a developing field of study* (pp. 145–183). San Francisco: Jossey-Bass.

Peterson, D. A. (1983). *Facilitating education for older learners*. San Francisco: Jossey-Bass.

Peterson, E. A. (Ed.). (1996). *Freedom road: Adult education of African Americans*. Malabar, FL: Krieger.

Peterson, E. A. (Ed.). (2002). *Freedom road: Adult education of African Americans* (2nd ed.). Malabar, FL: Krieger.

Phillips, D. C. (1995). The good, the bad, and the ugly: The many faces of constructivism. *Educational Researcher, 24*(7), 5–12.

Phillips, L., and Associates (Summer 1994). Status of mandatory continuing education for selected professions, *Newsletter*. Athens, GA: Louis Phillips and Associates.

Pietrykowski, B. (1996). Knowledge and power in adult education: Beyond Freire and Habermas. *Adult Education Quarterly, 46*(2), 82–97.

Pittman, V. (1989). What is the image of the field today? In B. A. Quigley (Ed.), *Fulfilling the promise of adult and continuing education*. New Directions for Continuing Education, No. 44. San Francisco: Jossey-Bass.

Polanyi, M. (1967). *The tacit dimension*. New York: Doubleday.

Pole, T. A. (1967). *A history of the origin and progress of adult schools*. London: Woburn Press. (Original work published in 1816.)

Porter, D. R. (1993). Improving administrative efficiency through technology. In P. Mulcrone (Ed.), *Current perspectives on administration of adult education programs*. New Directions for Adult and Continuing Education, No. 60. San Francisco: Jossey-Bass.

Pratt, D. D. (1993). Andragogy after twenty-five years. In S. B. Merriam (Ed.), *An update on adult learning theory*. New Directions for Adult and Continuing Education, No. 57. San Francisco: Jossey-Bass.

Quigley, B. A. (1993). To shape the future: Towards a framework for adult education social policy research and action. *International Journal of Lifelong Education, 12*(2), 117–127.

Rachal, J. R. (1988). Taxonomies and typologies of adult education. *Lifelong Learning: An Omnibus of Practice and Research, 12*(2), 20–23.

Rachal, J. R. (1989). The social context of adult and continuing education. In P. Mulcrone (Ed.), *Handbook of adult and continuing education* (pp. 3–14). San Francisco: Jossey-Bass.

Reed, H. B., and Loughran, E. L. (Eds.). (1984). *Beyond schools: Education for economic, social and personal development*. Amherst: School of Education, University of Massachusetts.

Reich, R. (2001). *The future of success*. New York: Knopf.

Resnick, L. B. (1987). Learning in school and out. *Educational Researcher, 16*(9), 13–20.

Rice, J. K., with Meyer, S. (1989). Continuing education for women. In S. B. Merriam and P. M. Cunningham (Eds.), *Handbook of adult and continuing education* (pp. 550–568). San Francisco: Jossey-Bass.

Ritter, H. (1986). *Dictionary of concepts in history*. Westport, CT: Greenwood Press.

Roberts, H. (1982). *Culture and adult education: A study of Alberta and Quebec*. Edmonton: University of Alberta Press.

Robinson, J. H. (1924). *The humanizing of knowledge*. New York: Doran.

Rocco, T. (2006). Disability as an issue of marginalization. In S. B. Merriam, B. C. Courtenay, and R. M. Cervero (Eds.). *Global issues and adult education: Perspectives from Latin America, Southern Africa, and the United States* (pp.169- 181). San Francisco: Jossey-Bass.

Rogers, C. R. (1969). *Freedom to learn*. Columbus, OH: Charles E. Merrill.

Rogers, C. R. (1983). *Freedom to learn for the 80s*. Columbus, OH: Charles E. Merrill.

Rohfeld, R. W. (Ed.). (1990a). *Expanding access to knowledge: Continuing higher education*. Washington, DC: National University Continuing Education Association.

Rohfeld, R. W. (1990b). James Harvey Robinson: Historian as adult educator. *Adult Education Quarterly, 40*(4), 219–228.

Rose, A. D. (1989a). Beyond classroom walls: The Carnegie Corporation and the founding of the American Association for Adult Education. *Adult Education Quarterly, 39*(3), 140–151.

Rose, A. D. (1989b). Nontraditional education and the assessment of prior learning. In S. B. Merriam and P. M. Cunningham (Eds.), *Handbook of adult and continuing education* (pp. 211–220). San Francisco: Jossey-Bass.

Rose, A. D. (1991). Preparing for veterans: Higher education and the efforts to accredit the learning of World War II servicemen and women. *Adult Education Quarterly, 42*(1), 30–45.

Rose, A. D. (1995). Exploring the potential of distance education. *Adult Learning, 7*(7), 5, 8.

Rose, A. D., and Mason, R. (1990). *Survey of graduate programs in adult education.* Unpublished manuscript, Graduate Studies in Adult/Continuing Education, Northern Illinois University.

Ross-Gordon, J. M. (1990). Serving culturally diverse populations: A social imperative for adult and continuing education. In J. M. Ross-Gordon, L. G. Martin, and D. B. Briscoe (Eds.), *Serving culturally diverse populations.* New Directions for Adult and Continuing Education, No. 48. San Francisco: Jossey-Bass.

Ross-Gordon, J. M., Martin, L. G., and Briscoe, D. B. (Eds.). (1990a). *Serving culturally diverse populations.* New Directions for Adult and Continuing Education, No. 48. San Francisco: Jossey-Bass.

Ross-Gordon, J. M., Martin, L. G., and Briscoe, D. B. (1990b). Conclusion. In J. M. Ross-Gordon, L. G. Martin, and D. B. Briscoe (Eds.), *Serving culturally diverse populations.* New Directions for Adult and Continuing Education, No. 48. San Francisco: Jossey-Bass.

Ross, L. Q. (Leo Rosten). (1937). *The education of H*Y*M*A*N K*A*P*L*A*N.* Orlando: Harcourt Brace.

Rothwell, W., and Sredl, H. J. (1992). *Professional human resource development roles and competencies.* Amherst, MA: HRD Press.

Rowden, D. (Ed.). (1936). *Handbook of adult education in the United States.* Washington, DC: American Association for Adult Education.

Rowden, R. W. (Ed.). (1996). *Workplace learning: Debating five critical questions of theory and practice.* New Directions for Adult and Continuing Education, No. 72. San Francisco: Jossey-Bass.

Rubenson, K. (1989). The sociology of adult education. In S. B. Merriam and P. M. Cunningham (Eds.), *Handbook of adult and continuing education* (pp. 51–69). San Francisco: Jossey-Bass.

Rutkoff, P. M., and Scott, W. B. (1986). *New School: A history of the New School for Social Research.* New York: Free Press.

St. Clair, R., and Sandlin, J. A. (2004). Editors' notes. *Promoting critical practice in adult education* (pp. 1–4). New Directions for Adult and Continuing Education, No. 102. San Francisco: Jossey-Bass.

St. Pierre, E. A. (2006). Scientifically based research in education: Epistemology and ethics. *Adult Education Quarterly, 56*(4), 239–266.

Scanlan, C. S., and Darkenwald, G. G. (1984). Identifying deterrents to participation in continuing education. *Adult Education Quarterly, 34*(3), 155–166.

Schaie, K. W., and Willis, S. L. (1986). *Adult development and aging* (2nd ed.). Boston: Little, Brown.

Schied, F. M. (1993). *Learning in social context: Workers and adult education in nineteenth century Chicago.* DeKalb: LEPS Press, Northern Illinois University.

Schied, F. M. (1994). From workers to trade unionists: Transformation and instrumentalism in workers and adult education after the First World War. In M. Hyams, J. Armstrong, and E. Anderson (compilers), *Proceedings of the 35th Annual Adult Education Research Conference* (pp. 318–323). Knoxville: University of Tennessee.

Schied, F. M. (1995). [Review of the book *The pursuit of knowledge under difficulties: From self-improvement to adult education in America, 1750–1990.*]. *Adult Education Quarterly, 45*(4), 232–235.

Schied, F. M. (2001). Struggling to learn, learning to struggle: Workers, workplace learning, and the emergence of human resource development. In V. Sheared and P. A. Sissel (Eds.), *Making space: Merging theory and practice in adult education* (pp. 125–137). Westport, CT: Bergin & Garvey.

Schied, F. M. (2006). In the belly of the beast: Globalization and adult education in the United States. In S. B. Merriam, B. C. Courtenay, and R. M. Cervero (Eds.), *Global issues and adult education: Perspectives from Latin America, Southern Africa, and the United States* (pp. 53–63). San Francisco: Jossey-Bass.

Schmidt-Boshnick, M., and Scott, S. M. (1995). Participation for empowerment: The Candora experience. *Convergence, 28*(3), 63–69.

Schoeffel, P. (1995). Adult education in the Pacific Islands: An overview. Supplement to *Adult Education and Development, 43*, 44–52.

Schön, D. A. (1983). *The reflective practitioner.* New York: Basic Books.

Schön, D. A. (1987). *Educating the reflective practitioner.* San Francisco: Jossey-Bass.

Schroeder, W. L. (1970). Adult education defined and described. In R. M. Smith, G. F. Aker, and J. R. Kidd (Eds.), *Handbook of adult education* (pp. 25–44). New York: Macmillan.

Schroeder, W. L. (1980). Typology of adult learning systems. In J. M. Peters and Associates (Eds.), *Building an effective adult education enterprise* (pp. 41–77). San Francisco: Jossey-Bass.

Schwartz, B. (2004). *The paradox of choice: Why more is less.* New York: Harper-Collins.

Seller, M. (1978). Success and failure in adult education: The immigrant experience 1914–1924. *Adult Education, 28*(2), 83–99.

Senge, P. M. (1990). *The fifth discipline: The art and practice of the learning organization.* New York: Doubleday.

Sheared, V., and Sissel, P.A. (Eds.). (2001). *Making space: Merging theory and practice in adult education.* Westport, CT: Bergin & Garvey.

Sheehy, G. (1976). *Passages.* New York: Dutton.

Sheehy, G. (1995). *New passages.* New York: Random House.

Shor, I. (1992). *Empowering education: Critical teaching for social change.* Chicago: University of Chicago Press.

Shor, I., and Freire, P. (1987). *A pedagogy for liberation: Dialogues on transforming education.* South Hadley, MA: Bergin and Garvey.

Singarella, T., and Sork, T. (1983). Questions of values and conduct: Ethical issues for adult education. *Adult Education Quarterly, 33*(4), 244–251.

Skinner, B. F. (1971). *Beyond freedom and dignity.* New York: Knopf.

Skinner, B. F. (1974). *About behaviorism.* New York: Knopf.

Smith, D. H. (2006). Adult continuing education and human resource development: Present competitors, potential partners. *New Horizons in Adult Education, (20)*1, 12–20.

Smith, D. H., and Offerman, M. J. (1989). The management of adult and continuing education. In S. B. Merriam and P. M. Cunningham (Eds.), *Handbook of adult and continuing education* (pp. 246–259). San Francisco: Jossey-Bass.

Smith, H. W. (1978). *Opening vistas in workers' education: An autobiography of Hilda Worthington Smith.* Washington, DC: H. W. Smith.

Smith, M. K. (1994). *Local education: Community, conversation, praxis.* Philadelphia: Open University Press.

Smith, R. M. (Ed.). (1987). *Theory building for learning how to learn.* Chicago: Educational Studies Press.

Smith, R. M., Aker, G. F., and Kidd, J. R. (Eds.). (1970). *Handbook of adult education.* New York: Macmillan.

Smith, W. L., Eyre, G. A., and Miller, J.W. (1982). Join your professional organizations. In C. Klevins (Ed.), *Materials and methods in adult and continuing education* (pp. 384–389). Los Angeles: Klevens Publications.

Soares de Moraes, F. D. (1995). Environmental education in San Miguel Teotongo, Mexico: A project and its methods. *Adult Education and Development, 44,* 239–249.

Somerville, M. (2004). Somatic knowledge and qualitative reasoning: From theory to practice. *Journal of Aesthetic Education, 38*(4), 80–96.

Sork, T. J., and Busky, J. H. (1986). A descriptive and evaluative analysis of program planning literature, 1950–1983. *Adult Education Quarterly, 36*(2), 86–96.

Sork, T. J., and Caffarella, R. S. (1989). Planning programs for adults. In S. B. Merriam and P. M. Cunningham (Eds.), *Handbook of adult and continuing education* (pp. 233–245). San Francisco: Jossey-Bass.

Sork, T. J., and Welock, B. A. (1992). Adult and continuing education needs a code of ethics. In M. W. Galbraith and B. Sisco (Eds.), *Confronting controversies in challenging times: A call for action.* New Directions for Adult and Continuing Education, No. 54. San Francisco: Jossey-Bass.

Spaulding, S. (1987). Policy and planning in adult education: The international dimension. In W. M. Rivera (Ed.), *Planning adult learning: Issues, practices and directions* (pp. 142–168). London: Croom Helm.

Stacy, W., and Duc-Le To. (1994). Adult education and training markets. In T. Husen and T. N. Postlethwaite (Eds.). *The international encyclopedia of education* (2nd ed., Vol. 1, pp. 106–111). New York: Pergamon Press.

Stalker, J. (1996). Women and adult education: Rethinking androcentric research. *Adult Education Quarterly, 46*(2), 98–113.

Stanage, S. (1987). *Adult education and phenomenological research: New directions for theory, practice, and research.* Malabar, FL: Krieger.

Stanford, M. (1994). *A companion to the study of history.* Cambridge, MA and Oxford: Blackwell.

Sternberg, R. J. (1985). *Beyond I.Q.: A triarchic theory of human intelligence.* Cambridge, UK: Cambridge University Press.

Sternberg, R. J. (1988). *The triarchic mind: A new theory of human intelligence.* New York: Viking Penguin.

Stewart, D. W. (1987). *Adult learning in America: Eduard Lindeman and his agenda for lifelong learning.* Malabar, FL: Krieger.

Stewart, D. W. (1993). *Immigration and education: The crisis and the opportunities.* San Francisco: New Lexington Press.

Strewe, B. (1994). Adult education in transition in Central Europe, the CIS and the Baltic States. *Adult Education and Development 43,* 286–302.

Stubblefield, H. W. (1982). Histories of adult education: An interpretation of Adams, Grattan, and Knowles. *Proceedings of the 23rd Annual Adult Education Research Conference.* Lincoln, NE, April 1982.

Stubblefield, H. W. (1988). *Towards a history of adult education in America.* London: Croom Helm.

Stubblefield, H. W. (1991a). Making the most of professional reading. In R. G. Brockett (Ed.), *Professional development for educators of adults*. New Directions for Adult and Continuing Education, No. 51. San Francisco: Jossey-Bass.

Stubblefield, H. W. (1991b). Learning from the discipline of history. In J. M. Peters, P. Jarvis, and Associates (Eds.), *Adult education: Evolution and achievements in a developing field of study* (pp. 322–343). San Francisco: Jossey-Bass.

Stubblefield, H. W., and Keane, P. (1994). *Adult education in the American experience*. San Francisco: Jossey-Bass.

Stubblefield, H. W., and Rachal, J. R. (1992). On the origins of the term and meanings of 'adult education' in the United States. *Adult Education Quarterly, 42*(2), 106–116.

Summer courses in adult education. (1938). *Journal of Adult Education, 10*(2), 210–212.

Tamayo, R. (1994). Indigenous education and social organization: Case study of three ethnic groups in Colombia. *Adult Education and Development, 42*, 187–203.

Taylor, E. W. (2001). Adult Education Quarterly from 1989 to 1999: A content analysis of all submissions. *Adult Education Quarterly, 51*(4), 322–340.

Taylor, R., Rockhill, K., and Fieldhouse, R. (1985). *University adult education in England and the USA*. Beckenham, Kent, UK: Croom Helm.

Taylor, R., and Ward, K. (1988). Adult education with unemployed people. In T. Lovett (Ed.), *Radical approaches to adult education: A reader* (pp. 242–262). London: Routledge.

Tennant, M., and Pogson, P. (1995). *Learning and change in the adult years: A developmental perspective*. San Francisco: Jossey-Bass.

Thach, L., and Murphy, K. L. (1994). Collaboration in distance education: From local to international perspectives. *The American Journal of Distance Education, 8*(3), 5–21.

Thomas, A. M. (1991a). *Beyond education*. San Francisco: Jossey-Bass.

Thomas, A. M. (1991b). Relationships with political science. In J. M. Peters, P. Jarvis, and Associates (Eds.), *Adult education: Evolution and achievements in a developing field of study* (pp. 301–321). San Francisco: Jossey-Bass.

Thomas, J. E. (1985). *Learning democracy in Japan: The social education of Japanese adults*. London: Sage.

Thorndike, E. L. (1935). *Adult interests*. New York: Macmillan.

Thorndike, E. L., Bregman, E. O., Tilton, J. W., and Woodyard, E. (1928). *Adult learning*. New York: Macmillan.

Tisdell, E. J. (1993a). Feminism and adult learning: Power, pedagogy, and praxis. In S. B. Merriam (Ed.), *An update on adult learning theory*. New Directions for Adult and Continuing Education, No. 57. San Francisco: Jossey-Bass.

Tisdell, E. J. (1993b). Interlocking systems of power, privilege, and oppression in adult higher education classes. *Adult Education Quarterly, 43*(4), 203–226.

Tisdell, E. J. (1995). *Creating inclusive adult learning environments: Insights from multicultural education and feminist pedagogy*. Columbus, OH: ERIC Clearinghouse on Adult, Career, and Vocational Education, Series No. 361.

Tisdell, E. J. (1999). The spiritual dimension of adult development. In M.C. Clark and R. S. Caffarella (Eds.), *An update on adult development theory: New ways of thinking about the life course*. New Directions for Adult and Continuing Education, No. 84 (pp. 87–95). San Francisco: Jossey-Bass.

Tisdell, E. J. (2003). *Exploring spirituality and culture in adult and higher education*. San Francisco: Jossey-Bass.

Titmus, C. J. (1989a). Comparative studies in adult and lifelong education. In C. J. Titmus (Ed.), *Lifelong education for adults: An international handbook* (pp. 541–544). New York: Pergamon Press.

Titmus, C. J. (Ed.). (1989b). *Lifelong education for adults: An international handbook*. New York: Pergamon Press.

Tolliver, D. E., and Tisdell, E. J. (2006). Engaging spirituality in the transformative higher education classroom. In E. W. Taylor (Ed.), *Teaching for change: Fostering transformative learning in the classroom*. New Directions For Adult and Continuing Education, No. 109 (pp.37–48). San Francisco: Jossey-Bass.

Tough, A. (1967). *Learning without a teacher*. (Educational Research Series No. 3.) Toronto: Ontario Institute for Studies in Education.

Tough, A. (1979). *The adult's learning projects: A fresh approach to theory and practice in adult learning* (2nd ed.). Austin, TX: Learning Concepts. (Original work published in 1971.)

Tough, A. (1991). *Crucial questions about the future*. Lanham, MD: University Press of America.

Tyler, R. W. (1949). *Basic principles of curriculum and instruction*. Chicago: University of Chicago Press.

United Nations. (1993). *World population prospects: The 1992 revision*. New York: United Nations.

United Nations Educational, Scientific and Cultural Organization. (1977). *The general conference adopts a recommendation on adult education*. (Adult Education Information Notes No. 1.)

U.S. Department of Education, National Center for Education Statistics. (1994). *The condition of education*. Washington, DC: U.S. Department of Education.

U.S. Government. (2005). Scientifically based research methods. *Federal Register, 70*(15), 3585–3589.

Usher, R., and Bryant, I. (1989). *Adult education as theory, practice and research.* London: Routledge.

Vaillant, G. (1977). *Adaptation to life.* Boston: Little, Brown.

Valentine, T., and Darkenwald, G. G. (1990). Deterrents to participation in adult education: Profiles of potential learners. *Adult Education Quarterly, 41*(1), 29–42.

Van Tilburg, E., and Moore, A. B. (1989). Education for rural adults. In S. B. Merriam and P. M. Cunningham (Eds.), *Handbook of adult and continuing education* (pp. 537–549). San Francisco: Jossey-Bass.

Velazquez, L. C. (1994–1995). Addressing migrant farmworkers' perceptions of schooling, learning, and education. *The Rural Educator, 16*(2), 32–36.

Vella, J. (1994). *Learning to listen, learning to teach: The power of dialogue in educating adults.* San Francisco: Jossey-Bass.

Vella, J. (2000). A spirited epistemology: Honoring the adult learner as subject. In L. English and M. Gillen (Eds.), *Addressing the spiritual dimensions of adult learning: What educators can do* (pp. 7–16). New Directions for Adult and Continuing Education, No. 85. San Francisco: Jossey-Bass.

Verner, C. (1964). Definition of terms. In G. Jensen, A. A. Liveright, and W. Hallenbeck (Eds.), *Adult education: Outlines of an emerging field of university study* (pp. 27–39). Washington, DC: Adult Education Association of the U.S.A.

Verner, C., and Booth, A. (1964). *Adult education.* New York: The Center for Applied Research in Education.

Vernon, S., Lo Parco, L. B., and Marsick, V. J. (1993). Satisfying accountability needs with nontraditional methods. In P. Mulcrone (Ed.), *Current perspectives on administration of adult education programs.* New Directions for Adult and Continuing Education, No. 60. San Francisco: Jossey-Bass.

Vio Grossi, F. (1994). Make it global—make it local but always do it democratically. Adult education for democracy in the world today. *Adult Education and Development, 42,* 65–79.

Vosko, R. S. (1984). *The reactions of adult learners to selected instructional environments.* Unpublished doctoral dissertation, Syracuse University, Syracuse, NY.

Wain, K. (1993). Lifelong education and adult education—the state of the theory. *International Journal of Lifelong Education, 12*(2), 85–99.

Wang, M., Lin, W., Sun, S., and Fang, J. (Eds.). (1988). *China: Lessons from practice.* New Directions for Continuing Education, No. 37. San Francisco: Jossey-Bass.

Watkins, K. E., and Marsick, V. J. (1993). *Sculpting the learning organization*. San Francisco: Jossey-Bass.

Welton, M. (1986). An authentic instrument of the democratic process: The intellectual origins of the Canadian Citizens' Forum. *Studies in the Education of Adults*, April, 35–49.

Welton, M. (Ed.). (1987). *Knowledge for the people*. Toronto: OISE Press.

Welton, M. (1993). The contribution of critical theory to our understanding of adult learning. In S. B. Merriam (Ed.), *An update on adult learning theory*. New Directions in Adult and Continuing Education, No. 57. San Francisco: Jossey-Bass.

Welton, M. (1993). In search of the object: Historiography and adult education. *Studies in Continuing Education*, *15*(2), 133–148.

West, C. (1993). *Race matters*. Boston: Beacon Press.

Whipple, J. B. (1964). The uses of history for adult education. In G. Jensen, A. A. Liveright, and W. Hallenbeck (Eds.), *Adult education: Outlines of an emerging field of university study* (pp. 201–213). Washington, DC: Adult Education Association of the U.S.A.

White, B. A. (1992). Professional certification is a needed option for adult and continuing education. In M. W. Galbraith and B. Sisco (Eds.), *Confronting controversies in challenging times: A call for action*. New Directions for Adult and Continuing Education, No. 54. San Francisco: Jossey-Bass.

White, C., and Merrifield, J. (1990). *A foot in the door: Rural communities involved in social change*. Knoxville: Center for Literacy Studies, University of Tennessee.

Willis, V. J. (1996). Human resource development as evolutionary system: From pyramid building to space walking and beyond. In R. W. Rowden (Ed.), *Workplace learning: Debating five critical questions of theory and practice*. New Directions for Adult and Continuing Education, No. 72 (pp. 31–39). San Francisco: Jossey-Bass.

Wilson, A. L. (1993a). The common concern: Controlling the professionalization of adult education. *Adult Education Quarterly*, *44*(1), 1–16.

Wilson, A. L. (1993b). The promise of situated cognition. In S. B. Merriam (Ed.), *An update on adult learning theory*. New Directions for Adult and Continuing Education, No. 57. San Francisco: Jossey-Bass.

Wilson, A. L. (1995). Telling tales out of school: Whose story needs telling? *Adult Education Quarterly*, *45*(4), 240–244.

Wilson, A. L., and Hayes, E. R. (Eds.). (2000a). *Handbook of adult and continuing education*. San Francisco: Jossey-Bass.

Wilson, A. L., and Hayes, E. R. (2000b). A selective history of the adult education handbooks. In A. L. Wilson and E. R. Hayes (Eds.), *Handbook of adult and continuing education* (pp. 3–14). San Francisco: Jossey-Bass.

Wilson, A. L., and Melichar, K. E. (1994). History as critique: Collective representation in constructing the pasts of adult education. In M. Hyams, J. Armstrong, and E. Anderson (compilers), *Proceedings of the 35th Annual Adult Education Research Conference* (pp. 401–406). Knoxville: University of Tennessee.

Wise, M., and Glowacki-Dudka, M. (Eds.) (2004). *Embracing and enhancing the margins of adult education.* New Directions for Adult and Continuing Education, No. 104. San Francisco: Jossey-Bass.

Withnall, A.M.E., and Kabwasa, N. O. (1989). Education for older adults. In C. J. Titmus (Ed.), *Lifelong education for adults: An international handbook* (pp. 319–321). New York: Pergamon Press.

Yates, E. (1958). *Pebble in a pool: The widening circles of Dorothy Canfield Fisher's life.* New York: Dutton.

Youngman, F. (1986). *Adult education and socialist pedagogy.* London: Croom Helm.

Zeph, C. P. (1991). Graduate study as professional development. In R. G. Brockett (Ed.), *Professional development for educators of adults.* New Directions for Adult and Continuing Education, No. 51. San Francisco: Jossey-Bass.

Ziegahn, L. (2000). Adult education, communication, and the global context. In A. L. Wilson and E. R. Hayes (Eds.), *Handbook of adult and continuing education* (pp. 312–326). San Francisco: Jossey-Bass.

Zinn, L. (1990). Identifying your philosophical orientation. In M. W. Galbraith (Ed.), *Adult learning methods: A guide for effective instruction* (pp. 39–77). Malabar, FL: Krieger.

Name Index

Subject Index

A

Access and opportunity, 187–189; age restrictions on, 192–193; cultural determinants of, 198–200; educational responses to, 204–208; geographic limitations on, 189–192; political responses to, 201–204; sex restrictions on, 193–195; socioeconomic restrictions on, 195–198; technological responses to, 208–212. See also Participation

Action inquiry technologies, 155

Action research, 155, 273

Adult basic education (ABE), 11–12

Adult development, 143–146; and life events, 144–145; phase theories of, 143–144; and psychosocial development of women, 145; and sequential patterns of change, 144; stage theories of, 144; and transitions, 145

Adult education: definitions of, 7–10; informal, and globalized mass media, 293; and focus on individuals or society, 89–94; and the future of the field, 286–289; globalization trends and impacts on, 291–296; goals and purposes of, 17–22, 82; historical terms for, 8–9; holistic conceptions of, 301–306; human

capital theory of, 297; and human resource development (HRD) practice, 296–301; imbalances of power and privilege in, 310–311; institutionalization of, 86–88, 95; international terms for, 13–15; marginal status of, 23, 86, 110–111, 201; program, 16; and related terms, 10–13; typologies of, 18–22, 104–109

Adult Education Association of the United States of America (AEA/USA), 36, 61, 223–224, 228, 268

Adult education field: adult education's alignment with, 84–89; critical theory analysis in, 306, 307–310; diversity in, 306–311, 315; graduate study trends in, 313–315; knowledge base growth in, 311–313; phases of development in, 306–307; professionalization of, 311–313; reflection and critique in, 307; unity and diversity in, 78–84

Adult education program planning, critical perspective in, 308–309

Adult Education Research Conference (AERC), 260, 313

Adult education for social change, 248–249; and collaborative learning, 249–251; and knowledge